Other Books in the Jossey-Bass Nonprofit and Public Management Series:

Human Resources Management for Public and Nonprofit Organizations

Human Resources Management for Public and Nonprofit Organizations

Joan E. Pynes

Jossey-Bass Publishers • San Francisco

Jossey-Bass books and products are available through most bookstores. To contact Jossey-Bass directly, call (888) 378-2537, fax to 800 605-2665, or visit our website at www.josseybass.com.

Substantial discounts on bulk quantities of Jossey-Bass books are available to corporations, professional associations, and other organizations. For details and discount information, contact the special sales department at Jossey-Bass.

 Manufactured in the United States of America on Lyons Falls Turin Book. This paper is acid-free and 100 percent totally chlorine-free.

Library of Congress Cataloging-in-Publication Data

Pynes, Joan.
   Human resources management for public and nonprofit organizations
/ Joan E. Pynes.
     p. cm. — (The Jossey-Bass public administration series)
(The Jossey-Bass nonprofit sector series)
   Includes bibliographical references and index.
   ISBN 0-7879-0808-8 (alk. paper)
   1. Public administration—United States—Personnel management.
2. Nonprofit organizations—United States—Personnel management.
I. Title. II. Series. III. Series: The Jossey-Bass nonprofit
sector series.
HF5549.2.U5P96   1997
352.6'0973—DC21   96-50184

FIRST EDITION
HB Printing 10 9 8 7 6 5 4 3

The Jossey-Bass Nonprofit
and Public Management Series

Consulting Editor
Public Management and Administration
James L. Perry
Indiana University

Contents

List of Tables, Figure, and Exhibits

Preface

Government and nonprofit organizations are facing many changes. They are confronted with tighter budgets brought about by shifts in federal and state funding priorities and by tax levy limits. These changes have occurred simultaneously with increasing demands for efficiency with no loss in effectiveness. In many public services, employees have been forced to compete with the private and non-profit sectors, which has resulted in the privatization of some of these services. Outsourcing, franchise agreements, vouchers, and the purchase of service contracting are just some of the means used by the public sector in the privatization of services. All of these alternatives have human resources management (HRM) implications.

Changing demographics have resulted in an increasingly diverse workforce composed of increasing numbers of employees who have disabilities, who are women, and who are members of ethnic and racial minorities. These changes have forced organizations to review their HRM practices to make sure that employees are treated fairly and evaluated on job-related performance rather than according to stereotypes or biases. Training programs have been implemented in many agencies to expedite a change in attitudes.

Changes in information technology and automation have rendered many jobs obsolete. At the same time, in many cases advances in technology have enabled employees to work from their homes, provided opportunities for more flexible work hours, and increased the employment options for disabled individuals. These changes in technology have also encouraged the restructuring of public agencies. Computer networks, modems, fax machines, and videoconferencing have changed communication patterns, often resulting in flatter organizations through the elimination of layers of managers or administrators. This flattening of the hierarchy has led to fewer promotional opportunities, and the need for organizations to review their reward systems.

Organizations must do more than just adapt to internal changes. They must also seek better ways to meet the expectations held by citizens, clients, funding sources, elected officials, boards of directors, interest groups, and the media. All public agencies are under pressure to improve the quality of their services while also controlling labor costs, and to increase productivity without increasing taxes or the costs of services rendered.

In summary, declining revenues combined with demographic changes, changes in employees' values, workforce diversity issues, and the need to retain effective workers with limited advancement opportunities are some of the forces that have compelled public and nonprofit organizations to become concerned with their survival (Bryson, 1988; Klingner, 1993). These changes require a more flexible and skilled workforce. To survive, organizations need employees with new skills. *Hard Truths/Tough Choices* (National Commission on the State and Local Public Service, 1993) identified five skill areas that are needed by the new public manager: competency in team building, competency in communication, competency in involving employees, commitment to cultural awareness, and commitment to quality. These skills have HRM implications for employee recruitment, selection, and training. Public and nonprofit sector jobs are increasingly professional in nature, requiring higher levels of education. At the same time, there is a decrease in jobs that are physically demanding. Employees in public and nonprofit agencies often deal with a variety of people, many of whom have a stake in the agency. Taxpayers, clients, customers, elected officials, donors, contractors, board members, and special interest groups are just some of the stakeholders concerned about agency performance. Employers must ask themselves how to meet the public's objectives and satisfy the organization's stakeholders.

Public and nonprofit agencies must be flexible and attuned to the needs of society. They must seek to improve the quality of their services by engaging in strategic human resources management (SHRM). Recruitment and selection strategies must be innovative, career development opportunities must be provided, work assignments must be flexible, and policies must reward superior performers and hold accountable marginal employees. These policies must be developed and administered according to the principles of equity, efficiency, and effectiveness. Performance standards must be designed to promote the goals and values of organizations.

Historically, HRM has been seen as Cinderella—on the periphery, not integrated into the core of agency functions. Fitz-enz (1996, p. 3) notes that historically personnel departments were either dumping grounds for "organizational casualties"—likable employees who were not proficient in other tasks—or they were staffed with employees from line functions, neither of whom had any formal education in personnel administration. He also attributes the peripheral relationship of HRM departments to other functional departments to the fact that for years it was believed that organizations could not measure or quantify what the HRM department accomplished or contributed to the organization's bottom line. HRM departments did not speak in financial terms, the common denominator of business language, nor were they very good at communicating the relationship between successful HRM programs and organizational success. As a result, most HRM departments were denied access to the organization's strategic planning processes and forced into reactive activities instead of being allowed to collaborate with the other management teams to formulate policies and determine future objectives. This approach has been a mistake. Research in the private sector has found that returns on wise HRM policies can surpass returns from other resources (Cascio, 1991a; Fitz-enz, 1996). In the public and nonprofit sectors, where 60 to 80 percent of expenditures are for personnel, SHRM is even more important than in the private sector.

Purpose and Audience

This book addresses HRM issues found in nonprofit and public agencies. While there are many textbooks on public personnel management, none address the nonprofit sector, thus omitting a significant partner that provides services that benefit society. Topics such as recruiting and managing volunteers or working with a board of directors have not been addressed. There are other omissions as well, such as a discussion of nonprofit labor relations. For example, nonprofit labor relations are governed by the amended National Labor Relations Act (the Labor-Management Relations Act) while most federal employees fall under the Federal Service Labor-Management Relations Statute (Title VII of the Civil Service Reform Act of 1978) and state employees are guided by their respective public employee relations statutes. In the public sector, an applicant's or employee's religion is irrelevant, and discrimination because of religion is prohibited. However, religiously affiliated nonprofits that provide services of a religious nature may in special circumstances discriminate against applicants or employees on the basis of their religion.

Because service-provider nonprofits are typically the recipients of government contracts and grants, a new intergovernmental environment has emerged as nongovernment organizations have increasingly been used to implement public policy. Kramer and Grossman (1987) and Salamon (1992, 1995) refer to this new interorganizational environment as the "new political economy," the "contract state," or "nonprofit federalism."

The emphasis in this book will be on nonprofits that are closely associated with providing a public benefit or service or with solving a problem on behalf of the public interest. It will focus on nonprofits that are responsible for delivering health care, social services, education, arts, and research. The objectives of these nonprofits often parallel those of many government agencies in terms of the individual and community services they provide.

Public organizations and nonprofits are similar in that they define themselves according to their missions or the services they offer. These services are often intangible and difficult to measure. The clients receiving public or nonprofit services and the professionals delivering them make very different judgments about the quality of those services. Both sectors are responsible to multiple constituencies—nonprofits are responsible to supporters, sponsors, clients, and government sources that provide funding and impose regulations; and public agencies are responsible to their respective legislative and judicial branches, and to taxpayers, cognate agencies, political appointees, clients, the media, and other levels of government (Kanter & Summers, 1987; Starling, 1986).

Lipsky and Smith (1989–1990) comment that public and private service organizations share many characteristics: the need to process clients through systems of eligibility and treatment, the need to maintain a competent staff to be effective, and the need to account for financial expenditures. These organizations are also expected to be fair (equitable), to accommodate likely and unanticipated complexities (responsive), to protect the interests of sponsors in minimizing costs (efficient), to be true to their mandated purposes (accountable), and to be honest (fiscally honorable) (pp. 630–631).

The conceptual foundation of this book is strategic human resources management. SHRM is the integration of human resources management with the strategic mission of the organization. It adapts human resources policies and practices to meet the challenges faced by agencies today, as well as those they will face in the future. Human resources departments must take a proactive role in guiding and supporting agency efforts to meet the changing demands of their environments. The information provided in this book is to be used to improve the effectiveness of HRM activities.

In many organizations, HRM policies and practices develop on an ad hoc basis, with little integration of the organization's future needs. Often policies are developed to solve an immediate problem, with no thought to their long-term implications. Such policies and practices lock the agency into inflexible modes of operation, leaving them unable to see that other strategies might be more appropriate.

This book emphasizes the importance of HRM functions, revealing them as major contributors to the accomplishment of the agency's mission both in the present and as the agency changes. The purpose of the book is to provide practitioners, policymakers (such as elected officials), and board members of local, state, federal, and nonprofit organizations with an understanding of the importance of SHRM in managing change. It provides the guidance necessary to implement effective HRM strategies.

The book was also written to be a textbook for use in public administration and nonprofit management graduate programs that offer courses in personnel administration, human resources management, strategic planning, and nonprofit management. While the literature on nonprofit management has increased in recent years, little information exists that addresses nonprofit HRM concerns. This book should help fill that void.

Recently, the National Association of Schools of Public Affairs and Administration has redefined the "public" in "public administration" to include the nonprofit sector, and the Academy of Management Division for the Public Sector has recently changed its name to the Division for Public and Nonprofit Sectors. Both changes illustrate the increasing focus on the management of nonprofit agencies by practitioners and academics in public administration. Despite the growth of nonprofit management in many public administration curriculums, none of the current public personnel textbooks address the nonprofit sector. As more public administration programs offer a specialization in nonprofit management, it is important that resources be available that target the challenges faced by both the public and nonprofit sectors.

Overview of the Contents

Part One introduces the reader to the context and environment of human resources management. Chapter One discusses how society and workplaces have changed, and the HRM implications of those changes. Chapter Two explains how SHRM and human resources planning are imperative if agencies are going to remain competitive and be able to accomplish their missions; it also explains how SHRM is consistent with reinventing government. Chapter Three discusses the importance of managing diversity if organizations expect to prosper. Chapter Four presents the legal environment of equal employment opportunity.

Part Two presents the techniques and functional areas of human resources management. Examples are provided in each chapter. Chapter Five explains the importance of job analysis before executing HRM policies or developing job descriptions, performance appraisal instruments, training and development programs, and recruitment and selection criteria. A variety of job analysis techniques are discussed. In Chapter Six recruitment and selection techniques are explained. Drug testing, physical ability tests, psychological examinations, and other selection techniques used in the public and nonprofit sectors are summarized. At the end of the chapter, important psychometric concepts are explained.

Evaluating employees' performance is the focus of Chapter

Seven. Different performance appraisal techniques are explained, and their strengths and weaknesses are identified. The importance of rater training and documentation is noted. Ethical issues in performance appraisal are discussed, as are merit pay and 360-degree evaluations. Conflicts between total quality management and performance evaluation are also addressed. Chapter Eight identifies the internal and external factors that influence compensation policies and practices. The techniques used to develop pay systems are discussed. Examples of job evaluation systems are provided and nontraditional pay systems are explained. In Chapter Nine, employer-provided benefits and pensions are discussed.

The focus of Chapter Ten is training and development activities. Changes in technology and demographics and the development of new responsibilities and expectations have made training and career development more important than ever. Identifying training needs, developing training objectives and the curriculum, and the evaluation of training are explored. Different training formats are summarized. The chapter concludes with examples of management training and career development programs. Chapter Eleven, the last chapter in Part Two, discusses collective bargaining in the public and nonprofit sectors. The legal environment of labor-management relations for nonprofit, federal, state, and local employees is explored. Definitions and explanations are provided for concepts such as unit determination, union security, unfair labor practices, management rights, impasse resolution, and grievance arbitration. The reasons that unions exist in the public and nonprofit sectors are examined.

Part Three moves away from HRM practices and focuses on the pending HRM challenges in public and nonprofit organizations. Chapter Twelve discusses the importance of managing volunteers, and how HRM practices can assist in making the volunteer experience productive for the agency and satisfying to the volunteer. Chapter Thirteen summarizes some of the emerging issues that have begun to affect HRM practices and that are likely to become more important in the future. Topics such as contracting-out services, violence in the workplace, alternative dispute resolution techniques, and changes in information and computer technology are examined. The last chapter provides an overall conclusion for the book. It summarizes the key lessons presented in the preceding chapters, which hopefully will convince public and nonprofit administrators of the importance of proactive HRM practices.

Edwardsville, Illinois   JOAN E. PYNES
December 1996

Acknowledgments

A number of people have made valuable contributions to this book. First, I would like to thank Alan Shrader and Susan Williams from Jossey-Bass as well as James L. Perry and two anonymous reviewers for their helpful comments and suggestions.

Many colleagues provided assistance by contributing anecdotes, reviewing earlier chapters, or both. I would like to thank Lynn Bartles of the Department of Psychology at Southern Illinois University at Edwardsville; Anne Goldyche Dailey, Berkshire Farm Center and Services for Youth; Patricia Goldstein, formerly of Parents of Special Children; Jeanene Harris, United Way of Greater St. Louis; September McAdoo, formerly of Places for People; and Patricia Murray, New York State Division for Youth. I would also like to thank Theresa Wasylenko for her patience and ceaseless good humor while preparing and revising the tables and exhibits. Special acknowledgment goes to my husband, Mike McNaughton, for his never-ending editorial assistance.

I would also like to express my appreciation to my family for their support and encouragement. Mom, Dad, Robyn, and Mike: thanks! This book is dedicated to my mother, who has always inspired to me to do my best.

The Author

JOAN E. PYNES is associate professor of public administration and policy analysis at Southern Illinois University at Edwardsville. She received her B.A. degree (1979) in public justice from SUNY Oswego, and her M.P.A. degree (1983) and Ph.D. degree (1988) in public administration from Florida Atlantic University.

Pynes is coauthor (with J. M. Lafferty) of *Local Government Labor Relations: A Guide for Public Administrators* (1993). She has also published articles in *Review of Public Personnel Administration, Public Personnel Management, Journal of Applied Psychology, Journal of Management Systems, Journal of Criminal Justice, American Journal of Police, Public Productivity and Management Review, Journal of Collective Negotiations in the Public Sector, Public Administration Quarterly,* and *Journal of Business and Psychology.*

Human Resources Management for Public and Nonprofit Organizations

Part One

Human Resources Management in Context

Public and nonprofit organizations are finding themselves having to confront a variety of economic, technological, legal, and cultural changes with which they must cope effectively if they are to remain viable. The key to viability is well-trained and flexible employees. To be responsive to the constantly changing environment, agencies must integrate their human resources management (HRM) needs with their long-term strategic plans. This part of the book consists of four chapters that explain how society and workplaces have changed and what the HRM implications of these changes are for organizations.

Chapter One reviews some of the external factors that impact the internal operations of an organization, such as changes in economic conditions and the fiscal uncertainty that such changes can bring to an agency, and the social and cultural changes affecting the demographic composition of the workforce. In most organizations today there is a more diverse group of employees than there used to be in the 1970s and 1980s that is bringing new expectations into the organization. Technological changes such as the increased use of computers, computer databases, and telecommunications and networking have changed the way agencies are structured and work is organized and managed. Organizations need to recruit and hire people who have the skills and orientation to fit the new culture. The legal environment must always be monitored for change. Equal employment opportunity, labor relations, and compensation and benefits are all regulated by law.

There is also an emphasis on reinventing today's public and nonprofit organizations so that they can improve the quality of their services. Staff need to have the critical knowledge skills, abilities, and other characteristics to perform specific jobs, but they also need to be flexible and willing to deal with rapid and unstructured change. To make this possible, HRM needs to be more closely integrated with the organization's objectives and mission.

Chapter Two addresses the strategic side of HRM and the importance of strategic human resources and human resources planning. It explains why strategic human resources management (SHRM) and human resources planning are critical if agencies are going to accomplish their missions. SHRM believes that realistic planning is not possible unless strategic planning takes into consideration information on current and potential human resources. Human resources planning requires the assessment of past trends, an evaluation of the present situation and the projection of future events. The external and internal environments must be scanned and changes that might affect an organization's human resources must be anticipated if organizations wish to remain viable.

Chapter Three is devoted to exploring the issues of managing a diverse workforce. As already noted, the demographic composition of public and nonprofit workforces has changed. Women, racial and ethnic minorities, and older, disabled, and homosexual workers are more visible in today's workplace and may not always be accepted by other employees and managers. This diversity must be understood if organizations want to deal effectively with all employees regardless of their different characteristics. When diversity is well managed, all employees are supported, valued, and included. A supportive work environment enables employees to achieve their fullest potential.

Chapter Four focuses on the federal laws governing equal employment opportunity. Equal employment opportunity requires that employers not discriminate in the administration and execution of all HRM practices, such as recruitment, selection, promotion, training, compensation, career development, discipline, and labor-management relations. To understand the legal environment of equal employment opportunity, one must be familiar with the laws and regulations that govern its implementation.

Chapter One

Human Resources Management in a Dynamic Environment

Many external and internal environmental factors affect an organization's human resources management (HRM). The public and nonprofit sectors are increasingly being influenced by external factors that impact the internal operations of the organization. The following examples illustrate some of the external and internal pressures facing public and nonprofit organizations. The common thread running through each example is that it confronts an HRM challenge:

- The Bureau of Indian Affairs plans a reduction in force that will affect between 2,600 and 4,000 of its 12,000 workers. Jobs that will be affected include law enforcement, fisheries, social workers, and accountants ("Where Things Stand," 1995).
- The American Red Cross has borrowed $15 million from its disaster relief fund and transferred $34 million from funds used to support chapter operations to help its blood services program. Besides transferring money the agency is cutting staff, merging some operations, and expanding others (Rose, 1995).
- The Governor of Missouri signed a teacher retirement bill that gives some public school teachers the option of retiring as early as forty-seven years of age. It allows teachers to draw half their salary as a pension after twenty-five years of service, regardless of age. The previous law required retirees to be at least fifty-five or to have thirty years of service (Bell, 1995).

The organizations in the previous examples must contend with internal HRM issues brought about by external factors. The Bureau of Indian Affairs, for example, must reduce its workforce because of a lack of federal funds. A reduction in force that extensive will require services to be reduced and/or programs to be eliminated. The employees who survive the layoffs are likely to face increased workloads and longer hours, resulting in higher stress and possibly less commitment to the organization.

An internal Red Cross memo dated April 24, 1995, indicated that the American Red Cross blood program was expected to report a deficit of $76 million. The memo also said that the Red Cross had been hurt by a government hold on plasma products, a major revenue source. The Red Cross supplies approximately half of the blood used in U.S. hospitals, and blood is the agency's primary revenue source. To help resolve the financial crunch, regional offices must do all they can to reduce costs and improve procedures, including focusing on large-scale blood drives. Other efforts to reduce costs include restrictions on hiring, purchasing, and travel as well as cuts in consulting contracts and other reductions in staff costs (Rose, 1995).

School districts across the State of Missouri can expect to see an increase in teacher retirements as a result of the new law signed by Governor Carnahan. As school districts lose many experienced teachers, the number of new teachers they will have to recruit, select, train, and supervise will increase.

This chapter reviews some of the challenges affecting nonprofit and public agencies, and then briefly addresses how proactive HRM practices can make a difference in helping organizations achieve their missions despite these changes.

Economic Changes

Public and nonprofit organizations are confronting reductions in federal funding. The Republican Congress's "Contract with America" has attempted to scale back the size of the federal government and its involvement in the lives of Americans. Movement is afoot to distribute monies to state governments, which would then be responsible for disseminating it to local governments and nonprofit organizations based on each state's individual assessment of need. This approach to funding results in increased discretion at the state level, but it also brings uncertainty to local governments and nonprofit organizations that are already receiving federal funds to provide services. Social service programs and services provided primarily to the poor, elderly, sick, and disabled are likely to be the first programs affected by this new strategy.

Proponents of returning this authority to the states believe that state officials are in a better position than federal bureaucrats to assess what services are needed. Opponents of the idea believe that states often neglect the compassion that would warrant their being entrusted with federal funds. For example, Carol Kamin, the executive director of the Children's Action Alliance, a statewide advocacy group in Arizona, stated the following: "Block-grants appear to be a response to calls for local control, but what they really do is destroy assurances that Arizona children will receive the help they need when threatened by severe deprivation" (in Stehle, 1995, p. 32). Kamin and others believe that state neglect of the needy is what encouraged federal involvement in the first place. Leaders of social service groups in Arizona worry that shifting spending authority to the state will increase the competition across nonprofits competing for funds not earmarked for specific purposes or programs (Stehle, 1995).

Public employees are also concerned as more governments attempt to privatize what were previously public services. Becker, Silverstein, and Chaykin (1995) noted the obstacles confronted by a county in southern Florida when it attempted to privatize its mental health services. The incumbent public employees resisted the privatization efforts; their resistance was motivated by concerns for job security and decreases in employer-provided benefits such as health insurance, retirement pensions, and paid days off. The authors concluded that the resistance faced by the county could be generalized to the attempted privatization of other social service programs—that public employees are reluctant to see their jobs transferred to nonprofit or for-profit organizations because they fear losses in compensation and benefits.

State employees working in mental health for the state of Massachusetts were not able to resist the state's privatization efforts. In the 1970s, Massachusetts began a partnership between the state government and nonprofits providing mental health services.

Through the partnership, the state assigned state employees to work for nonprofit agencies or provided state contract dollars to supplement the nonprofits own third-party monies. State employees working for the nonprofits were paid by the state, but the nonprofits billed the state for their services. The nonprofits were allowed to keep this "retained revenue" so they could expand services and programs (Brotman, 1992, p. 543). In 1992, when Massachusetts began to privatize its mental health services, state employees who were assigned to nonprofit vendors were summarily discharged from state employment. This resulted in the layoff of more than eight hundred employees working in a variety of outpatient and residential facilities. The Department of Mental Health extended to nonprofit agencies 80 percent of the value of the salaries of employees formerly on the payroll of the state. No funds were appropriated for employee fringe benefits. The nonprofits were then told to reorganize without cutting any services. Because of the prior billing arrangement in which the state paid nonprofits for the services performed by state employees, for every state employee transferred to the nonprofit payroll approximately one and one-half salaries were lost. Most vendors had to decrease their staff substantially in order to adhere to this new arrangement. As a result of the loss of revenue to pay staff salaries, clinics were merged or closed, productivity standards were increased, criteria for treatment became more restrictive, and attention to the bottom line became more critical (Brotman, 1992, pp. 543–544). The Massachusetts experience illustrates how a change in funding can affect both public and nonprofit agencies, and both employees and services.

Public and nonprofit employees are not the only workers facing an uncertain future. Many large private-sector companies, such as I.B.M., AT&T, Sprint, Prudential, 3M, McDonnell Douglas, and Boeing, have laid off employees. Uncertain financial times place additional stress on public and nonprofit organizations. Increased unemployment often requires the expansion of financial assistance, medical aid, and job training or retraining services. These services are typically provided by the public and nonprofit sectors, which must absorb an increase in demand for services without increasing their staffs.

Nonprofit and public agencies are impacted by economic

uncertainty in other ways. Individuals who have been or might be laid off are less inclined than more securely employed people to spend dollars on cultural activities such as visiting museums, the theater, or the symphony. They are also likely to reduce the level of their contributions to charitable nonprofits or to services such as National Public Radio or the Public Broadcasting Service, exacerbating the financial pressures on these already fiscally stressed agencies. In 1995, the House of Representatives voted to cut $141 million from the Corporation for Public Broadcasting's budget between 1995 and 1997, and the Senate voted to freeze spending at current levels for the next two years. Even in the best of times, private contributions could not make up for such losses in public funding.

Because of a decline in private contributions, the United Way of Central Indiana was forced to lay off nine full-time employees from its payroll in the wake of corporate reductions that cost the agency thousands of dollars. There was a loss of 7,300 jobs at area companies, and approximately 4,000 of the displaced workers had previously contributed to the United Way ("Indiana United Way," 1995).

Uncertain financial times cause citizens to focus more on the performance of the public sector. People with less money to spend want assurances that their tax dollars are spent wisely and without waste. This provokes greater scrutiny of the performance outcomes of government. More and more citizens are demanding a voice in the way public monies are allocated.

Social and Cultural Changes

The demographic composition of the American workforce has changed. Reports such as Workforce 2000 (Hudson Institute, 1987) and Civil Service 2000 (Johnson, 1988) have projected that by the twenty-first century white males will be a minority in the workplace, and they will be working beside increased numbers of women, minorities, and immigrants. Employers will need to manage a diverse workforce. They will need to ensure that agency rewards such as promotional opportunities and compensation are determined by job performance, initiative, or special skills, not by racism or sexism.

There has also been a shift in the attitudes and values of employees. Employees are seeking a balance between their personal lives and work lives. They are demanding more leisure time to spend with their families. There has also been a change in what constitutes a family; a father, mother, and two children is no longer the norm. Nontraditional families are now prevalent. Divorce, death, domestic partners, and different generations of the same family living together have become commonplace and have a significant impact on the work environment. Because of the increase in single-parent families, families in which both parents work, and employees taking care of elderly parents and young children, organizations need to provide employees with more flexibility and options in choosing work schedules and benefits. Issues such as day care, elder care, assistance with family problems, and spousal involvement in career planning have become important.

Attitudes toward work have also changed; a greater number of employees want challenging jobs and the opportunity to exercise discretion in the performance of their tasks. Improving the quality of work life has become important. Empowerment, teamwork, quality improvement, job design, labor-management cooperation, and participative management are expected. Organizational cultures will need to be changed if organizations wish to attract, motivate, and retain a competent workforce.

Technological Changes

The increased use of computer databases, telecommunications, and networking are changing the way organizations are structured and how work is organized and managed. Rocheleau (1988, p. 165) posed the following questions in regard to the changes introduced by computer technology:

How well does the new information technology mesh with the old structures?

How do existing structures have to be modified, and what structures have to be created in order to manage the new information technology?

How does the degree of centralization within organizations affect the implementation of the new information technology?

Does the new information technology spur centralization or decentralization?

Perry and Kramer (1993) noted that most of the changes necessary to accommodate greater use of information technology will need to occur in personnel systems. "High demand in many technological specialties will necessitate rapid assessment and hiring of applicants. This is likely to require streamlining government hiring practices and shifting merit system controls from input practices (for example, testing) to post audit" (p. 240). Thus information technology is creating new challenges for HRM systems.

Computers and automation now play a major role in the redesign of traditionally routine jobs and are expected to be a major contributor to productivity in the future (Hudson Institute, 1987). For example, the introduction of computers into offices has changed the nature of even clerical jobs (McIntosh, 1990), including the management of more information. Stenographic talents such as speed and accuracy in typing and dictation have become less relevant than problem solving, decision making, and critical thinking (McIntosh, 1990). Computers and information technology are also being used to design and manage public sector programs. Andersen, Belardo, and Dawes (1994) note that strategic information management is already a powerful tool for service integration. They cite as one example how the state of Pennsylvania has developed a food stamp program that issues ATM cards to its food stamp recipients for purchasing groceries. No paper changes hands; instead, all accounting information is kept on-line, eliminating the need for the merchants, the banks, and the agency to reconcile separate paper-bound transactions each month. Other examples include New York State's automated fingerprint system, which speeds criminal investigations and court proceedings throughout the state, and the San Francisco Bay Area's use of geographic information systems to manage the effects of the October 1989 earthquake. Information technology is not only being used to automate routine tasks, but it is increasingly being used to restructure and integrate service delivery procedures and programs.

Organizations need to recruit and hire people with a new set of skills and orientation to fit the new culture. Key challenges facing organizations will be the ability to attract and hire qualified applicants and to provide training for incumbent employees so that the benefits of high technology can be realized.

The Legal Environment

Public and nonprofit agencies must comply with federal, state, and local laws, with executive orders and the rules and regulations promulgated by administrative agencies such as the Equal Employment Opportunity Commission, as well as with federal and state court decisions. Equal employment opportunity, labor relations, and employer contributions to benefits such as retirement plans and pensions, workman's compensation, and unemployment insurance are regulated by law. The legal environment must be monitored because it is always changing. For example, there are a number of bills pending before Congress that, if passed, will make changes to the Fair Labor Standards Act, eliminate affirmative action programs, prohibit discrimination against gays and lesbians, and permit the mandatory retirement of police and firefighters when they reach a certain age.

Reinventing Organizations

To meet the challenges just identified, public and nonprofit agencies must be flexible and attuned to the needs of society. They must seek to improve the quality of their services by engaging in strategic human resource management. Recruitment and selection strategies must be innovative, career development opportunities must be provided, work assignments must be flexible, and policies must reward superior performers and hold accountable marginal employees. These policies must be developed and administered with the principles of equity, efficiency, and effectiveness. Performance standards must be designed to promote the goals and values of organizations.

Creating a Government That Works Better and Costs Less, the report of the National Performance Review (1993), acknowledged the need to redesign, reinvent, and reinvigorate the federal government. It proposed to do this by "cutting red tape," "putting customers first," "empowering employees," and "cutting back to basics." Specific HRM proposals were to create a flexible and responsive hiring system, reform the pay and classification systems, improve performance and award programs, and improve labor-management relations.

Hard Truths/Tough Choices: An Agenda for State and Local Reform (1993)—the first report of the National Commission on the State and Local Public Service, more commonly referred to as the "Winter Commission Report," after William F. Winter, who was the commission's chairman—recommended changes to revitalize state and local governments. HRM-related reforms included flattening the bureaucracy by reducing the number of management layers and thinning the ranks of the managers who remain. The report recognized that responsive government needs to transfer personnel dollars to the front line, and that the demands placed on employees who provide direct services, such as social workers, public health nurses, and job counselors, are usually unrealistic and inhibit quality performance.

The report recommended that personnel systems should be deregulated, that civil service systems should be reformed, and that the use of veterans preference and seniority should be minimized. It questioned the efficacy of most civil service systems. The cornerstones of such systems typically include a rule of three, which means that supervisors can only select one of the top three candidates among the many who are qualified. The report recommended that preference granted for years of seniority should also be scrutinized. It questioned how merit can exist when based on years employed instead of performance. The commission believed that merit can best be realized through a decentralized system that permits departments to address issues of selection, career mobility, pay, diversity, and terminations.

To survive, organizations need employees with new skills. The changes suggested in these reports should result in a more flexible and skilled workforce. The Winter Commission Report identified five skill areas that are needed by the new public manager: competency in team building, competency in communication, competency in involving employees, commitment to cultural awareness, and commitment to quality. These skills have HRM implications in regard to recruitment, selection, and training.

Governments should create a learning environment by restoring employee training and education budgets, creating a new skills package for all employees, basing pay increases on skills rather than on time in position, insisting on a new kind of problem-solving public manager rather than merely a paper pusher, and encouraging a new style of labor-management communication. Employers must ask themselves how to meet the public's objectives, satisfy the organization's stakeholders, and be more responsive to the public it serves. These recommendations acknowledge that organizations need to invest in their human capital. Employees need continuous training so they can acquire the new skills that will enable them to perform more challenging tasks. To be successful, all employees, regardless of their positions and technical expertise, need to have communication skills, to be competent in team building, and to possess a sense of cultural awareness and a commitment to quality. Training can be used to teach and refine those skills.

Other task force reports suggest that government at the federal, state, and local levels needs to be reinvented and reengineered if the public sector is to fulfill its missions (see, for example, Columbia University Graduate Program in Public Policy and Administration, 1993; Governor's Human Resources Advisory Council, 1993; Ingraham & Rosenbloom, 1990; National Commission on the Public Service, 1989; Office of Personnel Management, 1993). Threads running consistently through these reports are the need to restructure centralized personnel systems, to attract and retain energetic and competent personnel with technical and professional skills, to reengineer management systems to best utilize the workforce, and to improve the quality of service and productivity of workers.

It is not just public agencies that have to deal with change. Nonprofits, dependent upon government for most of their revenue, must compete with other nonprofits, government agencies, and for-profit agencies for shrinking dollars. Faced with the same changes that are confronting public organizations, nonprofits must demonstrate that they are capable of providing cost-effective professional services. The nature of work has changed, and like public agencies, nonprofit organizations require their employees to have more professional and technical skills than they used to need. In both sectors there is a greater reliance on technology. Advances in technology call for advanced education, continuous training, and possibly the addition of new benefits, such as educational leaves or tuition reimbursement. Jobs may have to be redesigned in order to take advantage of employee skills and to enhance job satisfaction. Job rotation, job enlargement, and job enrichment have become critical HRM components.

Strategic Human Resources Management

Due to this increasing turbulence, organizations must think strategically as never before, and they must translate their insights into effective strategies for meeting future challenges (Bryson, 1988). Human resources functions must be active components in these responses. Strategic planning and HRM activities must be integrated and work together so that agencies can confront and manage impending challenges and change. Problems need to be diagnosed and strategies need to be implemented. HRM departments must be linked with the strategy of the organization, and HRM activities must be integrated into the everyday work of line managers and employees (Perry, 1993a).

Conventional HRM departments are thought of by most employees and managers as regulators and enforcers, concerned with compliance to rules and regulations, rather then as partners working in sync with them. Line managers typically view personnel specialists as obstructionists, while personnel specialists see line managers as uncooperative, disinterested, and antagonistic to merit principles (Perry, 1993b, p. 14). At the federal, state, and local levels, HRM departments are not perceived as being integrated into the strategic planning and policy development (Oppenheimer & Paguta, 1993; Ospina, 1992; Perry, 1993a, 1993b; Sampson, 1993; Hays & Kearney, 1992).

HRM departments need to expand their scope of activities beyond being just functional specialists concerned with staffing, evaluation, training, and compensation. Instead, they need to be concerned with how the organization can be more competitive and effective. By soliciting ideas from employees and managers and by listening to their concerns, HRM departments can become valuable members of the management team (Schuler, 1990).

Summary

An uncertain external environment coupled with changing needs for organizational skills have facilitated a shift in the importance of HRM functions. Organizations need individuals with the right technical knowledge, skills, abilities, and other characteristics, but they also need people who are flexible and willing to deal with rapid and unstructured changes. Public and nonprofit sector jobs are increasingly more professional in nature, requiring higher levels of education. At the same time there is a decrease in jobs requiring manual labor. Employees in public and nonprofit agencies need to be able to deal with a variety of people, many who have a stake in the agency. Taxpayers, clients, customers, elected officials, donors, contractors, board members, and special interest groups are just some of the stakeholders concerned about agency performance. HRM specialists should be team players working with line managers to identify such employees. Together they should identify any political, technological, financial, and social changes affecting the organization, and assist current employees in adapting to those changes.

The next chapter demonstrates how strategic human resources management can prepare today's organizations for the challenges they will be confronting tomorrow.

Chapter Two

Strategic Human Resources Management and Planning

Traditional human resources management (HRM) starts *after* agencies have developed their basic missions and strategic objectives. Management seldom considers the talents and capabilities of its present staff or the availability of new hires when establishing strategic plans. As a result, HRM departments and line managers are forced to react to the strategic plans instead of taking proactive postures.

Strategic human resources management (SHRM) is based on the belief that realistic planning is not possible unless it takes into consideration information on current and potential human resources. Organizational objectives should be formulated after relevant data on the quantity and potential of available human resources have been reviewed. Are there human resources available for short and long-term objectives? To compete, organizations must be able to anticipate, influence, and manage the forces that impact their ability to remain competitive. In the service sector, this means they must be able to manage their human resource capabilities. All too often agencies have relied on short-term service requirements to direct their HRM policies and practices. Little thought has been given to long-term implications. By invoking SHRM, agencies are better able to match their human resources requirements with the demands of the market and the needs of the organization. The human resources focus is not just on individual employee issues; it also focuses on integrating human resources into the organization's strategy. It becomes part of the visionary process.

This chapter defines SHRM, strategic planning, and human resources planning, and illustrates their importance to organizational vitality and success.

Strategic Human Resources Management

SHRM recognizes the role that employees play in contributing to an organization's success. It becomes part of the strategic planning and policy development process, guiding and supporting agency efforts as attempts are made to meet the demands imposed on the agency from its external and internal environments. SHRM is driven by an organization's strategy instead of by its functional or administrative activities (Perry, 1993a).

For Schuler (1992, p. 18), "SHRM is about integration and adaptation. It ensures that (1) HRM is fully integrated with the strategy and the strategic needs of the organization, (2) human resource policies cohere across both policy areas and hierarchies, and (3) human resource practices are adjusted, accepted, and used by line managers and employees as part of their everyday work."

For public and nonprofit organizations to remain viable, adapting to change is critical, otherwise they risk stagnation. No one will deny the unsettling nature of change. With change comes insecurity and uncertainty. However, change is an important part of growth, and organizations need to manage change. HRM departments must work with employees and managers to confront impending change. They should be partners in the design of staffing requirements, the identification of employee development needs and career opportunities, and the development of benefit packages and evaluation instruments. HRM specialists need to be connected to and knowledgeable about organizational objectives, and to be perceived as credible by line managers (Schuler, 1992 p. 27).

In an effort to transform its HRM department from a reactive department to a proactive one, the Minnesota Department of Transportation established the Human Resource Planning Board (HRPB). The HRPB is composed of managers from each division and personnel from the office of human resources who are responsible for identifying and prioritizing trends and opportunities that will impact the agency. Planning strategically for emerging human resources issues is a key responsibility of the planning board—particularly, identifying external and internal trends that may have human resources consequences for the agency. To do this the HRPB

Solicits issues and opportunities from internal management

Screens and prioritizes issues, trends, and opportunities

Assigns responsibility to develop strategies, solutions, and alternatives that satisfy or address the issues

Evaluates and selects from strategies, solutions, and alternatives, and recommends action to the deputy commissioner's staff

Implements, markets, and provides sustained support for selected strategies and solutions

Revisits and modifies strategies and solutions as needed (International Personnel Management Association, 1993, pp. 1–2)

When asked by the International Personnel Management Association why the HRPB is important, the staff of the office of human resources responded that it is more effective for managers to identify and address human resources issues on a long-term strategic basis than only on a short-term basis. Also, when managers are not involved in the HRM process, they tend to be suspicious of the HRM office's ideas. In addition, involving managers gives them a better understanding of the various HRM issues and the difficulty in solving some problems, such as what the Department of Transportation will become in twenty years. Will it continue to build roads or will it be more multimodel? If changes are made, how many engineers will be needed? With changes in technology causing many skills to become obsolete, how will the agency keep its employees trained?

Strategic Planning

Strategic planning is used by many public and nonprofit organizations to guide their future endeavors and the use of their available resources, as well as to identify needed additional resources, whether finances, physical facilities, equipment, or human resources. Strategic planning determines organizational purposes and objectives. It begins by asking the following questions:

1. Why does the organization exist?
2. What contribution does it make?
3. Who are the customers/clients now and who will they be in the future?
4. How would the current operations of the agency be characterized?
5. What are the key assumptions (legislative, technological, competitive, and financial) supporting current operations?
6. What are the organization's core competencies and how can they be maximized (Ulrich, 1992, p. 55)?

Once these questions have been answered, the external environment needs to be scanned for opportunities and threats. The external forces that will affect the organization and the people in it need to be considered. These forces include workforce patterns, economic conditions, competition, regulation, social values, and technological developments. The availability and stability of financial support; the advancement of technological changes, legal regulations, and social and cultural changes; and the evolution of human resources requirements must be considered when developing strategic plans. After the external factors are assessed, the internal strengths and weaknesses of the organization's incumbents must be identified. Factors to include in an internal assessment are current workforce skills, retirement patterns, demographic profiles, and human resources capabilities. This information can be used to forecast the organization's capabilities to confront its future opportunities and threats. The ultimate feasibility of strategic planning depends on the people who make it operational.

An example of a community-based nonprofit that has bravely confronted its external and internal environments with an SHRM plan is Places for People (PFP) (McAdoo, 1992; McAdoo & Pynes, 1995; Places for People, 1991–1992, 1993). PFP is a private, nonprofit organization dedicated to serving people in the St. Louis metropolitan area who have or are impacted by serious and persistent mental illness. It provides rehabilitative, support, and referral services. PFP began in 1972 with a supported housing program and now provides supported housing services for 165 residents. People live in apartments of their own choosing—some with roommates, some alone. A continuous treatment team works with the clients from the point of initial screening, intake, and development of an individualized treatment plan, through the process of moving into an apartment. The team provides a range of services, such as assistance with shopping, cooking, and budgeting, medication monitoring, and twenty-four-hour crisis intervention. Employees meet regularly with their clients to help them work toward their personal goals and to provide support during the difficult times.

Three years after establishing its supported housing program, PFP expanded to include a psychosocial rehabilitation center. The center is organized on the clubhouse model. Clients are considered members, and they contribute their time, energy, and talents to preparing meals, operating a thrift store, answering the phones, and performing building maintenance or clerical work. The center offers workshops in art, exercise, crafts, social skills, and health and nutrition. It also offers field trips such as visits to sporting and cultural events, and activities such as camping and canoeing.

PFP expanded again in 1983, when it began to provide services supporting a group home. The group home is a transitional, residential facility staffed twenty-four hours a day. Residents preparing for community living spend up to eighteen months working on independent living and vocational rehabilitation skills. Individual goals are set for residents, with the objective of preparing them for independent living.

Until 1992, each program functioned separately within the agency; each had its own staff, director, and program policies. In 1992, the agency went through a restructuring incited by information revealed during strategic planning sessions. The purpose of the planning sessions was to identify critical issues facing the agency, possible directions for the future, opportunities or threats, strengths and weaknesses, and potential allies and competitors.

The strategic planning sessions were attended by representatives from all agency programs, the board of directors, consumers, and executive staff. The planning process was facilitated by an outside consultant. The following critical goals were identified (McAdoo, 1992, pp. 167–168):

1. To identify new services that the agency must provide in order to continue to meet the needs of a changing population in difficult economic times

2. To identify new funding sources and other resources that will be necessary to provide these services
3. To identify and hire the staff necessary to provide these additional services
4. To identify ways to involve clients and/or consumers at all levels of the organization and in the agency's decision-making process
5. To increase community awareness about Places for People and the needs of individuals with severe and persistent mental illness

As a result of the strategic planning process, some serious internal personnel issues came to light. Employees did not feel involved in the agency or a sense of ownership in the success of the organization; they did not feel that they had the authority to do their jobs or that they were responsible or accountable for the work they performed; they did not feel that policies were administered equitably across program lines, that management was interested in the success of line staff, or that mutual trust and respect existed among coworkers or between management and line staff; they did not feel that they had a voice in the agency decisions that affected them, or that information was communicated effectively throughout the organization.

In response to these concerns, a focus group was created to examine job enrichment issues within the agency. Three guidelines were stipulated by the executive director: (1) the group could not suggest ideas that would cost the agency more money; (2) the group must be mindful of the needs of the agency as a whole, as well as the needs of the clients; and (3) the suggestions put forth for correcting or improving the situation must be practical and realistic.

This internal evaluation caused PFP to reexamine its philosophical values and prompted the agency to begin to restructure its organizational design. As a result, PFP's program components were combined so that all services are now provided by four integrated teams of professionals. Each team now provides both rehabilitative and community support services. Staff are no longer divided along programmatic lines, and everyone is involved in providing the full range of services, including treatment planning, resource management, assistance in the activities of daily living, problem solving, social skills, substance abuse education, medication management, budgeting, community integration, advocacy, and crisis assessment. The agency is open seven days a week and the staff are available twenty-four hours a day to respond to crisis situations. Team members are responsible for planning their own work schedules, which are designed to meet the needs of a diverse client population. Teams are responsible for setting their own goals and objectives in the areas of productivity, client services, and paperwork.

Staff are invited to meetings of the board of directors, and staff representatives participate on board committees. Team members meet daily to review activities, and team leaders meet weekly with other executive staff for updates on client and personnel issues. The agency meets together as a whole on a monthly basis for ongoing training, problem solving, and discussions of new developments in the community mental health field.

These changes were not without controversy. Many employees who were unable to make the transition to a team approach resigned from the agency. Their vacancies, however, enabled the agency to hire new staff members with expertise that the incumbents lacked, such as skills in vocational rehabilitation, substance abuse, and dual diagnosis. Seventeen months after the restructuring, both the staff and clients believed that the agency had become more responsive to the needs of its clients, staff, and community (McAdoo & Pynes, 1995).

Given the turbulence of the health care field and the shift in many states to managed-care mental health systems patterned after the medical model, PFP and other community health care providers will have to continue to reevaluate their futures. Managed care is just one of the many changes affecting public and nonprofit agencies. Organizations need to monitor the changes in their external environments and understand what human resources capabilities will be needed to remain competitive.

Human Resources Planning

Public sector organizations often have a crisis orientation rather than a strategic focus. Public agencies often cope with changes rather than plan for them (Ospina, 1992). Human resources planning is a way to develop a strategic approach to preventing problems.

Agencies need to anticipate their personnel requirements so that they are prepared to deal with changing situations. As described earlier in this chapter, SHRM forces managers to identify future organizational needs and to review the demand for and the readily available supply of skills in the organization and workforce; it can also assist in the development of programs. An immediate outcome of strategic human resources planning could be a shift from reactive to assertive organizations.

SHRM closely monitors an agency's external environment for changes that will impact the organization's ability to fulfill its mission. These changes may be societal trends like those discussed in Chapter One, or they may be changes restricted to the agency's immediate surroundings, such as an election that changes the composition of the city council, or a decision by elected officials to eliminate funding for specific programs (for example, a state or local government decision to rescind its funding for a shelter that provides services to the homeless). Government programs are also affected by the political whims of elected officials trying to be responsive to their constituents.

Changes in an agency's external environment will impact its internal environment. If programs are eliminated, will staff need to be laid off? Will employees receive training when new technology is introduced? If services are expanded, will new staff be recruited, or might paraprofessional staff be encouraged to apply for the positions?

Human resources planning is a critical component of SHRM. It is the process of analyzing and identifying the need for and availability of human resources to meet the agency's objectives. Forecasting is used to assess past trends, evaluate the present situation, and project future events. Forecasting and planning complement each other because forecasts identify expectations while plans establish concrete goals and objectives.

Agencies must consider how to allocate people to jobs over long periods. Attempts must be made to anticipate expansions or reductions in programs or other changes that may affect the organization. Based on these analyses, plans can be made for the recruitment and selection of new employees, the shifting of employees to different programs or units, or the retraining of incumbent employees.

Forecasting human resources requirements involves determining the number and types of employees needed by skill level. First, agencies need to audit the skills of incumbent employees and determine their capabilities and weaknesses. Positions must also be audited. In most organizations there are likely to be jobs that are vulnerable, that technology or reengineering are ready to replace. Job analyses must be conducted to provide information on existing jobs. The basic requirements of a job should be defined and converted to job specifications that specify the minimum knowledge, skills, abilities, and other characteristics (KSAOCs) necessary for effective performance. The skill requirements of positions do change, so any changes that occur must be monitored and reflected in the job specifications.

It is not enough to monitor changes in positions. Organizations must also keep abreast of the skills that their employees possess. Human resources planning uses data inventories to integrate the planning and utilization functions of SHRM. Data inventories compile summary information, such as the characteristics of employees, the distribution of employees by position, employees' performance, and career objectives. Specific data that are typically catalogued are age, education, career path, current skills, work experience, aspirations, performance evaluations, years with the organization, and jobs for which one is qualified. Expected vacancies due to retirement, promotion, transfer, sick leave, relocation, or termination are also tracked. Using a computerized human resources information system to compile these data makes the retrieval of this information readily available for forecasting human resources needs.

When forecasting the availability of human resources, agencies need to consider both the internal and the external supply of qualified candidates. The internal supply of candidates is influenced by training and development, and by transfer, promotion, and retirement policies. A succession analysis should be prepared that forecasts the supply of people for certain positions. Succession plans should be used to identify potential personnel changes, to select backup candidates, and to keep track of attrition. The external supply of candidates is also influenced by a variety of factors, including developments in technology, the actions of competing employers, geographic location, and government regulations.

SHRM attempts to match the available supply of labor with the forecasted demand in light of the strategic plan of the agency. If necessary skills do not exist in the present workforce, employees will need to be trained in the new skills, or external recruitment must be used to bring those skills to the agency. If the necessary skills are not available within the organization, the employer must identify where employees with those skills are likely to be found and recruitment strategies must be developed.

Many techniques are available for forecasting human resources needs. They range in sophistication from computer simulations to human best guesses. In most instances, forecasting is a combination of quantitative methods and subjective judgments.

The Importance of Strategic Human Resources Management

As discussed in Chapter One, many changes have taken place in the public and nonprofit sectors that impact the financial stability and viability of agencies and programs. This has lead to increased scrutiny on the part of the public, stakeholders, clients, and funding sources as to the efficiency and effectiveness of services and programs. This scrutiny has led to an understanding of the importance of the staff who provide the services in the nonprofit and public sectors. Agencies need to ask the following questions: What kinds of skills do employees need? What is the best way to identify and select employees? What kind of training and education will be needed? Human resources needs must continuously be reappraised relative to agency plans and objectives.

The future viability of an organization and its human resources capabilities are interrelated and must be considered together. HRM must be vertically integrated with strategic planning and horizontally integrated with other human resources functions, such as training and development, compensation and benefits, recruitment and selection, labor relations, and the evaluation of the human resources planning process, to allow for adjustments to be made to confront rapidly changing environmental conditions. SHRM guides management in identifying and implementing the appropriate human resources learning activities for resolving organizational problems or adapting to meet new opportunities.

SHRM determines the human resources needs of the agency and ensures that qualified personnel are recruited and developed to meet organizational needs. Should there be a shift in demand for services, agencies must know whether there are potential employees with the requisite skills available to provide these services and whether the agency's finances can afford the costs associated with additional compensation and benefits. Forecasting an agency's human resources supply reveals the characteristics of its internal supply of labor; it also helps to assess the promotability of incumbent employees, implement succession planning and salary planning, and identify areas in which external recruitment and/or training and development are necessary.

Training and development are essential to the effective use of an organization's human resources and are an integral part of its human resources planning. Training is used to remedy immediate needs, while development is concerned with long-term objectives and the ability to cope with change. Training should be viewed as a continuous process. There will always be new employees, new positions, new problems, and changes in technology and in the external and internal environments, which will require a planned approach to training and development and its integration with other HRM functions. Training and development influence recruitment, selection, career planning, and the compatibility between agency goals and employee aspirations. Training and development programs must be integrated in order to complement the organization's mission and operations.

Organizations used to hire employees to fit the characteristics of a particular job. Now it is important for organizations to select employees who fit the characteristics not only of the position but also of the organization (Bowen, Ledford, & Nathan, 1991). HRM specialists must work with managers to assess human resources needs. Together they must project the demand for services, develop new resources, and determine the appropriate reallocations of services. Recruitment and training must be tied to the organization's mission. Turnover and retirements must be anticipated and planned for. HRM departments must track the skills of incumbent employees and keep skill inventories. They must also provide for employee development, education, and specialized training if organizations are going to successfully meet the future.

Summary

The role that employees play in meeting the challenges of today's workplace cannot be underestimated. Both the nonprofit and public sectors are part of the service sector economy and are judged on the basis of the performance of their staffs. Because of this reliance on staff, agencies must build closer ties between strategic planning and HRM if they are to be successful. SHRM is such a bridge. Agencies must adapt their human resources needs to fit their modified missions and the forces brought on by external demands.

SHRM is the result when HRM is vertically integrated with strategic planning and horizontally integrated with other human resources functions, such as training and development, compensation and benefits, recruitment and selection, labor relations, and the evaluation of the human resources planning process. The integration of human resources techniques with the forecasting elements of human resources planning allows an organization's day-to-day human resources activities to be consistent with the organization's long-term focus.

Chapter Three

Managing a Diverse Workforce

The demographic composition of the American workforce has changed since the 1970s and 1980s. Women, persons of color, persons of different ethnic and religious backgrounds, persons with physical and mental disabilities, and homosexuals are more visible in the workplace. The civil rights movements of the past and present have called attention to the historical patterns of discrimination that resulted in social, economic, and political inequality across America. These movements have resulted in the passage of a variety of federal, state, and local laws in an attempt to remedy what was perceived to be unfair and unequal treatment. For organizations to remain viable, not only must they comply with the laws governing equal employment opportunity, but in today's multicultural workplace they must also understand the role that cultural differences can play in an organization. Employers must learn how to manage diversity and capitalize on each member's contributions to enhance the organization's effectiveness. This chapter discusses new management challenges, such as valuing organizational diversity as a vital organizational resource (Loden & Rosener, 1991). The federal laws governing equal employment opportunity will be discussed in the following chapter.

Consider the following examples:

• The Maryland state police department agreed to pay approximately $243,000 in back pay to ninety-eight white men and a white woman who charged that they were unlawfully passed over for promotions given to minorities. The department will also promote seventeen employees, provide increased retirement benefits, and pay $50,000 in attorneys' fees (*Liebno v. Maryland State Police,* 1995).

•   A California university agreed to pay $1 million to settle a claim by an Asian American professor that she was denied tenure based on her race and gender. She was denied tenure in the architecture department despite being highly qualified (*Wang v. University of California,* 1996).

•   An employer revoked the offer of a maintenance supervisor job to an individual with a history of epilepsy who had not had a seizure in more than ten years.

•   A white Drug Enforcement Administration (DEA) agent was awarded $180,000 in damages after being suspended for ten days without pay for speaking up for his black partner, who had been harassed by white agents because of his race. The agent sued under Title VII of the Civil Rights Act of 1964, alleging that his black partner had been subject to racial slurs to his face and on the telephone. The award included an order that all references to the suspension be removed from his file (*Probst v. Reno,* 1995).

•   The U.S. Court of Appeals at Atlanta held that the state of Georgia unlawfully burdened a woman's first amendment right to intimate association by withdrawing a job offer when it learned she planned to marry her lesbian partner in a Jewish ceremony. The woman was offered a job in the state's attorney general's office, where she had previously worked as a law clerk. When the attorney general became aware that she was marrying another woman, a practice not recognized by Georgia law, he withdrew the offer, writing that inaction would constitute tacit approval and "jeopardize the proper function" of his office. The court held that the state must show it had a compelling interest in denying her employment after it learned of her wedding plans (*Shahar v. Bowers,* 1995).

These examples demonstrate some of the complexities that arise in managing a diverse workforce. Despite the integration into the workforce of women, racial and ethnic minorities, persons with disabilities, and homosexuals, individuals and employers have much to learn in regard to diversity. Although members of protected classes and homosexuals have received the most attention in the literature, diversity can also include differences in underlying attributes or nonobservable differences, such as working styles, values, and personality types, as well as differences in culture, socioeconomic background, educational background, occupational background or professional orientation, industry experience, organizational membership, and group tenure (Milliken & Martins, 1996).

Fairness in recruitment, selection, promotion, performance evaluation, training and development, and compensation are just some of the challenges facing strategic human resources management. Organizations must find ways to provide advancement opportunities for the increasing numbers of minorities and women without placing white males at an unfair disadvantage. Dissatisfaction with traditional affirmative action programs will necessitate that organizations develop new programs to ensure that diversity enhances the work environment. Not only must obvious differences in race, gender, age, disability, and national origin be recognized, but differences in personality types, working styles, and professional training and orientations (for example, creative, technical, legal, and scientific) must also be considered as organizations move toward more collaborative, team-based strategies to provide services. The diversity literature and research has tended to focus on women, racial and ethnic minorities, and the disabled because, over the years, legislation, executive orders, and administrative rulings have been executed to eliminate discrimination against these groups and to promote their advancement in the workplace. No laws exist that prohibit discrimination against people relative to the underlying attributes—such as personality type, working style, professional training, and orientations—noted earlier. Because of this distinction, this chapter emphasizes diversity as it relates to members of protected classes, but it still recognizes that the commitment to workforce diversity is broader and includes the encouragement of dissimilar viewpoints.

Glass Ceilings

The term *glass ceiling* refers to the artificial barriers that block the advancement of women and minorities to upper-level managerial and executive positions within organizations. Such obstacles must be eliminated.

Studies have shown that African Americans, Asian Americans, Hispanics, and women are underrepresented in upper-level supervisory, management, and senior executive positions of federal employment (Cornwell & Kellough, 1994; Guy, 1993; Kim, 1993; Kim & Lewis, 1994; Lewis, 1988, 1994; Naff, 1994; Page, 1994; Sisneros, 1992; Swift, 1992–1993; U.S. Merit Systems Protection Board, 1991). Other studies confirm the existence of a glass ceiling at the state and local levels (Bullard & Wright, 1993; Guy, 1993, Rehfuss, 1986; Slack, 1987). The commitment of women and minorities to their jobs is typically questioned because of their family responsibilities or inability to relocate, or because of doubts about their leadership styles (Swift, 1992–1993; Naff, 1994). The assumption that they are less committed often results in their being bypassed for important assignments and developmental opportunities.

Hodgkinson, Weitzman, Toppe, and Noga (1992) report that in 1990, 69 percent of employees in the nonprofit sector were female. But Michael O'Neill (Odendahl & O'Neill, 1994) questions whether the influence of women in and through the nonprofit sector is as great as their statistical predominance. Steinberg and Jacobs (1994) and Odendahl and Youmans (1994) suggest that the nonprofit sector is in reality controlled by an elite male power structure, and that within the sector occupations are distributed according to gender. For example, men are financial officers and doctors while women are teachers and nurses. Women may constitute the majority of the nonprofit workforce, but they are typically prevented from reaching top executive and policymaking positions.

Research by Preston (1990) indicates that women can often be found in executive positions in nonprofit organizations. However, Preston attributes this finding to women willing to work for lower salaries in exchange for the increased skill development opportunities and responsibilities provided by the nonprofit sector.

Regardless of the employment sector, subtle assumptions, attitudes, and stereotypes exist in the workplace, manifesting as organizational cultures that affect the mobility patterns of women and minorities. The rest of this chapter discusses the difference between equal employment opportunity and affirmative action, and the implications for managing a diverse workforce. Strategies that employers can implement to accommodate multicultural differences are reviewed.

Equal Employment Opportunity and Affirmative Action

Many statutes, executive orders, court decisions, and administrative regulations exist that prohibit employment discrimination against persons due to their race, color, sex, national origin, religion, or disability. Employment decisions are to be based on merit and job-related qualifications, not on one's membership in a certain classification. Equal employment opportunity requires employers not to discriminate in the administration and execution of all human resources management (HRM) practices such as recruitment, selection, promotions, training, compensation, career development, discipline, and labor-management relations. An overview of these laws is provided in Chapter Four. In passing the laws Congress assumed that outlawing deliberate discrimination and punishing employers found guilty of unfair practices was sufficient to eradicate the vestiges of years of discrimination.

Although the passing of these laws meant that overt discrimination was no longer tolerated, women and minorities were still underrepresented in the workforce. A more assertive strategy was needed to correct for past and present discrimination. That strategy was affirmative action. Executive Order 11246 states that "an affirmative action program is a set of specific and results-oriented procedures to which the contractor commits itself to apply every good faith effort. The objective of those procedures plus such efforts is equal employment opportunity" (60–2.10).

In 1965, President Johnson signed Executive Order 11246, which prohibits discrimination in federal employment on the basis of race, creed, color, or national origin. In 1968, this order was amended by Executive Order 11375, in which the word "creed" was changed to "religion" and sex discrimination was added to the list of prohibited items. The executive order applies to all federal agencies, contractors, and subcontractors, including all of the facilities of the agency holding the contract, regardless of at which plant the work is conducted. Contractors and subcontractors with more than $50,000 in government business and fifty or more employees are not only prohibited from discriminating but must also take affirmative action to ensure that applicants and employees are not treated differently because of their sex, religion, race, color, and national origin. The Rehabilitation Act of 1973 and the

Vietnam Era Veterans Readjustment Act of 1974 also require federal contractors or subcontractors to take affirmative action for the employment and advancement of qualified disabled persons and veterans, and qualified veterans of the Vietnam era.

Affirmative action has often been interpreted and criticized as requiring the implementation of quotas regardless of an individual's qualifications and ability to perform a job. In reality, affirmative action may refer to several strategies, including active recruitment of groups underrepresented in an organization, eliminating irrelevant employment practices that bar protected groups from employment, and the most controversial one, granting preferential treatment to protected groups. The effectiveness of affirmative action is represented by the extent to which employers make an effort through their personnel practices to attract, retain, and upgrade members of protected classes as a condition of doing business with the government.

Affirmative action is presently under review by the Clinton administration, the U.S. Congress, and many state governments, such as Massachusetts, Michigan, Pennsylvania, Colorado, Texas, and Oregon. On June 1, 1995, Governor Pete Wilson of California dismantled some of the affirmative action programs intended to help women and minorities in his state. He cut in half the number of state highway contracts targeted for minority-owned businesses, limited some seasonal programs that employed large numbers of minorities, and eliminated about 150 boards across the state that advised agencies on affirmative action and hiring goals for some 150,000 full-time state workers. He urged the citizens of California to vote in favor of the California Civil Rights Initiative, a proposal to eliminate affirmative action in state jobs and higher education enrollment, which was passed in November 1996.

Critics of affirmative action claim that it results in reverse discrimination and that the costs of complying with its guidelines are too expensive. Claims of reverse discrimination suggest that special advantages or preferential treatment given to women and minorities promote unfair treatment against white males and are thus still discrimination. A second argument against affirmative action is that the dollar costs associated with complying with the regulations are high and that compliance results in lower productivity because of a less qualified workforce. There is, however, little evidence to validate these arguments. Alfred W. Blumrosen analyzed federal court decisions issued between 1990 and 1994 and found that reverse discrimination cases accounted for only 1 to 3 percent of some three thousand employment bias cases. Many of the claimants were found to be less qualified for the job than the chosen woman or minority applicant. When affirmative action programs were challenged as unfair to white men, the courts looked at the facts in each case and either upheld the programs, invalidated them, or called for reexamination of them in light of current conditions ("Reverse Bias Not Widespread," 1995). Despite the lack of empirical evidence that affirmative action plans have led to the selection or promotion of extensive numbers of "unqualified" women and minorities, research has found that women and minorities are stigmatized as less competent than white men (Heilman, Lucas, & Block, 1992). Although Executive Order 11246, the Rehabilitation Act of 1973, and the Vietnam Era Veterans Readjustment Act apply only to organizations receiving federal funds, many public and nonprofit organizations have decided to implement voluntary affirmative action programs to redress previous discriminatory employment practices, or to make their workforce more representative of the constituents or clients they serve.

The Difference Between Compliance with Laws and Managing Diversity

Equal employment opportunity and affirmative action are legal requirements designed to bring women and minorities into the workforce. Managing diversity requires more than just compliance with laws. The management of diversity consists of "management processes to create a supportive work environment for employees already on board, and to develop and fully include all of them in order to make the organization more productive" (U.S. Merit Systems Protection Board, 1993, p. xiii).

To manage diversity, employers must first understand and then manage their organizational cultures. *Organizational culture* is defined as the values, beliefs, assumptions, expectations, attitudes, and norms shared by a majority of the organization's members. Wilson (1989, p. 91) believes that "every organization has a culture, that is a persistent, patterned way of thinking about the central tasks of and human relationships within an organization. Culture is to an organization what personality is to an individual. Like human culture generally, it is passed from one generation to the next. It changes slowly, if at all."

Organizations possess not only a dominant culture, but subcultures can also emerge. Subcultures often develop to reflect common problems, situations, or experiences that employees face. Wilson (1989) notes that within the U.S. Navy, different subcultures exist for naval personnel assigned to submarines, aircraft carriers, or battleships.

Organizational culture is perceived to be valuable when it helps to orient new employees to expected job-related behaviors and performance levels. A strong culture can minimize the need for formal rules and regulations because values, traditions and rituals, heroes and heroines, and the informal communication network that provides information and interprets messages sent through the organization serve to reduce ambiguity (Deal & Kennedy, 1982). Employers must be aware that an entrenched organizational culture can be a liability when the shared culture will not react to change, or change to enhance the organization's effectiveness. At the International Association of Chiefs of Police conference held in October 1995, one of the topics discussed was changing the "code of silence" that protects racist and corrupt police officers (Lantigua, 1995). The Central Intelligence Agency (CIA) is an example of an agency that possessed a culture unfair to women. The CIA agreed to pay $940,000 to settle a suit that alleged that it was biased against women holding or seeking positions as basic-category officers. The settlement included back pay, salary increases, and retroactive placements. The CIA was also required to revise its employment practices to include management training, to monitor future promotion rates, and to increase the level of feedback given to female employees (*Conway v. Studeman*, 1995).

The increase of women and minorities in the workforce is going to continue. The attitudes, beliefs, values, and customs of people in society are an integral part of their culture, and affect their behavior on the job. Research has found that men, women, and minorities do not have a common culture or organizational life; rather, each group identifies, defines, and organizes its experience in the organization in unique ways that influence group members' reactions to work assignments, leadership styles, and reward systems (Fine, Johnson, and Ryan, 1990). These differences create the potential for communication problems, which lead to increased organizational conflict.

Management must balance two conflicting goals: get employees to accept the dominant values, and encourage acceptance of differences. Robbins (1994, p. 259) calls this the "paradox of diversity." It is important for new employees to accept the organization's culture; otherwise they are not likely to be accepted. But at the same time, management must acknowledge and demonstrate support for the differences that these employees bring to the workplace. Valuing diversity means recognizing and appreciating that individuals are different, that diversity can be an advantage if it is well managed, and that diversity should be encouraged. Accepting diverse ideas encourages employees to be more creative, which leads to greater flexibility and problem-solving capabilities (Fine, Johnson, & Ryan, 1990; Ospina, 1996).

Human Resources Implications for Managing Diversity

Employers must understand that compliance with equal employment opportunity and affirmative action does not necessarily mean that incumbent employees will respect or accept the new entrants. HRM policies and procedures must adjust to cope with an increasingly diverse workforce. Employers will be under constant pressure to ensure equality with respect to employment, advancement opportunities, and compensation. Employers need to value diversity. Many times diversity is addressed in terms of visible differences, such as race, gender, age, or disability. But an employee's sexual orientation, religion, inconspicuous disability, education, work style, lifestyle, and culture are not as readily visible, and various combinations of differences of these less visible differences can exist in one person. Even differences such as parenthood or responsibility for elderly relatives are components of employee diversity, needing accommodation through parental leaves, flexible work schedules, or child/elder care assistance. Employers and employees must understand that there are many dimensions of diversity.

Training management and employees to welcome diversity is essential. Cox and Blake (1991) identified awareness training and skill building as two popular types of training. Awareness training focuses on creating an understanding of the need for and means of managing and valuing diversity. It is designed to increase the participants' awareness of diversity-related issues such as stereotyping and cross-cultural insensitivity.

Skill-building training educates employees on specific cultural differences and how to respond to such differences in the workplace. To reinforce the organization's commitment to valuing diversity, Cox and Blake (1991) suggest that employers conduct cultural and systems audits. These audits consist of comprehensive analysis of the agency's organizational culture and HRM systems such as recruitment, performance appraisals, career patterns, and compensation. The objective of the audits is to uncover whether there are sources of potential bias that may inadvertently put some employees at a disadvantage. If changes are made, they should be monitored and evaluated. Continued training and modifications in rewards and sanctions may need to be institutionalized (Cox & Blake, 1991).

Sexual harassment and discrimination against gays and lesbians are topics that should be included in multicultural diversity training curriculums along with the traditional topics of race, gender, disability, religion, and national origin. Over the last few years, allegations of sexual harassment and unfair treatment towards homosexuals have increased. Brief discussions of both topics follow.

Sexual Harassment

If women are going to contribute to an organization's effectiveness, their daily routines must be free from intimidation and the distraction brought about by sexual harassment. Employers have become more sensitive to the growing need for policies and procedures to eliminate sexual harassment in the workplace. Today, most organizations have sexual harassment policies in place and are demanding that managers and supervisors enforce them.

The Supreme Court ruled in *Meritor Savings Bank v. Vinson* (1986) that sexual harassment is a form of sexual discrimination, illegal under Title VII. Any workplace conduct that is "sufficiently severe or pervasive to alter the conditions of employment and create an abusive working environment" constitutes illegal sexual harassment. Sexual harassment is illegal because it constitutes discrimination with respect to a person's conditions of employment. The Equal Employment Opportunity Commission (1989, p. 197) has defined sexual harassment as

> unwelcome sexual advances, requests for sexual favors, and other verbal or physical conduct of a sexual nature when (1) submission to such conduct is made either explicitly or implicitly a term or condition of an individual's employment, (2) submission to or rejection of such conduct by an individual is used as the basis for employment decisions affecting such individual, or (3) such conduct has the purpose or effect of unreasonably interfering with an individual's work performance or creating an intimidating, hostile, or offensive working environment.

There are two forms of sexual harassment: *quid pro quo harassment,* a Latin term meaning "this for that," or *one thing in return for another* and *hostile environment harassment.* Quid pro quo harassment exists where the employer places sexual demands on the employee as a condition of that person receiving employment benefits—for example, when a supervisor requires that a subordinate go out on a date as a condition of receiving a promotion or a pay increase. The reverse is also considered quid pro quo harassment—for example, because a subordinate will not date a supervisor, the supervisor retaliates by assigning work of a less desirable nature to the employee or lowers the employee's performance evaluation rating.

Hostile environment sexual harassment does not require the loss of a tangible employment benefit. Instead, the focus is on unwelcome contact that is sufficiently severe or pervasive to alter the conditions of the employee's employment and create an abusive working environment. In *Ellison v. Brady* (1991), the ninth circuit federal appellate court created a "reasonable woman" standard that it applied to the issue of whether sexually oriented conduct constituted a hostile or offensive environment. The court believed that it was important to examine the behavior from the perspective of a reasonable woman since "a sex-blind reasonable person standard tends to be male-biased and tends to systematically ignore the experiences of women." Since research demonstrates that women and men differ in their responses to sexually oriented behavior, the court believed that it was inappropriate to use the viewpoint of a man (or men in general) to determine whether a reasonable woman would have found the conduct to be unwelcome, a requirement that the woman must meet in order to prevail. The standard moved from the "reasonable person" perspective to the "reasonable victim" perspective.

The most recent Supreme Court case addressing sexual harassment was *Harris v. Forklift Systems* (1993). In this case the Supreme Court reversed the decision of the U.S. Court of Appeals at Cincinnati that held that Theresa Harris was not the victim of sexual harassment because she did not prove that she suffered any psychological harm. The Supreme Court said that "Title VII comes into play before the harassing conduct leads to a nervous breakdown. . . . The conduct's effect on the employee's psychological well-being is just one factor that may be considered along with all other circumstances to be considered in determining hostile environment harassment, including the frequency of the discriminatory conduct, its severity, whether it is physically threatening or humiliating, or a mere offensive utterance, and whether it unreasonably interferes with an employee's work performance."

Sexual Orientation

No federal laws presently exist that prohibit discrimination on the basis of sexual orientation. On September 10, 1996, the United States Senate defeated the Employment Non-Discrimination Act by the margin of 50 to 49. The bill would have prohibited discrimination on the basis of sexual orientation. It defines sexual orientation as "lesbian, gay, bisexual, or heterosexual orientation, real or perceived, as manifested by identity, acts, statements or association." If the bill were to be passed, employers, employment agencies, and labor unions would be prohibited from using an individual's sexual orientation as the basis for an employment decision. The bill would not apply to employers with fewer than fifteen employees, to religious institutions, or to the military.

Although no federal protection presently exists, many state and local governments have enacted their own laws that prohibit discrimination against gays and lesbians. As of April 1996, nine states prohibit discrimination on account of sexual orientation. For example, Minnesota and Rhode Island have both amended their state human rights acts specifically to prohibit discrimination in employment on the basis of actual or perceived sexual orientation. In other states, governors have issued executive orders. More than one hundred counties and municipalities prohibit such discrimination. The National League of Cities has a constituency support group called Gay, Lesbian, and Bisexual Local Officials, and within the state of California, the Golden State Peace Officers Association has a support group called PRIDE Behind the Badge.

Federal employees are protected by the Civil Service Reform Act of 1978. It prohibits job discrimination for any non-job-related issue. In 1980, the Carter administration issued a policy statement specifically including sexual orientation bias. The statute covered executive branch offices and the Government Printing Office, but not the General Accounting Office or intelligence agencies. There is a support group for gay, lesbian, and federal employees called Federal GLOBE; and as of October 1994, at least twenty federal agencies had their own GLOBE groups (Walker, 1994).

On August 4, 1995, President Clinton issued Executive Order 12968, which forbade federal agencies from using sexual orientation as a reason for denying security clearances to lesbians and gays. The executive order extended coverage to private citizens working for defense contractors, engineering firms, and high-tech industries involved with the government. This order created the first uniform standard for U.S. agencies in granting security clearances, and requires federal agencies to recognize one another's security clearances. The Defense, Energy, and State Departments, the Office of Personnel Management, the U.S. Information Agency, the Federal Bureau of Investigation, the Secret Service, and the U.S. Customs Service already had stopped using homosexuality as a reason for denying security clearances for civilian workers.

Many nonprofit and private employers were at the forefront of prohibiting discrimination against gays and lesbians. They willingly promulgated their own personnel policies that protected the rights of gay and lesbian employees. Not fearing reprisals, many gay, lesbian, and bisexual support groups were first founded in those organizations. In addition to nondiscrimination policies, many nonprofit and private employers initiated the extension of domestic partnership benefits to homosexual couples.

Employer Liability

Employers are generally liable for the acts of their supervisors and managers, regardless of whether the employer is aware of these people's acts. If an employer knew or should have known about a supervisor's or manager's harassment of a coworker and did nothing to stop it, the employer will be liable. The employer may also be liable for behaviors committed in the workplace by nonemployees, clients, or outside contractors if the employer knew or should have known about the harassment and did not take appropriate action. The courts have made it clear that an organization is liable for sexual harassment when management is aware of the activity, yet does not take immediate and appropriate corrective action.

An employer is likely to minimize its sexual harassment liability under the following circumstances: (1) if it has issued a specific policy against sexual harassment; (2) if it establishes a sexual harassment complaint procedure with multiple avenues for redress (an employee who is harassed by his supervisor must be able to go elsewhere in the organization to file a complaint and not only to his supervisor); (3) if the employer educates supervisors and employees as to the actions and behaviors that constitute sexual harassment and alerts the supervisors and employees that the organization will not tolerate such behavior; (4) if charges of sexual harassment are investigated promptly and thoroughly; and (5) if the employer takes immediate and appropriate corrective action.

The Civil Rights Act of 1991 provides for compensatory damages in addition to back pay for intentional discrimination and unlawful harassment. Private and nonprofit employers may also be liable for punitive damages.

Summary

Changes in society and the workplace have resulted in diversity becoming an important issue for strategic human resources management. Current personnel systems must be reviewed and interrelated to produce and retain a diverse workforce. The organization's culture must be evaluated. This can be done through the review of formal documents, HRM policies and procedures, rewards systems, recruitment and selection procedures, and succession planning. These components should all be inter-related, and attention should be paid to the provision of flexible benefits and alternative work schedules or flextime as they relate to work and family life.

When diversity is well managed, all workers are valued and included. As a result, productivity is improved because the work environment is supportive and nurturing, and contributions are appreciated. The successful management of diversity leads to enhanced interpersonal communication among employees, responsiveness to social and demographic changes, a reduction in equal employment litigation, and a climate of fairness and equity. Diverse groups offer a wider range of ideas because different individuals are likely to perceive problems in a different light and to develop alternative solutions.

Employees who are mistreated tend to be less productive. Energy is spent feeling anxious, angry, frustrated, or fearful instead of concentrating on job-related tasks. Mistreated employees tend to have greater rates of absenteeism and, when possible, will seek other employment opportunities.

Organizations also suffer when their work environments are hostile. Higher turnover rates result in increased recruitment and selection expenses, as well as increased training and retraining costs. Often a divisive "us versus them" atmosphere evolves, which manifests as decreased cooperation and teamwork and increased distrust among employees. Organizations that promote diversity will be able to attract and retain the best employees. Workforces that are representative of the constituents they serve will also be more successful in expanding their constituent and customer base and will be poised to capture new markets.

A supportive environment in which employees can contribute and achieve their fullest potential is necessary. All managers and supervisors should be held accountable for making the workplace supportive. Diversity programs will not be successful unless top managers provide leadership and exemplify the commitment to diversity.

Chapter Four

Equal Employment Opportunity

Public and nonprofit personnel administration is influenced by myriad laws governing equal employment opportunity. Equal employment opportunity has implications for all aspects of human resources management (HRM), from human resources planning, recruitment and selection, training and career development, compensation and benefits, and performance evaluation to labor-management relations. This chapter explains the federal legal environment that governs equal employment opportunity.

The following examples illustrate how dynamic and complex the legal environment of equal employment opportunity has become:

• A court awarded an attorney more than $650,000 in back wages and interest for sexual harassment and race bias by the Securities and Exchange Commission. The attorney claimed that she was not considered fairly in her work assignments and that she was denied a promotion after rejecting her supervisor's sexual advances (*Barnes v. Breedon,* 1996).

• An employee who was terminated due to excessive absenteeism after she took off five consecutive days to care for her son who had an ear infection sued her employer, contending that her discharge violated the Family and Medical Leave Act.

• A sixty-three-year-old administrative employee of a synagogue was terminated and replaced by a younger man. The sixty-three-year-old sued the synagogue, claiming that he was the victim of age discrimination and protected by the Age Discrimination in Employment Act.

• Settling an AIDS discrimination suit, the Chicago Police Department agreed to discontinue testing new recruits for the HIV virus and requiring their HIV status. The settlement resolved a class action filed by the American Civil Liberties Union in July 1994, alleging that the police department violated the Americans with Disabilities Act and the Rehabilitation Act when it denied employment to individuals who were HIV-positive (*Doe v. City of Chicago*, 1995).

These examples are all concerned with violations of federal laws. Administrators must understand the federal, state, and local laws that impact HRM. These laws are designed to eradicate discrimination in the workplace for non-job-related or performance-related reasons. However, many employers either do not understand the laws, misapply them, or choose to ignore them. Employers must consider these laws when developing employment policies and practices.

Federal Equal Employment Opportunity Laws

This section explains the federal laws governing equal employment opportunity. It is recommended, however, that you check with your state and local governments' fair employment practice agencies for additional laws and regulations that may impact the equal employment opportunity practices of your agency.

Civil Rights Acts of 1866 and 1871

The Civil Rights Act of 1866 was based on the Thirteenth Amendment to the U.S. Constitution and prohibits racial discrimination in the making and enforcement of contracts, which could include hiring and promotion decisions. Nonprofit and private employers, unions, and employment agencies fall under its coverage. The Civil Rights Act of 1871 covers state and local governments. It is based on the Fourteenth Amendment and prohibits the deprivation of equal employment rights under state laws.

Title VII of the Civil Rights Act of 1964

The Civil Rights Act of 1964 was signed by President Johnson. It covers all employers having more than fifteen employees, except private clubs, religious organizations, and places of employment connected to an Indian reservation. Title VII of the act deals specifically with discrimination in employment and prohibits discrimination based on race, color, religion, sex, or national origin. The passage of this law was not without controversy. Many politicians (mostly in the South) thought that a federal law forbidding discrimination would usurp states' rights. Congressman Howard Smith of Virginia tried to defeat the bill by including sex as one of the protected classifications. He hoped that the insertion of sex would render the bill foolish and lead to its defeat. The act passed with the inclusion of sex, and today litigation concerning sex discrimination is very common.

The Civil Rights Act of 1964 created the U.S. Equal Employment Opportunity Commission (EEOC) to investigate complaints and to try to resolve disputes through conciliation. The act was amended in 1972 by the Equal Employment Opportunity Act, which extended coverage to state and local governments and to educational institutions. At this time the EEOC was granted enforcement powers to bring action against organizations in the courts if necessary to force compliance with Title VII.

The EEOC requires that most organizations submit annual EEO forms. Data from these forms are used to identify possible patterns of discrimination in particular organizations or segments of the workforce. The EEOC may then take legal action against an organization based on this data.

Employers are required to make periodic reports. All employers with one hundred or more employees and all government contractors and subcontractors with fifty or more employees and a federal contract over $50,000 are required to fill out the Employers Information Report EEO–1. The EEO–1 report summarizes employees by job category, race, color, and sex. Nonprofit organizations that meet the criteria must also comply with the reporting requirements. The Association of Community Organizations for Reform Now (ACORN), which serves low- and moderate-income people, has employed about two hundred people since 1990. It has refused to file the EEO–1 report, claiming that to file would impede its members' right of association under the First Amendment. It has also claimed that it is not an "industry affecting commerce" and thus not subject to Title VII. The EEOC sued ACORN for noncompliance with the reporting requirement. A federal district court in Louisiana ruled that the requirement of reporting pertinent information regarding an organization's employees does not in and of itself operate to suppress the free exchange of ideas. Furthermore, the court stated that Congress intended "industry affecting commerce" to cover all activities affecting commerce whether they are operated for profit or for nonprofit or charitable purposes. The court found that ACORN's nonprofit status "in no way decreases the significance of its business activities (*Equal Employment Opportunity Commission v. Association of Community Organizations for Reform Now,* 1995). Other organizations that must file EEO reports are apprenticeship committees (EEO–2), local unions (EEO–3), state and local governments (EEO–4), elementary and secondary educational institutions (EEO–5), and institutions of higher education (EEO–6).

Title VII does not prohibit discrimination based on seniority systems, veterans' preference rights, national security reasons, or job qualifications based on test scores, backgrounds, or experience, even when the use of such practices may be correlated with race, sex, color, religion, or national origin. Section §703(e)(1) of Title VII permits an employer to discriminate on religion, sex, or national origin in those instances where religion, sex, or national origin is a "bona fide occupational qualification" (BFOQ) reasonably necessary to the normal operation of that particular business or enterprise. For example, a BFOQ that excludes one group (for example, males or females) from an employment opportunity is permissible if the employer can argue that the "essence of the business" requires the exclusion, that is, when business would be significantly affected by not employing members of one group exclusively. A recent case dealing with this issue was *United Automobile Workers v. Johnson Controls* (1991). Johnson Controls is a car battery manufacturer that excluded fertile women from jobs where there was high exposure to lead. Fertile men, however, were not automatically excluded and were given a choice as to whether they wanted to risk their reproductive health. The company argued that this policy fell within the BFOQ exception to Title VII. In its 1991 decision, the Supreme Court disagreed. The Court found that the policy was discriminatory since only women employees were affected by the policy. "Respondent's fetal protection policy explicitly discriminates against women on the basis of their sex. The policy excludes women with childbearing capacity from lead-exposed jobs and so creates a facial classification based on gender. . . . Despite evidence in the record about the debilitating effect of lead exposure on the male reproductive system, Johnson Controls is concerned only with the harms that may befall the unborn offspring of its female employees." The Court stated that women who are as capable of doing the job as their male counterparts may not be forced to choose between having a child and having a job. In general, the position of the courts regarding BFOQs clearly favors judgments about the performance, abilities, or potential of specific individuals rather than discrimination by class or categories. The Supreme Court has said that the BFOQ exception to Title VII is a narrow one, limited to policies that are directly related to a worker's ability to do the job. The burden of proof is on the employer to justify any BFOQ claim.

For most public sector jobs, it is very difficult to substantiate the necessity of gender, race, religion, national origin, age, or disability as a BFOQ. However, there are some instances where a BFOQ case can be made. Recently, the U.S. Court of Appeals at Philadelphia ruled that gender can be considered a BFOQ for the purposes of staffing a psychiatric hospital's unit that treats emotionally disturbed and sexually abused children. A female childcare worker was assigned to work the night shift because the hospital needed a balance of men and women to provide therapeutic care to female and male patients who may want to talk with a staff member of their own sex. The court held that Title VII excuses discrimination that is justified as a BFOQ when it is reasonably necessary to the normal operation of a business. The essence of the hospital's business requires consideration of gender in staffing decisions because if there are not members of both sexes on a shift, the hospital's ability to provide care to its patients is impeded (*Healey v. Southwood Psychiatric Hospital,* 1996).

The question of whether race, religion, national origin, color, and sex constitute a BFOQ does arise often in the nonprofit sector. Is gender a legitimate BFOQ for an executive director position at a rape and sexual abuse center? Can a qualified male perform the administrative and leadership tasks, or does the executive director need to be a female? Would race be a BFOQ for a leadership position in a community-based nonprofit that provides services to racial minorities? If a BFOQ is challenged, the burden is on the employer to justify its position.

Laws That Address Religious Discrimination

Under Section 701(j) of the Civil Rights Act of 1964 employers are obligated to accommodate their employees' or prospective employees' religious practices. Failure to make accommodations is unlawful unless an employer can demonstrate that it cannot reasonably accommodate the employee because of undue hardship in the conduct of its business. In *Trans World Airlines, Inc., v. Hardison* (1977), the Supreme Court ruled that the employer and the union need not violate a seniority provision of a valid collective bargaining agreement, that the employer has no obligation to impose undesirable shifts on nonreligious employees, and that the employer has no obligation to call in substitute workers if such accommodation would require more than de minimis cost.

Nonprofit organizations that provide secular services but that are affiliated with and governed by religious institutions are exempt from the law under Section 702 of the Civil Rights Act of 1964, which states: "This title shall not apply to an employer with respect to the employment of aliens outside any State, or to a religious corporation, association, educational institution, or society with respect to the employment of individuals of a particular religion to perform work connected with the carrying on by such corporation, association, educational institution, or society of its activities" (as amended by P.L.92–261, eff. March 24, 1972).

Educational institutions such as universities, schools, or other institutions of learning are also exempt from the law. Section 703(e)(2) of the Civil Rights Act of 1964 states that

> it shall not be an unlawful employment practice for a school, college, university, or other educational institution or institution of learning to hire and employ employees of a particular religion if

such school, college, university, or other educational institution or institution of learning is, in whole or in substantial part, owned, supported, controlled, or managed by a particular religion or by a particular religious corporation, association, or society, or if the curriculum of such school, college, university, or other educational institution of learning is directed toward the propagation of a particular religion.

In *Mormon Church v. Amos* (1987) the Supreme Court upheld the right of the Mormon Church to terminate a building engineer who had worked at its nonprofit gymnasium for sixteen years, because he failed to maintain his qualification for church membership. The Court claimed that the decision to terminate was based on the precepts of the organization's religion and thus exempt from the Title VII prohibition against religious discrimination (Twomey, 1994). Twomey observes that the Section 703(e)(2) exemption is broad and is not limited to the religious activities of the institution (p. 16).

Pregnancy Discrimination Act of 1978

The Pregnancy Discrimination Act of 1978 prohibits employment practices that discriminate on the basis of pregnancy, childbirth, or related medical conditions. A woman is protected from being fired or refused a job or promotion simply because she is pregnant. She also cannot be forced to take a leave of absence as long as she is able to work.

Under the law, employers are obligated to treat pregnancy as though it were a disability. For example, if other employees who are on disability leave are entitled to return to their jobs when they are able to work again, then so should women who have been unable to work due to pregnancy.

The Pregnancy Discrimination Act also requires that employers must provide full benefits coverage for pregnancy. A woman unable to work for pregnancy-related reasons is entitled to disability benefits or sick leave on the same basis as employees unable to work for other medical reasons.

States may pass their own laws requiring additional benefits for pregnant employees beyond the scope of the federal law. The

Supreme Court upheld a California law that required employers to provide up to four months of unpaid pregnancy disability leave with guaranteed reinstatement, even though disabled males were not entitled to the same benefit (*California Federal Savings & Loan Association v. Guerra*, 1987).

The Age Discrimination in Employment Act of 1967

The Age Discrimination in Employment Act (ADEA) was enacted by Congress in 1967 to prohibit discrimination because of age in matters pertaining to hiring, job retention, compensation, and other terms and conditions of employment. Congress intended to promote the employment of older persons based on their ability rather than on their age, and to prohibit arbitrary age discrimination in employment. In 1974, the ADEA was amended to extend coverage to state and local government employees as well as to most federal employees. The ADEA protected workers between the ages of forty and sixty-five. Employers were granted four exemptions to the act: (1) where age is a BFOQ reasonably necessary to normal operation of a particular business; (2) where differentiation is based on reasonable factors other than age; (3) to observe the terms of a bona fide seniority system or a bona fide insurance plan, with the qualification that no seniority system or benefit plan may require or permit the involuntary retirement of who is covered by ADEA; and (4) where an employee is discharged or disciplined for good cause.

The ADEA was amended in 1978 by raising the upper limit to seventy years of age, and again in 1986 to prohibit compulsory retirement for most jobs. Exemptions to the 1986 amendment included tenured college and university professors, high level executives and policymakers who held such positions for more than two years and whose pension and benefits amounted to at least $40,000 per year, and law enforcement officers and firefighters. The exemptions for tenured professors and public safety officers expired on December 31, 1993. The House of Representatives in April 1995 passed HR 849, which reinstates the public safety exemption. However, until the Senate passes similar legislation, the retirement of police or firefighters may not be required solely because of their age. Instead they must meet one of the four exemptions listed earlier. The ADEA now applies to employers with twenty or more employees, unions of twenty-five or more members, employment agencies, and federal, state, and local governments.

On April 1, 1996, the Supreme Court ruled that an individual claiming age discrimination need not show that the replacement worker was under age forty to pursue the claim. An ADEA worker claimant must show a logical connection between his or her age and his or her discharge, but there is no requirement to show that the replacement was under forty. Justice Scalia wrote that "the fact that one person in the protected class lost out to another person in the protected class is thus irrelevant, so long as he has lost out because of his age" (*O'Connor v. Consolidated Coin Caterers Corporation*, 1996).

Earlier in this chapter religious freedom was discussed under Title VII of the Civil Rights Act of 1964 as guaranteed to all Americans under the First Amendment to the U.S. Constitution. If, however, an administrative employee is discharged from a religious organization because of alleged age discrimination, can he or she sue under the ADEA? Or would that be an infringement of the organization's First Amendment guarantee of religious freedom? A suit was brought by a sixty-three-year-old employee who was replaced by a thirty-seven-year-old. The elder employee sued for age bias under the ADEA. A federal district court dismissed the suit, finding that the employee's administrative duties were inextricably intertwined with the synagogue's religious purpose. The court's recognition of the case would have violated the synagogue's First Amendment guarantee of religious freedom. However, on October 28, 1994, the United States Court of Appeals for the Eighth Circuit (*Weissman v. Congregation Shaare Emeth*, 1994) reversed the district court's decision. The appellate court ruled that the employee was not a member of the clergy and that the discharge was not based on religious grounds but on dissatisfaction with his job performance. Unsatisfactory job performance cannot be characterized as a religious reason. The fact that a lay employee has religious duties does not shield a religious employer from an ADEA claim. The age discrimination claim was reinstated.

The Americans with Disabilities Act of 1990

In 1990, Congress passed the Americans with Disabilities Act (ADA). Title I of the ADA provides that qualified individuals may not be discriminated against on the basis of disability in all aspects of the employment relationship, from the application stage through retirement. The law took effect on July 26, 1992, for organizations of twenty-five or more employees and on July 26, 1994, for organizations with fifteen to twenty-four employees. Employment practices covered by ADA include job application procedures, hiring, firing, advancement, compensation, training, and other terms and conditions and privileges of employment.

The ADA recognized the following categories of disabilities:

1. Individuals with a physical or mental impairment that substantially limits one or more major life activities. This could include walking, seeing, hearing, and speaking. Examples of other physical and/or mental impairments that might be considered disabilities include speech impediments, learning disabilities, AIDS, mental retardation, chronic mental illness, and epilepsy.
2. Having a record of such an impairment. This could include people who have recovered from a heart attack, cancer, a back injury, or mental illness.
3. Being regarded as having an impairment. This would include individuals who are perceived as having a disability, such as individuals suspected of having the HIV virus.

Under the ADA, to be considered qualified, an individual must be able to perform the "essential functions of the position," meaning that the individual must satisfy the prerequisites for the position and be able to perform the essential functions of the job with or without reasonable accommodation.

Employers must provide the disabled with "reasonable accommodations" that do not place an undue hardship on the organization. Undue hardship is defined as an adjustment related to an employer's operation, financial resources, and facilities that requires significant difficulty or expense. Undue hardship and reasonable accommodation are to be determined on a case-by-case basis, taking into account such things as the size of the employer, the number of employees responsible for a particular job or task, and the employer's ability to afford the accommodation. Accommodations may include interventions such as reassignment, part-time work, and flexible schedules, or modifications in equipment and the work environment such as acquiring a special telephone headset or larger computer screen or moving a training workshop to a location accessible to wheelchairs.

Civil Rights Act of 1991

The Civil Rights Act of 1991 (CRA) was passed by Congress on November 7, 1991, and signed into law by President Bush on November 21, 1991. The CRA provides additional remedies to protect against and deter unlawful discrimination and harassment in employment and to restore the strength of federal antidiscrimination laws that many felt had been weakened by several Supreme Court decisions. The CRA of 1991 amended five civil rights statutes: Title VII of the Civil Rights Act of 1964, the Americans with Disabilities Act of 1990, the Age Discrimination in Employment Act of 1967, the Civil Rights Act of 1866, and the Civil Rights Attorney's Fee Awards Act of 1976. In addition, three new laws were created: Section 1981A of Title 42 of the U.S. Code, the Glass Ceiling Act of 1991, and the Government Employee Rights Act of 1991. Compensatory and punitive damages were made available to the victims of private and/or nonprofit employers. Public employees are now entitled to only compensatory damages. There is now a cap on damages permitted under the law that is determined by the number of workers employed by an organization.

Family and Medical Leave Act of 1993

The Family and Medical Leave Act (FMLA) was signed by President Clinton shortly after his inauguration and took effect on August 5, 1993. FMLA applies to all public agencies, including state, local, and federal employers; educational institutions; business entities engaged in commerce or in an industry affecting commerce; and private sector employers who employ fifty or more employees in twenty or more work weeks in the current or preceding calendar year, including joint employers and successors of covered employers.

Family and medical leave is available for the birth or adoption of a child or the placement of a child in foster care; to care for a spouse, child, or parent with a serious health condition; or to accommodate the disabling illness of the employee. To be eligible for the leave, an employee must have worked for at least twelve months and for at least 1,250 hours during the year preceding the start of the leave.

The law requires employers to maintain coverage under any group health plan under the condition that coverage would have been provided if no leave was taken. When the leave ends, employees are entitled to return to the same jobs they held before going on leave, or to equivalent positions. An equivalent position is defined as a position having the same pay, benefits, and working conditions and that involves the same or substantially similar duties and responsibilities. Employees must be restored to the same or a geographically proximate worksite.

Not all employees are eligible for leave under FMLA. An employee who qualifies as a key employee may be denied restoration to employment. A key employee is salaried and is among the highest paid 10 percent of the employees at the worksite. Employees must be notified by the employer of their status as a key employee if there is any possibility that the employer may deny reinstatement. Employees are required to give employers thirty days advance notice of the need to take family and medical leave when it is foreseeable for the birth of a child or the placement of a child for adoption or foster care, or for planned medical treatment. When it is not possible to provide such notice, employees must give notice within one or two business days of when the employee learns of the need for leave.

Employers can require medical certification from a health care provider to support leave requests. Employees who are denied leave or who are denied reinstatement at the end of leave in violation of the law may file a complaint with the Department of Labor. Employees may also file a private lawsuit against the employer to obtain damages and other relief. The FMLA does not supersede any state or local law that provides greater family or medical leave rights. Employers covered by both federal and state laws must comply with both.

Proving Employment Discrimination

Cases of alleged discrimination in violation of federal or state statutes can be made under one of two theories: disparate treatment and disparate impact.

Disparate Treatment

Disparate treatment occurs when an employer treats a protected-class employee differently than a non-protected-class employee in a similar situation. For example, deliberately using different criteria for selection depending on the candidate's sex or race would constitute disparate treatment, such as an employer asking female applicants questions about their marital status or child-care arrangements that are not asked of male applicants, or an employer requiring African American applicants to take pencil-and-paper preemployment tests that white applicants applying for the same positions and possessing the same qualifications are not required to take.

The following procedures established in *McDonnell Douglas v. Green* (1973) require plaintiffs to show that an employer treats one or more members of a protected group differently than the employer treats members of another group.

1. The applicant/employee is a member of a class protected by the statute alleged to be violated (sex, race, age, national origin).
2. The applicant/employee applied for the vacancy and is qualified to perform the job.
3. Although qualified, the applicant/employee was rejected.
4. After rejection, the vacancy remained and the employer continued to seek applications from persons of equal qualification.

The Supreme Court established that in disparate treatment cases the burden is on the plaintiff to prove that the employer *intended* to discriminate because of race, sex, color, religion, or national origin. In *St. Mary's Honor Center v. Hicks* (1993), the Supreme Court ruled that in addition to showing that all of the employer's legal reasons are false an employee must prove that the employer was motivated by bias. The plaintiff must show direct evidence of discrimination.

Disparate Impact

Disparate impact occurs when an employer's policy or practice, neutral on its face and in its application, has a negative effect on the employment opportunities of protected-class individuals. "Neutral" means that the employer requires all applicants or employees to take the same examination or to possess the same qualifications for the positions. Unlike in the examples provided under disparate treatment, in which the employer deliberately treated males and females or black and white applicants and employees differently, under disparate impact all applicants and employees are treated the same but protected-class members are not hired or promoted. Such impact is illegal if the employment practice is not job related or related to the employment in question. For example, if an agency hired fifty whites and no Hispanics from one hundred white and one hundred Hispanic applicants, then disparate impact has occurred. Whether or not the employer had good intentions or did not mean to discriminate is irrelevant to the courts in this type of lawsuit. After the plaintiff shows evidence of disparate impact, the employer must carry the burden of producing evidence of business necessity or job relatedness for the employment practice. Finally, the burden shifts back to the plaintiff, who must show that an alternative procedure is available that is equal to or better than the employer's practice and has a less discriminatory effect.

The Uniform Guidelines on Employee Selection Procedures (1978) were jointly adopted by the EEOC, the U.S. Civil Service Commission, the U.S. Department of Labor, and the U.S. Department of Justice. While not administrative regulations, the guidelines are granted great deference by the courts. The purpose of the guidelines is to provide a framework for determining the proper use of tests and other selection procedures. They are applicable to all employers: federal, state, local, nonprofit, and private.

The Uniform Guidelines and many courts have adopted the "four-fifths rule" as a yardstick for determining disparate impact. This rule states that a selection rate (determined by the number of applicants selected divided by the number who applied) for a protected group should not be less than four-fifths, or 80 percent of the rate for the group with the highest selection rate.

Disparate impact theory has been used in many cases involving neutral employment practices such as tests, entrance requirements, and physical requirements. In 1988, the Supreme Court extended use of the disparate impact theory in cases involving "subjective" employment practices such as interviews, performance appraisals, and job recommendations (*Watson v. Fort Worth Bank and Trust,* 1988). Statistical data based on the four-fifths rule can be used in a disparate impact case to establish prima facie evidence of discrimination when decisions are based on subjective employment practices.

Affirmative Action: Executive Orders and Other Federal Laws

Chapter Three briefly discussed equal employment opportunity and the executive orders and federal laws that require employers to engage in affirmative action. This section explains in further detail affirmative action and the requirements imposed on employers through Executive Orders 11246 and 11375, the Rehabilitation Act of 1973, and the Vietnam Era Veterans Readjustment Act of 1974.

Executive Orders 11246 and 11375

In 1965, President Johnson signed Executive Order 11246, which prohibited discrimination in federal employment or by federal contractors on the basis of race, creed, color, or national origin. In 1961 it was amended by Executive Order 11375 to change the word "creed" to "religion" and to add sex discrimination to the other prohibited items. The order applies to all federal agencies, contractors, and subcontractors, including all the facilities of the agency holding the contract, regardless of at which plant the work is conducted. Contractors and subcontractors with more than $50,000 in government business and fifty or more employees are not only prohibited from discriminating but also must take affirmative action to ensure that applicants and employees are not treated differently as a function of their sex, religion, race, color, and national origin. The order also authorizes the cancellation of federal contracts for failure to meet the order's guidelines. It requires a contractor to post notices of equal employment opportunity and to document its compliance to the Department of Labor.

Executive Order 11246 is enforced by the Department of Labor through the Office of Federal Contract Compliance Programs (OFCCP). The OFCCP is a branch of the Department of Labor's Employment Standards Administration. It promulgates guidelines and conducts audits of federal contractors to ensure compliance with the executive order. The OFCCP is charged with processing complaints as well as compliance review. The OFCCP reviews complaints; it can visit an employer's worksite and review the affirmative action plans for compliance with the law. Minority availability is measured by the portion of qualified applicants (actual or potential) who are minorities. OFCCP defines "underutilization" as fewer minorities or women in a particular job group than would reasonably be expected by their availability. When a job group is identified as underutilized, the contractor must set goals to correct the underutilization. The goals for each underutilized group, together with the utilization analysis, becomes part of the written affirmative action plan. A federal contractor must monitor information about the status of employees when creating and using an affirmative action plan. The employer must demonstrate that its employment practices comply with Executive Order 11246 and with the OFCCP's guidelines by documenting employment decisions on hiring, termination, promotion, demotion, and transfer.

If noncompliance is found, the OFCCP generally first tries to reach a conciliation agreement with the employer. Special hiring or recruitment programs, seniority credit, or back pay may be some of the provisions included in the agreement. If an agreement cannot be reached, the employer is scheduled to have a hearing with a judge. If an agreement is still not reached, employers may lose their government contracts or have their payments withheld. They may also lose the right to bid on future government contracts, or be debarred from all subsequent contract work.

While equal employment opportunity is a legal duty, affirmative action can be voluntary or involuntary. Although Executive

Order 11246 applies only to organizations receiving federal funds, many public and nonprofit organizations have decided to implement voluntary affirmative action programs to redress previous discriminatory employment practices or because they wish to make their workforce more representative. Involuntary affirmative action is permitted under the Civil Rights Act of 1964, section 706 (g), which states that if a court finds that an employer has intentionally engaged in an unlawful employment practice, it may order appropriate affirmative action. Affirmative action is not required unless the employer has adopted the plan pursuant to a court order, if the employer has adopted the plan as a remedy for past discrimination, or if the employer must comply with an executive order or an order required by a federal or state agency requiring affirmative action as a condition of doing business with the government. Employers who are not the recipients of government contracts may be forced to develop affirmative plans if an investigation by a state or federal compliance agency finds that an employer's personnel practices discriminate against protected-class members.

There are three types of involuntarily affirmative action plans. They are presented here in order from least restrictive to most restrictive:

Conciliation agreement. After an investigation by a compliance agency, the employer may acknowledge that there is merit to the allegation of discriminatory employment practices and agree to change its practices to comply with the recommendations of the compliance agency.

Consent decree. A consent decree is an agreement between an employer and a compliance agency negotiated with the approval of a court and subject to court enforcement.

Court order. Court orders result if a compliance agency must take an employer to court because neither a conciliation agreement nor a consent decree can be agreed upon. If the court finds the employer guilty of discrimination, the judge may impose remedies. These can include hiring or promotion quotas, changes in personnel practices, and financial compensation for the victims of discrimination.

A summary of Supreme Court decisions pertaining to affirmative action programs is presented in Exhibit 4.1.

The Rehabilitation Act of 1973

The Rehabilitation Act prohibits discrimination on the basis of physical or mental disability. A disabled person is defined as one who (1) has an impairment that affects a major life activity, (2) has a history of such an impairment, or (3) is considered as having such an impairment. Major life activities are functions such as seeing, speaking, walking, and caring for oneself. Disabled individuals would also include those with mental handicaps, and may include those with illnesses that make them unfit for employment, such as contagious diseases (tuberculosis, heart disease, cancer, diabetes, drug dependency, or alcoholism, for example). The Supreme Court ruled in *Arline v. School Board of Nassau County* (1987) that individuals with contagious diseases who are able to perform their jobs are protected by the Rehabilitation Act of 1973. The Court stated that the assessment of risks cannot be based on "society's accumulated myths and fears about disability and disease." Most states have similar laws protecting disabled workers from discrimination.

Section 501 of the Rehabilitation Act requires the federal government as an employer to develop and implement affirmative action plans on behalf of disabled employees. Congress enacted this provision with the expectation that the federal government would serve as a model for other employers.

Section 503 requires all federal contractors or subcontractors receiving funds over $2500 to take affirmative action for the employment of qualified disabled persons. Enforcement is carried out by the Department of Labor's Employment Standards Administration. Under the Rehabilitation Act, as under the Americans with Disabilities Act of 1990, a disabled person is considered qualified for a job if an individual analysis determines that he or she can with reasonable accommodation perform the essential functions of the job. Employers must make such accommodations unless it can be shown that the accommodation would pose an undue hardship on the firm.

Section 504 prohibits federally funded programs and government agencies from excluding from employment an "otherwise qualified handicapped individual . . . solely by reason of handicap." The enforcement of Section 504 rests with each federal agency that provides financial assistance. The attorney general of the United

Exhibit 4.1. Summary of Supreme Court
Affirmative Action Decisions.

Adarand Constructors v. Pena (1995)
Federal affirmative action programs that favor racial minorities must meet the same "strict scrutiny" requirements applied to state and local programs; they must serve a compelling governmental interest and be narrowly tailored.

City of Richmond v. J. A. Croson Co. (1989)
Governments imposing set-aside programs for minorities have to prove a history of prior discrimination. Governments may only favor one race over the other when it is remedying identifiable discrimination. Declared unconstitutional, a Richmond, Virginia, ordinance set aside 30 percent of public work contracts for minority contractors.

Martin v. Wilks (1989)
A consent decree between one group of employees and its employer cannot possibly settle, voluntarily or otherwise, the connecting claims of another group of employees who do not join in the agreement. Consent decrees may be challenged by parties who were not originally involved in reaching the settlement.

Johnson v. Santa Clara Transportation Agency (1987)
Organizations may adopt voluntary affirmative action programs to hire and promote qualified minorities and women to correct a "conspicuous imbalance in job categories traditionally segregated by race and sex." Gender can be considered in promotional decisions even when there is no evidence of past discrimination.

United States v. Paradise (1987)
District federal judges may impose strict racial quotas where there is a history of "egregious" racial bias to remedy the effects of past discrimination.

Sheet Metal Workers' Local 28 v. Equal Employment Opportunity Commission (1986)
Two important rules emerged. First, a court may order a union to use quotas to overcome a history of "egregious

discrimination." Second, black and Hispanic applicants can benefit even if they themselves were not victims of past union bias.

Firefighters Local 93 v. City of Cleveland (1986)

The court held that trial judges may approve voluntary pacts between employee associations and public employers to give minorities hiring preferences. Because Local 93 was not a party to the consent decree, it could not protest the terms of that decree.

Wygant v. Jackson Board of Education (1986)

The court again upheld seniority, ruling that laying off more experienced white teachers violates the constitutional guarantee of equal protection. The court said that governments might be allowed to use race for hiring preferences to redress past discrimination but not for layoffs.

Firefighters Local 1784 v. Stotts (1984)

The justices held that seniority systems may not be abrogated to benefit individuals who were not proven victims of discrimination.

United Steelworkers of America v. Weber (1979)

In the first important private sector decision, the justices ruled 5 to 2 that private companies and unions could voluntarily adopt quotas to eliminate "manifest racial imbalance." Affirmative action plans are permissible that meet these four conditions: (1) the plan is temporary; (2) it is undertaken to eliminate manifest racial imbalance, (3) it is for nontraditional or traditionally segregated job categories, and (4) the plan does not require the discharge of white workers or create an absolute bar to their advancement.

Regents of the University of California v. Bakke (1978)

In the case of a rejected medical school applicant, the court held 5 to 4 that a public university could not use quotas to reserve a precise number of places for minority students. But the court also ruled 5 to 4 that race could be one of many factors in deciding admissions to university programs.

States has responsibility for the coordination of the enforcement efforts of the agencies.

In 1993, the United States Court of Appeals for the First Circuit ruled that an individual who suffered from morbid obesity was denied a job in violation of Section 504 of the Rehabilitation Act of 1973 (*Cook v. State of Rhode Island, Department of Mental Health, Retardation, and Hospitals,* 1993). Cook had worked as an institutional attendant for the mentally retarded from 1978 to 1980 and from 1981 to 1986. She reapplied for the position in 1988 and was rejected since she was found to be morbidly obese. She was five feet and two inches tall and weighed more than 320 pounds. The state claimed that her obesity limited her ability to evacuate patients in case of an emergency and put her at greater risk of developing serious ailments. She filed a lawsuit claiming that her rejection violated Section 504 of the Rehabilitation Act of 1973, which prohibits an otherwise qualified disabled individual from being discriminated against by a program or activity that receives federal financial assistance. The Court stated that to prevail in her claim it would be necessary to show that (1) she had applied for a job in a federally funded program, (2) she suffered from a disability, (3) she was qualified for the position, and (4) she was not hired due to her disability. The state argued that obesity was a condition that could be changed and that it was voluntary, and that it therefore did not constitute a disability. The Court found that even if people who are morbidly obese lose weight they still suffer from metabolic dysfunction. The Court stated that the Rehabilitation Act "contains no language suggesting that its protection is linked to how an individual became impaired, or whether an individual contributed to his or her impairment. The law applies to conditions such as alcoholism, AIDS, diabetes, cancer, and heart disease that can be made worse by voluntary conduct." Concern over excess absenteeism and increased workers compensation costs were prohibited reasons for rejecting Ms. Cook.

The Vietnam Era Veterans Readjustment Act of 1974

The Vietnam Era Veterans Readjustment Act of 1974 applies to employers with government contracts of $10,000 or more. Contractors are required to take affirmative action to employ and advance disabled veterans and qualified veterans of the Vietnam era. Enforcement of the act is by complaint to the Veterans Employment Service of the Department of Labor.

Summary

Equal employment opportunity has continued to evolve over the years so that it now prohibits not only race discrimination but discrimination against sex, religion, color, national origin, disability, and age. The equal employment opportunity and affirmative action laws create legal responsibilities for employers and affect all aspects of the employment relationship. Recruitment, selection, training, compensation and benefits, promotions, and terminations must all be conducted in a nondiscriminatory manner.

Whereas equal employment opportunity is a policy of nondiscrimination, affirmative action requires employers to analyze their workforces and develop plans of action to recruit, select, train, and promote members of protected classes, and to develop plans of action to correct areas in which past discrimination may have occurred.

Affirmative action is used by the federal government to promote a more diverse workforce. Recipients of federal funds are required to develop affirmative plans that encourage the recruitment, selection, training, and promotion of qualified disabled individuals, Vietnam War era veterans, and individuals who may have been discriminated against because of their race, sex, color, and national origin.

Affirmative action plans can be either involuntary or voluntary. Involuntary affirmative action plans have increasingly come under intense scrutiny, and affirmative action itself is presently being challenged.

The Equal Opportunity Act of 1996 (HR 2128, S 1085) was approved by the Republicans of the House Judiciary subcommittee on March 21, 1996, and now goes to the full committee. If passed, the act would prohibit the federal government from requiring or encouraging federal contractors from using race, color, national origin, or sex in hiring and promotion policies.

There have also been some recent federal court decisions concerning affirmative action. One case addressed affirmative action and the granting of federal contracts, and the second case dealt with affirmative action and law school admission policies. In *Adarand Constructors v. Pena* (1995), the U.S. Supreme Court ruled that federal programs that use race or ethnicity as a basis for decision making must be strictly scrutinized to ensure that they promote compelling government interest and that they are narrowly tailored to serve those interests. Federal affirmative action programs giving preference to minorities are subject to the same strict scrutiny applied to state and local programs.

In *Hopwood, et al., v. State of Texas, et al.* (1996), the Fifth Circuit Court of Appeals struck down the affirmative action program at the University of Texas Law School. The law school set up an admission system that viewed minorities and whites separately, resulting in an unconstitutional quota system. The court ruled that racial diversity can never be a compelling government interest, that racial diversity "may promote improper racial stereotypes, thus fueling racial hostility."

At this time, the Supreme Court has upheld the use of court-ordered affirmative action programs designed to eliminate egregious past discrimination (*United States v. Paradise,* 1986) and voluntary affirmative action plans designed to increase the representation of women and minorities in nontraditional jobs or in traditionally segregated positions (*Johnson v. Santa Clara Transportation Agency,* 1987; *United Steelworkers of America v. Weber,* 1979). Voluntary affirmative action plans are permitted as long as they meet four conditions: (1) the affirmative action plan is temporary, (2) it is undertaken to eliminate manifest racial imbalance, (3) it is for nontraditional jobs or traditionally segregated job categories, and (4) the plan does not require the discharge of white workers or create an absolute bar to their advancement.

The Supreme Court has not upheld the use of racial quotas when race serves as the only criterion for admission to universities and advanced graduate programs (*Regents of the University of California v. Bakke,* 1978) or when race is used to abrogate seniority systems in layoffs. Hiring and promotional preferences may be permissible to redress past discrimination but not layoffs (*Firefighters Local 1784 v. Stotts,* 1984; *Wygant v. Jackson Board of Education,* 1986).

The focus on equal employment opportunity and affirmative action programs has increased the importance of strategic human resources management and planning. Compliance with equal employment opportunity laws and affirmative action regulations are essential components of human resources planning and the effective utilization of all employees. One day affirmative action programs may be eliminated, and many of the paperwork requirements for compliance audits will no longer be necessary. However, organizations will still need to develop and implement progressive HRM strategies if they wish to successfully manage a diverse workforce.

Part Two

Methods and Functions of Human Resources Management

Strategic human resources management (SHRM) depends on the successful integration and execution of human resources management (HRM) methods and functions. The chapters in this part of the book explain the importance of job analysis, recruitment and selection, performance evaluation, compensation, benefits, training and career development, and collective bargaining.

Chapter Five discusses the importance of job analysis. A job analysis is a systematic process of collecting data for determining the knowledge, skills, abilities, and other characteristics (KSAOCs) required to successfully perform a job and to make judgments about the nature of a specific job. Information collected through a job analysis is applied to most HRM activities, such as recruitment and selection, development of compensation systems, human resources planning, career development and training, performance evaluation, risk management, and job design. The nature of work—how tasks, behaviors, and responsibilities are assigned to different jobs and how different jobs relate to one another—are explained.

Recruitment and selection are discussed in Chapter Six. SHRM depends on the successful recruitment and selection of qualified individuals. Recruitment is the process of attracting qualified candidates to apply for vacant positions within an organization. Selection is the final stage of the recruitment process, when decisions are made as to who will fill those positions. In public and nonprofit organizations, the recruitment and selection of competent employees are critical responsibilities because people are central to delivering the programs and services that constitute these organizations' reason for existence.

Selection techniques used to hire applicants must comply with federal laws and guidelines and be job-related; that is, they must not unfairly screen out protected-group members for non-job-related reasons.

The importance of performance evaluation is addressed in Chapter Seven. Performance evaluations provide management with essential information for making strategic decisions on employee advancement, retention, or separation. Evaluation links training and development with career planning and an agency's long-term human resource needs. Used to support job analysis and recruitment efforts, performance evaluations are an important component for forecasting the KSAOCs available within the organization.

Chapter Eight explains the development and maintenance of compensation systems. Compensation is the largest expense faced by public and nonprofit organizations. From 60 to 80 percent of the operating budget goes to employees' salaries and benefits. The design, implementation, and maintenance of compensation are therefore important parts of SHRM. Decisions about salaries, incentives, benefits, and quality-of-life issues are important in attracting, retaining, and motivating employees. Strategic decisions about pay levels, pay structures, job evaluation, and incentive pay systems influence the ability of an organization to compete in the marketplace to attract the most qualified and competent applications and to retain its most talented and productive employees. Compensation systems are influenced by federal laws and by external, internal, and employee equity considerations.

Benefits are part of the compensation system and are commonly referred to as indirect compensation. Benefits are an important part of the compensation package. An attractive benefit package can assist in the recruitment and retention of qualified employees. Chapter Nine discusses some of the more traditional benefits offered by employers, such as health insurance, retirement pensions, and paid time away from work, in addition to less traditional benefits such as child and elder care, flexible scheduling, and educational assistance. Changing demographics, family needs, and employee priorities require a greater range of employer-provided benefits than what was offered in the past.

The demands placed on organizations keep changing and technology has taken on much of the mentally and physically repetitive tasks once performed by employees. Positions today require employees to possess greater skills as they assume more challenging responsibilities. Jobs have become less specialized, forcing employees to work in teams to deliver services. New equipment and technology, the enactment of new laws and regulations, fluctuations in the economy, and the actions of competitors are just some of the variables that influence change. As organizations keep changing, they must implement training and development programs to ensure that their staff have the necessary KSAOCs to confront these new challenges. Chapter Ten discusses training and career development. Developing a comprehensive, long-range training program requires an SHRM plan and a recognition that employees are a most valuable resource. Training and development must become integrated into the core HRM functions.

Labor-management relations is an important component of SHRM. To remain competitive, management and unions have had to rethink their adversarial relationship and work together to creatively resolve problems and develop solutions that benefit both labor and management. Chapter Eleven explains the legal framework governing collective bargaining in the public and nonprofit sectors and provides some examples of the different types of benefits unions have negotiated for their members consistent with the workforce and workplace changes. Mental health and substance abuse benefits, child-care benefits, incentive awards, employee individual development plans, and flexible work schedules are just some examples of nontraditional benefits that have been negotiated.

Chapter Five

Job Analysis

For organizations to remain competitive, they must accurately identify and forecast their human resources needs. Organizations must assess past trends, evaluate their present situation, and project what human resources will be needed for them to meet the requirements of their strategic plans. Before informed decisions can be made about recruitment and development needs, compensation plans, training and career development objectives, performance management systems, and job design, data must first be collected and analyzed. The technique used to acquire the data necessary to make informed decisions is called job analysis.

A job analysis is a systematic process of collecting data for determining the knowledge, skills, abilities, and other characteristics (KSAOCs) required to successfully perform a job and to make judgments about the nature of a specific job. A job analysis identifies a job's activities, behaviors, tasks, and performance standards, the context in which the job is performed, and the personal requirements necessary to perform a job, such as personality, interests, physical characteristics, aptitudes, and job-related knowledge and skills. Each position is also analyzed in regard to its relationship to other positions in the organization.

Chapter Two, on strategic human resources management (SHRM), emphasized the need for human resources management (HRM) departments to assist their organizations in improving organizational effectiveness. Job analyses can be integral to SHRM planning. Schneider and Konz (1989, p. 53) define strategic job analysis as "the specification of the tasks to be performed and the knowledge, skills, and abilities required for effective performance for a job as it is predicted to exist in the future." Strategic job analyses recognize that most jobs will not remain stable but will change to meet future demands.

Consider the following examples:

- The State Universities Civil Service System wants to develop new statewide selection examinations for secretarial/clerical positions across twenty-six institutions. They want to be sure that the exams are job related and legally defensible.
- A nonprofit child-care facility wants to institute a performance evaluation system. Before instruments can be developed for each job, the most important job dimensions must be identified.
- A local government requires its maintenance employees to possess a valid driver's license when they are hired. An applicant for the position sued the city, alleging that the requirement is unnecessary and violates the Americans with Disabilities Act. He claims that driving is not an "essential function" of the job.
- The National Performance Review (1993) recommended that the federal government simplify its classification system by consolidating many similar job positions. This would require merging some existing positions or performing a large-scale consolidation of the job position structure. Before one of these things could be done, the KSAOCs, responsibilities, and tasks for each position and series would need to be reviewed.

Each of these situations requires that a job analysis be conducted to identify job duties and responsibilities, the types of technologies and equipment to be used, and the skills and experience required for successful performance.

Job analyses provide the foundation for most HRM activities. Following is a brief introduction to each area of activity:

Recruitment and selection. Job analysis identifies the knowledge, skills, abilities, and other characteristics (KSAOCs) required for each position. It identifies the minimum education, certification, or licensing requirements. A job analysis also identifies the tasks and responsibilities that are essential functions of the job. This information distinguishes the skills that will be needed by the people the agency recruits and hires. A job analysis is critical if an organization uses preemployment examinations for selection and promotion. Tests must be job related; the knowledge, skills, abilities, personality variables, and constructs to be tested need to be identified through an up-to-date job analysis. An organization does not know what knowledge, skills, and abilities to test for unless it knows what competencies are required for successful performance.

Developing compensation systems. Compensation is typically related to a job's requirements, such as education, the skills and experience needed to perform the job, and whether or not the employee is working in hazardous circumstances. A job analysis provides a standardized procedure for systematically determining pay and other benefits across the organization. It provides all employees with a basis for gaining a common understanding of the values of each job, of its relationship to other jobs, and of the requirements necessary to perform it.

Human resources planning, career development, and training. Job analysis information can help employers to design training and career development programs by identifying what skills are required for different jobs. Identifying the knowledge, skill, and responsibility requirements of each job makes it possible to train and develop employees for promotional opportunities. Available information assists all employees to better understand promotion and transfer requirements and to recognize career opportunities.

Performance evaluation. Performance standards should be derived from what employees actually do on the job. A job analysis identifies the tasks and responsibilities that employees perform in the course of their jobs. Areas of accountability can be identified and evaluation standards can be developed.

Risk management. A job analysis can be used to identify job hazards such as exposure to flammable materials or complicated machinery. Employers should use this information to develop training programs to alert employees to possible dangers.

Job design. Jobs are arranged around a set of work activities designed to enable the organization to carry out its mission. External and internal changes, however, often force organizations to rearrange or restructure work activities. Often the traditional tasks associated with a particular job change; a job analysis is necessary to identify and accommodate these changes.

This chapter discusses the legal significance of job analysis, the types of information obtained through a job analysis, the factors to consider when designing a job analysis program, and some of the advantages of strategic job analysis and generic job descriptions. The chapter concludes with the introduction of some of the job analysis techniques commonly used in the public and nonprofit sectors.

Legal Significance of Job Analysis Data

To demonstrate the validity and job relatedness of an employment test, the Uniform Guidelines on Employee Selection Procedures (1978) require that a job analysis be conducted. Content, criterion, and construct test validation strategies all must be based on a thorough and current job analysis. Employers must show that the requirements established for selecting workers are related to the job. When used as the basis for personnel decisions such as promotions or pay increases, performance evaluations are also considered to be examinations and fall under as rigorous scrutiny as employment tests. Furthermore, the Americans with Disabilities Act (ADA) defines a qualified applicant as one who can perform the essential functions of the job. Essential functions are the primary job duties intrinsic to the position; they do not include marginal or peripheral tasks that are not critical to the performance of the primary job functions. It is important that positions be analyzed to identify these functions. The applicant must then satisfy the prerequisites for the position and be able to perform the essential functions of the job with or without reasonable accommodation.

The most common reasons for conducting a job analysis are to gather information so that a job description can be written, so that job specifications can be identified, and so that the job can be placed within a job family classification. A job description is a summary of the most important features of a job. It states the nature of the work involved and provides information about tasks, responsibilities, and context. Information typically found in job descriptions includes job title, job family, job summary, task statements, reporting relationships, and job context indicators.

The ADA does not require employers to develop written job descriptions. However, a written job description that is prepared before advertising or interviewing applicants for the job should be reviewed to make sure that it accurately reflects the actual functions of the job. The Equal Employment Opportunity Commission (EEOC) and the Civil Rights Division of the Department of Justice recommend that job descriptions focus on the results or outcomes of a job function, not solely on the way it is customarily performed. This is because a person with a disability may be able to accomplish a job function, either with or without a reasonable accommodation, in a manner that is different from the way an employee who is not disabled may accomplish the same function.

Job specifications contain information about the KSAOCs of the position. While job descriptions are specific to a particular job, job specifications may be more general. They contain the minimum qualifications that a person should possess in order to perform the job. A job family is a collection of jobs that require common skills, occupational qualifications, technology, licensing, and working conditions.

Job Analysis Information and Methods

As noted earlier, job analysis is used as the basis for many HRM activities. However, different types of job analysis information, instruments, and procedures lend themselves more easily to different purposes. The first steps in conducting a job analysis are to define the purpose behind the analysis and then to determine what information is required.

Job Analysis Information

Different types of information are collected during a job analysis and a variety of methods can be used. The information most commonly collected are data on job activities, educational requirements, types of equipment or tools, working conditions, supervisory or management responsibilities, interpersonal or communication skills, agency contacts, external contacts, and the KSAOCs. *Knowledge* is the information required for the position. It can be factual, procedural, or conceptual, and is related to the performance of tasks, such as a general knowledge of accounting principles or of fund accounting as used in nonprofit organizations. *Skills* are the specific observable competencies required to perform the particular tasks of the position, such as the ability to input data accurately at one hundred characters per minute, or to diagnose and repair personal computers. *Abilities* are the applicant's aptitudes for performing particular tasks—what the applicant is able to do and how well—such as the ability to prepare and make presentations or to read city maps. *Other characteristics* include such things as attitudes, personality factors, or physical or mental traits needed to perform the job.

Methods of Collecting Job Data

Job analysis information can be obtained through a variety of methods. Data collection depends on the nature of the positions, the number of incumbents and supervisors of the positions being analyzed, the geographical dispersion of jobs, and the time available, as well as the type of information needed and the purpose of the analysis. The job analyst and the agency supervisors must work together to determine what will be the most effective method for collecting information. The job analyst can be an employee from the HRM department, an employee working for a consulting firm hired to perform job analysis studies, or—in a small organization—a support staff employee such as the administrative assistant to the city administrator or executive director of a nonprofit agency. The following paragraphs introduce the most common methods of data collection; a number of specific job analysis techniques are discussed later in the chapter.

Interview. The analyst interviews the incumbent performing the job, the immediate supervisor, or another subject matter expert (SME), or a combination of all three, about the essential functions of the position.

Questionnaire. SMEs are asked to complete an open-ended questionnaire. The job incumbent usually is asked to complete the questionnaire first and then the supervisor is asked to review it to add anything that may have been neglected or to clarify statements made by the incumbent. Exhibit 5.1 provides an example of a job analysis questionnaire.

Structured checklist. This is another form of questionnaire. The SMEs are asked to respond to information presented on the checklist. The SMEs check the responses most appropriate for their positions. Exhibit 5.2 presents an example of a structured checklist.

Observation. In this method the analyst actually observes the incumbent performing the job and records what he or she sees.

Exhibit 5.1. Job Analysis Questionnaire.

Name: _____ Date Completed: _____

Job Title: _____

A. Please specify the percent of your total time spent in performing each task. Work that is performed daily:

Essential Activities	Tasks	Percentage of Time

B. Indicate by "X" the organizational level of people in the agency and in other organizations with whom you come into contact. Also indicate the primary means by which you contact these individuals.

Within Agency (Employees of Agency)

a. _____ Contact mainly within own department or office.

b. _____ Regular contact with other departments or offices, furnishing and obtaining information.

c. _____ Regular contact with other departments or offices, requiring tact and the development of utmost cooperation.

d. _____ Regular contacts with major executives on matters requiring explanations and discussions.

Means of Contact

_____ Personal conversation   _____ Telephone   _____ Letter
_____ Other (specify)_____

Outside Agency (Nonemployees)

a. _____ Regular contact with persons outside the organization, involving effort that necessitates a great deal of tact and diplomacy.

b. _____ Regular contact with others by presenting data that may influence important decision.

c. _____ Regular contact with persons of high rank, requiring tact and judgment to deal with and influence these people.

Means of Contact

_____ Personal conversation   _____ Telephone   _____ Letter
_____ Other (specify)_____

C. What type of errors are possible on your job, and what would be the consequences of such errors in terms of additional expense to the organization, rework, and/or loss of good will?

Exhibit 5.2. Structured Task Questionnaire.

For each question, three responses are required:

A. Indicate the *frequency* with which this function is performed in this position.

B. Indicate how *important* this function is to the position.

C. Indicate whether *knowledge* of this function is essential for a newly hired employee in this position.

A	B	C
Frequency	Importance	Knowledge
0=Never	0=Not applicable	0=Not required for job
1=Rarely	1=Not important	1=Essential for newly hired employee
2=Sometimes	2=Somewhat important	2=Not essential at hire, can be learned on the job
3=Often	3=Important	
4=Very Often	4=Very Important	

Typing	A Frequency 0 1 2 3 4	B Importance 0 1 2 3 4	C Knowledge 0 1 2

1. Type/keyboard letters from handwritten rough drafts.

2. Type/keyboard letters to students, faculty, staff, applicants or outside individuals or companies.

3. Type/keyboard inventory reports or budget reports.

4. Type/keyboard monthly status reports.

5. Type/keyboard general office forms (such as purchase requisitions, work orders, travel vouchers, printing requisitions).

6. Type course materials, transparencies, syllabi, or tests for faculty.

7. Compose various letters and memos without written or verbal instructions.

8. Compose letters and memos from simple written outline of verbal instructions.

9. Proofread for spelling, grammar, and punctuation on all correspondence and reports.

10. Type/keyboard or edit manuscripts or drafts for supervisor.

11. Prepare manuscripts for publication, including correction of errors and consultation on other editing matters.

12. Lay out format and spacing for tables, charts, or other illustrations in preparation for typing.

This method works primarily for jobs in which activities or behaviors are readily observable. This method would not work well for intellectual or cognitive processes.

Diary/log. In this procedure employees are asked to keep track of and record their daily activities and the time spent on each.

Combination of all methods. Depending on the purpose of the job analysis and the targeted jobs it may be necessary to use a combination of all of the methods introduced here. Not all jobs lend themselves to observation. Many public and nonprofit incumbents sit behind desks, use personal computers, and talk on the telephone. An analyst can observe those behaviors but will not understand the cognitive processes that accompany them or the requisite educational requirements and knowledge that may be specific to each position.

Many organizations have a variety of positions, from very skilled to nonskilled. For example, a local government may have city planners, experts in computer applications, budgeting and finance personnel, clerk-typist positions, and groundskeeper and laborer positions. The analyst may use different methods of data collection for different positions. For example, the groundskeeper and laborer positions may not require reading and writing skills. To ask incumbents who may lack those skills to complete an open-ended written questionnaire may not provide the analyst with the information he or she is seeking. Instead, interviews and observation might be more appropriate data collection techniques. The city planner, however, might be asked to complete a questionnaire, followed by an interview to clarify any jargon or statements that the analyst does not understand. A follow-up interview also allows the incumbent to add information that she or he may have forgotten when completing the questionnaire.

In large organizations composed of many incumbents in the same position or in state or federal organizations with geographically dispersed locations the analyst may first want to meet with a small number of incumbents and supervisors and ask them questions or have them fill out an unstructured questionnaire. The analyst may then develop a structured questionnaire based on the information provided and distribute it to all of the incumbents who hold that position, and then analyze the data for common work activities and responsibilities.

Designing a Job Analysis Program

Why are you collecting job information? For what purpose will the data be used? The answer to these questions is important because different purposes require different information. For example, if the job analysis is to serve as the basis for determining compensation, the analyst would need to obtain information about educational requirements and level of experience and training. However, if the analysis is to serve as the basis for developing performance appraisal instruments, the job analyst will need to identify levels of task proficiency.

Another consideration is that employees may be sensitive to some of the purposes behind the job analysis. For example, employees are more likely to be more concerned about a job analysis when it will be used to develop a compensation system than when the information will be used to develop training and orientation material for new hires. Employees are thus likely to emphasize different information depending on the purpose of the analysis.

The analyst should work with representatives of the organization to determine the most effective method and procedures for collecting information. It is important for the analyst to understand how the organization operates and when would be the best time to obtain information from incumbents and supervisors, because not all jobs or tasks require the same intensity at the same times or for forty hours a week. Different tasks are likely to be performed on different days or at different times of the month or year. Also, some jobs have busy cycles during which the incumbents cannot be interrupted to visit with an analyst or to take the time to complete an extensive questionnaire.

The following factors should be taken into consideration when deciding on the most effective way to collect information:

Location and number of incumbents. Will a particular method or procedure enhance or restrict data collection because of a job's location? Will it be hazardous or too costly for an analyst to observe the job being performed? In the public sector many jobs are geographically dispersed throughout the city, state, or country. It might be too expensive and time-consuming for an analyst to visit and interview, for example, all of the child protective investigators across a state. Asking the investigators to complete a questionnaire instead would be more feasible.

Work conditions/environment. Would work need to shut down during interviews because of a dangerous working environment? Would the incumbent or analyst be at risk if work were disrupted? Are there distractions in the work environment such as noise, heat, hazardous materials, or risk management requirements that would impair the data collection?

Knowledge, technology, and personal factors. Do the knowledge, technology, or personal characteristics of the incumbents lend themselves to a particular method or procedure? As stated earlier, not all jobs or aspects of jobs are conducive to observation. A teacher's classroom performance can be observed. But what about the preparation? What would an analyst see? Can the thought processes be observed, or the knowledge required to prepare a lesson? Other factors to consider are whether the job consists of routine or unpredictable tasks and whether the complexity of the job favors a particular method. Will the SME prefer a particular method? Are there peer or organizational factors that may influence whether a procedure may be effective? For example, will a group interview inhibit employees from speaking up because they are intimidated by the presence of others? If supervisors and incumbents are asked to collaborate, will the supervisor dominate the conversation with the analyst?

After considering the factors just presented, the jobs to be studied need to be identified and the types of instruments that will be used to obtain relevant data and information need to be chosen. Management should notify the incumbents and supervisors in advance that a job analysis will be undertaken and explain to them the purpose or purposes behind the endeavor. The quality of the data collected depends on assistance from SMEs.

Strategic Job Analysis and Generic Job Descriptions

Advances in information technology have changed many public and nonprofit organizations. Positions are being redefined to mesh more congruently with new missions and services. Organizations have become less hierarchial as many managerial responsibilities have been transferred to employees and work teams. Positions have become more flexible, in the attempt to capitalize on improved information management capabilities as well as the changing characteristics of employees. Today many employees are expected to plan and organize their own work. One result of these changes is that employees are now expected to perform a variety of complex tasks that go beyond formal job descriptions. Positions today are more flexible and contingent upon changing organizational and job conditions (Carson & Stewart, 1996).

Traditional job analysis tends to focus on the KSAOCs required for performance of a position as it currently exists or as it has existed in the past. However, if agencies want to prepare for future changes, they must integrate into the job analysis strategic issues that may affect jobs in the future. Schneider and Konz (1989) recommend that a panel of SMEs be convened to discuss the kinds of issues that are likely to challenge positions as well as the organization in the future. Recommended SMEs include job incumbents, managers, supervisors, strategic planners, human resources staff, and experts in a technical field related to the job to be analyzed.

After potential future issues have been identified, tasks and KSAOCs need to be revised in anticipation of anticipated changes. The SMEs should then rate the jobs according to (1) the importance and time spent on each task or task cluster, (2) the importance of the KSAOCs, (3) the difficulty of learning the KSAOCs, and (4) when the KSAOCs will be learned. The result is that the KSAOCs based on the present job are reviewed based on the changes identified by the SMEs (Schneider & Konz, 1989, pp. 54–55). Implementation of this strategic job analysis process can assist HRM practitioners by anticipating and forecasting future organizational needs.

Cardy and Dobbins (1992) recognized that strategic job analysis may not be appropriate for organizations that desire to be more flexible but cannot anticipate or plan change. They recommend instead using a job analysis to develop generic position descriptions. They suggest moving away from a traditional job description in which specific job duties and tasks are enumerated, toward focusing instead on the level of general characteristics important for success in the organization's culture and for dealing with change. For example, the focus could be on general categories important for success, such as adaptability, self-motivation, and trainability, in addition to job context and specific technical skills. The job description could be on a broader set of KSAOCs instead of on specific tasks or behaviors (Carson & Stewart, 1996). Traditional job descriptions have been criticized for shackling management's ability to become more flexible. Generic job descriptions permit the flexibility to cross-train employees, reassign work, and reallocate decision-making responsibilities and authority when necessary. Cardy and Dobbins (1992) do caution that research needs to be conducted to make sure that generic job descriptions actually prepare organizations for the future, as well as comply with EEOC guidelines.

Job Analysis Techniques

A variety of job analysis approaches have been developed over the years. These approaches gather information on job content and/or worker characteristics that are common to jobs across a wide spectrum. They might describe how the incumbent does his or her job, the behaviors that are required to perform the job, or the activities that are performed. The following are some of the more common approaches used.

The Position Analysis Questionnaire (PAQ). The PAQ was developed by researchers at Purdue University. It is a structured job analysis questionnaire consisting of 187 worker-oriented job activities and work situation variables divided into the following six categories:

1. Information input (Where and how does the worker get the information that is used in performing the job?)
2. Mental processes (What reasoning, decision-making, planning, and information-processing activities are involved in performing the job?)
3. Work output (What physical activities does the worker perform and what tools or devices are used?)
4. Relationships with other people (What relationships are required in performing the job?)

5. Job context (In what physical and social contexts is the work performed?)
6. Other job characteristics (What activities, conditions, or characteristics other than those already described are relevant to the job?)

The PAQ items are rated using different scales, including importance, amount of time required, extent of use, possibility of occurrence, applicability, and difficulty. The PAQ is computer scored and a profile for the job is compared with standard profiles of known job families, enabling the comparison of one job to another. The quantitative nature of the PAQ enables it to be used for evaluating job worth and for identifying applicable exams for screening applicants (Henderson, 1989). An example of the PAQ is shown in Exhibit 5.3.

Department of Labor Procedure (DOL). The U.S. Department of Labor provides a standardized method to analyze jobs. Job tasks are analyzed and rated in terms of what an employee does with respect to data, people, and things (see Table 5.1). For example, the job of a counselor working with chronically mentally ill adults might be rated 1 under data, 3 under people, and 5 under things. These scores are translated into the tasks of coordinating, supervising, and tending. A personnel officer specializing in labor rela-

Table 5.1. Department of Labor Worker Functions.

Data	People	Things
0 Synthesizing	0 Mentoring	0 Setting up
1 Coordinating	1 Negotiating	1 Precision working
2 Analyzing	2 Instructing	2 Operating-controlling
3 Compiling	3 Supervising	3 Driving-operating
4 Computing	4 Diverting	4 Manipulating
5 Copying	5 Persuading	5 Tending
6 Comparing	6 Speaking-signaling	6 Feeding-offbearing
	7 Serving	7 Handling
	8 Taking instruction and helping	

tions might be rated 0 under data, 1 under people, and 0 under things. These scores indicate responsibility for synthesizing, negotiating, and setting up.

Functional Job Analysis (FJA). The FJA builds on the DOL approach by including four additional scales: (1) the scale of *worker instructions,* which identifies the extent to which specific instructions are necessary to perform the tasks and the levels of discretion exercised by employees; the scales of *educational development,* which are (2) the scale of *reasoning development,* which identifies the extent to which reasoning and judgment are required to perform the task, and (3) the scale of *mathematical development,* which measures the mathematical ability required to perform the tasks; and (4) the scale of *language development,* which measures the verbal and language skills required to perform the task.

Comprehensive Occupation Data Analysis Program (CODAP). The CODAP is a task inventory developed for Air Force specialties by the Air Training Command of the United States Air Force. Detailed task statements are written to describe the work. Each statement consists of an action, an object of the action, and essential modifiers. Job incumbents are asked to indicate the relative amount of time they spend on each task. Responses are then clustered by computer analysis into occupational groupings so that jobs having similar tasks and the same relative time-spent values are listed together.

Job Element Method (JEM). The JEM was developed by Ernest Primoff of the U.S. Office of Personnel Management. The purpose of the JEM is to identify the behaviors and their accompanying achievements that are significant for job success. A combination of behavior and achievements is referred to as an element. Elements may include job behaviors, intellectual behaviors, motor behaviors, and work habits.

A panel of SMEs identifies tasks significant to the job. Next the panel identifies the KSAOCs necessary to perform the job. At this stage the job tasks are turned into job elements. For example, the tasks "writes computer programs to perform statistical analyses, interprets the data, and writes reports" is transformed into the element "ability to write computer programs to perform statistical analyses, interpret data, and write reports."

The SMEs then rate the elements on four factors (Primoff, 1975, p. 3):

Exhibit 5.3. Position Analysis Questionnaire.

B1. Decision Making, Reasoning, and Planning/Scheduling
(continued)

38. Amount of planning/scheduling

Using the response scale below, indicate the amount of planning or scheduling the worker is required to do that affects his or her own activities and/or activities of others.

Amount of Planning/Scheduling

0 *Does not apply*
(has no opportunity to plan own activities, as activities are virtually predetermined)

1 *Very limited*
(has limited opportunity to plan or schedule own activities, for example, punch press operator or inspector)

2 *Limited*
(some planning is required, for example, that done by a lab technician or TV repair person)

3 *Moderate*
(a moderate amount of planning of own or other activities is required, for example, a carpenter who plans the best way to build a structure, an electrician, a police officer, or a dietician)

4 *Considerable*
(a fair amount of planning/scheduling is required, for example, a supervisor who plans the activities of subordinates, a teacher who prepares lectures or lesson plans, or a material coordinator who plans and schedules the arrival and distribution of materials)

5 *Extensive*
(substantial amount of planning/scheduling is required, for example, a department store manager, an executive who plans the activities of different work groups, an architect, or a scientist who makes comprehensive plans for experiments)

B2. Information-Processing Activities

In this section are various human operations involving information or data processing. Using the response scale at the left, rate each of the following items in terms of how important the activity is to the completion of the job.

Importance to This Job

0 Does not apply
1 Very minor
2 Low
3 Intermediate
4 High
5 Extreme

39. **Combining information**

Combining, synthesizing, or integrating information or data from two or more sources to establish new facts, hypotheses, theories, or a more complete body of *related* information, for example, an economist predicting future economic conditions, a pilot flying aircraft, or a judge trying a case

40. **Analyzing information or data**

Identifying underlying principles or facts by breaking down information into component parts, for example, interpreting financial reports or diagnosing mechanical disorders or medical symptoms

41. **Compiling**

Gathering, grouping, classifying, or arranging information or data in some meaningful order or form, for example, preparing various reports, filing correspondence on the basis of content, or selecting data to be gathered

42. **Coding/decoding**

Coding information or converting coded information back to its original form, for example, reading Morse code, translating foreign languages, or using other coding systems such as shorthand, mathematical symbols, computer languages, or drafting symbols

43. **Transcribing**

Copying or posting data or information for later use, for example, copying meter readings in a record book or entering transactions in a ledger

1. Barely acceptable: What relative portion of even barely acceptable workers are good in the element?
2. Superior: How important is the element in picking out the superior worker?
3. Trouble: How much trouble is likely if the element is ignored when choosing among applicants?
4. Practical: Is the element practical? To what extent can we fill our job openings if we demand it?

The ratings on these four factors are analyzed to identify those elements that have the greatest potential for selecting superior applicants. The premise behind the JEM is that the same elements may traverse different tasks and different jobs. The JEM is used by the federal government to establish selection standards and to validate selection examinations.

For a comprehensive compilation of different types of job analysis techniques and job analysis studies across a variety of occupations, please refer to *The Job Analysis Handbook for Business, Industry, and Government,* Volumes One and Two, by Sidney Gael (1988).

Summary

Forecasting human resources needs is a critical component of SHRM. Organizations must assess past trends, evaluate their present situation, and project their human resources needs. Before decisions can be made on recruitment and selection or training and development objectives, organizations need to audit the skills and positions of their incumbent employees. This audit will provide information on the inventory of KSAOCs and positions available within the agency and will call attention to any KSAOCs or positions that may be missing. Jobs change and the KSAOCs required to perform them also change. To remain competitive, agencies must keep abreast of changing skill and position requirements.

A job analysis is required not only for the planning and development of recruitment and selection strategies and for planning training and development programs; it also provides the foundation for other HRM functions. A job analysis is essential for the development of compensation systems, for identifying job-related competencies that can objectively evaluate employees' performance, for restructuring work activities, and for assessing risks in the workplace. An up-to-date job analysis is required to validate the job-relatedness of other human resources functions.

Chapter Six

Recruitment and Selection in the Public and Nonprofit Sectors

Strategic human resources management (SHRM) depends on the successful recruitment and selection of qualified individuals. Recruitment is the process of attracting qualified candidates to apply for vacant positions within an organization. Selection is the final stage of the recruitment process, when decisions are made as to who will be selected for the vacant positions. Both recruitment and selection require effective planning to determine the human resources needs of the organization. The organization must determine its immediate objectives and future direction, and it must forecast its employment needs so that those needs are aligned with the organization's strategies.

To fill positions, agencies have a variety of options. They can recruit new employees, they can promote or transfer incumbent employees who possess the skills necessary for the vacant positions, or they can provide training or educational support to lower level or paraprofessional employees in anticipation of future needs.

The recruitment and selection of qualified and competent employees is critical for public and nonprofit agencies because mission driven agencies are dependent upon their staffs. It is people who deliver the programs and services that public and nonprofit stakeholders expect; therefore, planning for and selecting qualified and competent employees must be done with a strategic purpose.

Consider the following situations:

- Funds have been appropriated for the Immigration and Naturalization Service to hire one thousand border patrol officers (Rivenbark, 1995a).
- Declining donations of food and cash have led local area food banks to broaden their missions. Besides distributing food, many have begun to provide child care and adult education, and to make job referrals. The executive director of one food bank, Hosea House, stated, "We have to get people out of the system if we are going to be able to feed the new people coming in." The expansion in services means that new positions need to be filled (Todd, 1994).
- The director of finance for a local government has notified the city manager that she plans to retire when she reaches sixty-five years of age, which is in eight months.
- The state division for youth needs to hire certified teachers, counselors, and maintenance and food service personnel to staff a new residential facility for delinquent youth.

These examples illustrate how important it is for public and nonprofit organizations to be able to attract applicants for their present and future staffing needs. Vacancies arise when employees are promoted or transferred to different positions within the agency, or when people retire or leave to seek employment in other agencies. Some departments or agencies may expand into new service or program areas requiring additional staff. Recruitment is an ongoing process in most organizations, however; often it is not planned and therefore is less successful than it could be. For recruitment to be successful, planning is essential. Recruitment efforts must be consistent with the agency's mission. Employers must understand how to determine the job requirements, where to seek and how to screen applicants so that qualified and competent individuals are selected.

This chapter introduces the reader to internal and external recruitment, applicant screening, selection methods, preemployment testing under the Americans with Disabilities Act (ADA), and executive/managerial recruitment and selection. An explanation of employment-test-related psychometric concepts is also provided.

Recruitment

As noted in Chapter Two, recruitment must be tied to the organization's mission, and attempts should be made to anticipate the future personnel needs of the agency. An SHRM plan should exist that will facilitate the agency's ability to accomplish its objectives.

Before recruitment for candidates begins, the human resources management (HRM) recruiter and the unit manager should review the qualifications needed for the vacant position or positions. This review enables them to identify the knowledge, skills, abilities, and other characteristics (KSAOCs) they will be looking for in the applicants, and it will guide them in developing an accurate job bulletin or advertisement.

Internal Recruitment

Public sector agencies often look at current staff first to fill vacancies in the workforce. In fact, many public agencies give extra credit or points to employees already working for the organization; the city of St. Louis, for example, gives additional points to candidates who already part of the workforce. In some cases there may be collective bargaining agreements in place that stipulate that incumbent employees should receive preferential consideration. Preference for incumbent employees may also exist in many nonprofit agencies in which program stability and connections to the community and funding sources are important. In these cases, employers would first consider the internal labor market.

For internal recruitment to work, agencies need to be proactive and incorporate strategic planning into their human resources practices. Organizations need to track the KSAOCs needed for the various jobs within the organization. Employees who possess those needed skills, whether they be administrative, managerial, or technological, should be identified. HRM departments and department managers should work together and make workforce projections based on the present level of employee skills. They should review transfers, retirements, promotions, and termination patterns. They should do succession planning, whereby individuals are identified who might fill positions when an incumbent leaves. This requires keeping track of and updating the records of each employee's KSAOCs and the demands required of each position.

Internal recruitment is favored by many organizations because administrators have the opportunity to review and evaluate the KSAOCs of internal applicants prior to selection. It also enables agencies to recoup the investment they have made in recruiting, selecting, training, and developing their current employees. Promoting qualified incumbent employees rewards them for their past performance and signals to other employees that the agency is committed to their development and advancement.

Before organizations limit recruitment efforts to internal recruitment, however, other factors should be considered. Some positions in public and nonprofit organizations require specialized skills that may not be found within the agency, and for such positions it may be necessary to recruit and hire from outside. Organizations with homogenous workforces—that is, agencies composed of all women, men, or Caucasians, for example—should also consider outside recruitment to increase the demographic diversity of their staff. Another important reason for the organization to consider external recruitment is when it wants to change its existing culture. Applicants hired from outside are not hampered by "sacred cows," relationships with colleagues, or the agency's history.

External Recruitment

External recruitment is when the organization seeks qualified applicants from outside the organization. Typically the agency would seek qualified applicants from the *relevant labor market*. A relevant labor market is defined by the skills required for the position and the location (geographical region) where those skills can be found. The nature of specific occupations or jobs often demarcates the labor market. Local labor markets, for example, are small areas, cities, or metropolitan statistical areas. Laborer, office and clerical, technical, and direct service provider positions are often filled from the local labor market. It is common for federal, state, and local governments and nonprofits to recruit clerical and trade employees, such as maintenance or custodial personnel, from the local labor market. Applicants for these positions are typically abundant and the salaries that accompany the positions preclude relocating new employees.

Regional labor markets are larger. They usually comprise a particular county or state or even several areas of a state. Depending on the skill supply in the region, technical, managerial, and professional workers as well as scientists and engineers may be recruited from a regional labor market. Agencies in the New England areas, for example, can use the regional labor market to recruit applicants for all kinds of positions because of the number and variety of colleges, universities, and industries located there.

State, local, and nonprofit agencies use the national labor market when critical skills are in short supply locally. Scientists, engineers, managers, professionals, and executives are most likely to be sought at the national level. The federal government, for example, recruits nationally through regional offices for all of its professional positions.

Public and nonprofit organizations need to develop a recruitment strategy. Decisions need to be made about when and where to look for qualified applicants, and action needs to be taken. Ban and Riccucci (1993) observed that the recruitment techniques most commonly used in the public sector are "passive" (pp. 83–84). Vacancies are posted but there is no recruitment plan, which is necessary in the increasingly competitive job environment. Ban and Riccucci recommend that public sector agencies anticipate their future needs, and actively and creatively promote the opportunities available in government. They also recommend integrating techniques such as internships, co-ops, and on-the-job training into the recruitment and selection process.

Recruitment planning and strategies at the federal and state levels are typically directed by central personnel offices, and for local governments by centralized civil service offices. It would be remiss to generalize any more than that because at this time many changes are taking place at all levels of government in regard to recruitment and selection. For example, the federal government has implemented many of the recruitment and selection recommendations from the National Performance Review (1993), such as eliminating the central hiring registers compiled by the Office of Personnel Management (OPM) and permitting managers to hire applicants for specific jobs without a written test. States such as Wisconsin have also made changes in the way applicants are recruited and selected.

Despite the well-deserved criticism of centralized personnel offices, they have begun to change with the times. Technology has made information more accessible to job seekers. The federal government has developed personal-computer-based kiosks that provide job seekers with current job information at the touch of a finger. Job seekers can access the Career America Connection, a twenty-four-hour voice response telephone system that provides callers with current nationwide information on federal jobs and application procedures. Callers can also request application materials. The Telephone Application Processing System enables job seekers to apply for federal employment by telephone. Voice prompts in the system enable applicants for specific occupations to respond to questions about their education and experience. The application process takes less than fifteen minutes, and callers can be referred to employing agencies the morning after ("Hiring Overhauled," 1994).

The state of Wisconsin's Department of Employment Relations (DER) has revised its recruitment and selection procedures through the implementation of four new programs. The Entry Professional Program and the Critical Recruitment Program enable state agencies to use alternatives to written examinations to hire college graduates as well as to select candidates for scientific and engineering positions that are difficult to fill. Another program permits applicants to take civil service exams without first making a reservation. Like the OPM, DER has also taken advantage of computer technology and created JOBS, an on-line bulletin board service that advertises job vacancies to state agencies and anyone with Internet access ("Personnel Department Eases," 1995).

Recruiting for Local Governments and Nonprofits

Recruitment efforts for local governments and nonprofit organizations should begin with a review of the competencies and skill levels of the positions that need to be filled. After these elements have been identified, the government or agency needs to develop a recruitment plan and target either the local, regional, or national labor market. Clerical, trade, and technical positions can typically be filled by the local and/or regional labor market. Executive, scientific, and medical positions such as executive directors of nonprofits, directors of development, city managers, police chiefs, and directors of large departments such as personnel, community development, public health, and finance may be recruited nationally. Some national recruitment sources used by the public and nonprofit sectors are general professional journals and newsletters such as the *PA Times, International City Manager's Association (ICMA) Newsletter, Public Personnel Management Newsletter, Community Jobs,* the *Nonprofit Times,* and the *Chronicle of Philanthropy.* There are also a variety of newsletters or job services targeted directly at special occupations. For example, positions in the arts and entertainment are targeted by such publications as the *National Arts Placement Affirmative Action Arts Newsletter, National Arts Placement, Entertainment Employment Journal,* and *Community Arts News.* An organization looking for social workers could advertise in *Social Service Jobs,* the National Association of Social Workers newsletter *NASW News,* or *Professional Opportunities Bulletin.* References to use for identifying sources to advertise in are books written by Daniel Lauber such as the *Nonprofits and Education Job Finder* (1997), the *Government Job Finder* (1997), and the *Professional's Job Finder* (1997). Lauber identifies job services and directories by occupational interests in twenty-four categories, including health care, social services, housing, science, transportation, and legal services.

When advertising is part of the recruitment process it should be written in a manner that will attract responses from qualified individuals and deter responses from those who are not qualified (Schofield, 1992). It is important for the advertisement to focus on the job qualifications that are required for the position so that only those candidates with qualifications matching the requirements of the position are attracted to apply for the position. To comply with the ADA, employers should inform applicants on an application form or job advertisement that the hiring process includes specific selection procedures (for example, a written test; demonstration of job skills such as typing, making a presentation, or editing a report; or interview). Applicants should be asked to inform the employer within a reasonable time period prior to the administration of the selection procedure of any reasonable accommodation needed to take a preemployment examination, accommodate an interview, or demonstrate a job skill. Employers may request from the applicant documentation verifying the need for an accommodation.

To ensure compliance with equal opportunity requirements it is important for agencies to scrutinize their recruitment procedures for practices that may result in discrimination. For instance, the recruitment strategies used should not exclude certain groups. The Equal Employment Opportunity Commission (EEOC) bans the use in recruitment of preferences based on age, race, national origin, religion, or sex. Some organizations, however, will undertake targeted recruitment. Targeted recruitment means that deliberate attempts are made to recruit protected-class members who have been identified as absent from or underutilized in an agency. This targeting may be done to comply with an affirmative action plan or conciliation agreement. Nonprofits that provide services to particular constituency groups, such as persons with AIDS, unwed mothers, or senior citizens, may deliberately target applicants from those groups during recruitment.

Screening Applicants

Once the organization has communicated its need to fill positions and applicants have responded, it then needs to screen the applicants to identify those with the requisite knowledge, skills, abilities, and other characteristics (KSAOCs).

Employment applications are often the first step in the screening process. Applicants fill out a form asking them to answer a variety of questions. The questions must not violate local, state, or federal employment discrimination laws. The rule followed by the EEOC, state agencies, and most courts is that if the employer asks a question on an employment application form, it is assumed that the answer is used in the hiring process. If the question does not pertain to the job applicant's qualification for the job in question, the question may be held illegal if it has a disparate impact on a covered group (Frierson & Jolly, 1988).

When developing an application, an organization should refer to the state's fair employment laws to eliminate any potential discriminatory questions. Questions about age, race, gender, and disability are permitted only when responding is voluntary and the information is required for recordkeeping purposes. Equal employment opportunity data should be collected by the personnel office and not used to screen out applicants.

Most applications are generic and not tailored for any one position. They usually provide limited space for applicants to provide detailed information about relevant work or educational experience. A supplemental questionnaire should be developed that asks questions related to the specific job to facilitate the screening process.

After individuals apply for a position, the applications need to be screened to eliminate applicants who are not qualified and to identify a list of qualified applicants. This process will be different for each position. It is not uncommon for a large urban government that is recruiting for police or fire personnel to have hundreds if not thousands of applicants. Positions typically inundated by applicants use multiple screening procedures to pare down the number of candidates. The first screen is to weed out applicants who do not meet the minimum requirements, such as age (for example, law enforcement positions require applicants to be at least twenty-one years old), level of education, or required certification. The second screen might include the elimination of applicants who lack the requisite experience.

For administrative or professional positions, which usually have more stringent education and experience requirements, there are likely to be fewer applicants. However, in today's competitive market it is still possible to have many applicants for such positions. A local government located in St. Louis County, Missouri, advertised in the *ICMA Newsletter* for a community development position and received resumes from one hundred interested candidates. A community nonprofit social service agency advertised for a development officer position and received sixty resumes.

To reduce the number of applicants to the most qualified, it is important to have preestablished criteria to facilitate the screening. Requiring previous experience as a city planner or community development specialist might be one standard. Previous fiscal management experience with a budget of two million dollars might be another. To screen resumes, an instrument such as a checklist might be developed to keep track of the relevant experience and education required. Anybody who has spent time reading many resumes knows that after the first ten or so fatigue sets in. You become less attentive as the review progresses. A checklist keeps you focused on the salient KSAOCs.

Employment screening techniques and tests must comply with the general principles and technical requirements of the Uniform Guidelines on Employee Selection Procedures (1978).

Preemployment testing is used to measure the KSAOCs of applicants and predict their ability to perform a job. It is an attempt to standardize the screening process and determine whether applicants possess the characteristics necessary to be successful on the job. Along with the Uniform Guidelines, the *Principles for the Validation and Use of Personnel Selection Procedures*—developed by the American Psychological Association, Division of Industrial and Organizational Psychology (1987)—broadly define tests as a variety of instruments or procedures used in the selection or promotion process. The following paragraphs introduce the types of selection techniques commonly used in employment settings, as well as alternative approaches.

Cognitive ability and aptitude tests. Tests of this sort are designed to reflect both the general and the specific capabilities and potentials of the individual applicant by measuring verbal, quantitative, nonverbal, and oral skills, or motor functions such as mechanical ability, numerical aptitude, finger dexterity, or perceptual accuracy. They are used to determine whether applicants possess the aptitude to learn the KSAOCs required in the position.

Achievement tests. These tests are designed to measure the degree of mastery of specific material, to assess whether an individual has profited from prior experience and learned specific materials. Most of the items on achievement tests assess whether the individual possesses specific knowledge of concepts considered critical for a job. Trade tests are examples of this type.

Personality inventories. Tests of this sort are designed to assess a person's typical behavioral traits and characteristics by measuring such traits as dominance, sociability, self-control, or introversion-extroversion. Some of the more common personality tests used in the public sector are the Minnesota Multiphasic Personality Inventory, the California Psychological Inventory, and the Edwards Personal Preference Schedule. They are used when interpersonal skills are key to successful performance.

Interest inventories. These tests are designed to predict job-choice behavior rather than job performance by ascertaining the occupational likes and dislikes of the individual and indicating the occupational areas that are most likely to be satisfying to that person. They are used to make a compatible person-job match.

Rating of experience and training (E & T). This procedure quantifies the education, experience, training, achievements, and other relevant data that applicants provide on job applications and questionnaires. Points are assigned to applicants based on the number of years of experience, education, and training relevant to the position. E & T exams are often referred to as unassembled examinations.

Structured oral exams. These exams are used to evaluate job requirements that are not easily assessed by paper-and-pencil measures, such as interpersonal, oral communication, and supervisory skills. While the specifics of the exams may differ, all structured oral exams share similar components. They are based on a job analysis that captures the critical KSAOCs necessary for the position. The questions are job-related and all applicants are asked the same questions. Rating scales are used to evaluate the responses, and the raters receive training prior to conducting the examination. Structured oral exams are used a great deal in the public sector. The U.S. Office of Personnel Management uses structured oral exams for a variety of positions from entry-level to senior, such as those in the Presidential Management Intern Program, and in the Administrative Law Judge selection process. The New York State court system uses oral exams for the hiring and placement of Spanish-speaking court interpreters. Many local governments use oral exams to determine promotions to supervisory positions in police and fire departments (Sproule, 1990).

Work sample or performance tests. These tests require applicants to demonstrate that they possess the necessary skills needed for successful job performance. Applicants are asked to perform tasks that are representative of actual job activities. For example, applicants applying for the position of editor of a nonprofit newsletter may be asked to actually edit and write copy, or applicants applying for a training position could be required to prepare and present a training module.

The Berkshire Farm Prevention Program in Onondaga County,

New York, screens applicants for the prevention worker position by requiring a Master of Social Work (M.S.W.) degree and five years of experience working with families. The prevention worker position is designed to help delinquent youth and status offenders stay out of residential placement facilities. The prevention worker's relationship is not only with the youth but also with their families and schools. The position requires clinical skills, advocacy skills, and the ability to work as a team member with other community care providers.

After the resumes have been screened, eligible applicants interested in the position must demonstrate their clinical and interpersonal skills by participating in counseling and crisis intervention role-playing exercises that are observed and evaluated by the program coordinator and incumbent prevention workers. Anne Goldych Dailey, the current program coordinator, established this screening procedure because she found that possession of an M.S.W. degree did not guarantee strong interpersonal and clinical skills. She believes that to be successful in this position, prevention workers need to be able to connect with and establish relationships. Such skills are not always obvious in an interview situation. While acknowledging that the role-playing simulations may be stressful for some candidates, the ability to function in stressful situations is key to effective performance. The client population is families or youth in crisis, and the workers are very autonomous, spending most of their time out in the field and not under direct supervision. Using this screening process has resulted in low turnover. Only one prevention worker has resigned in eleven years and that was because his wife was hired by a university out-of-state and the family relocated.

In-baskets. The in-basket is a written test designed to simulate administrative tasks. The exam is named after the in- and out-baskets that hold correspondence and memos delivered to or waiting to be picked up from desks or offices. The in-basket exercise consists of correspondence designed to be representative of the job's actual tasks. A set of instructions usually states that applicants should imagine that they have been placed in the position and must deal with the memos and other items that have accumulated. The test is used to measure such skills as task prioritization, written communication, and judgment.

Leaderless group discussions. This screening method is designed to assess attributes such as oral communication, leadership, persuasiveness, adaptability, and tolerance for stress. Applicants are assembled to work on solving a problem that requires cooperation. For example, they may be asked to compose a statement in response to charges that the agency's employees are treating clients unfairly, or they may be asked to work on a problem involving competition, such as deciding how to allocate a limited amount of money among a number of community projects. Nobody is designated as the group leader. Assessors evaluate the individual applicants' participation in the group's discussion.

Assessment centers. An assessment center is a special type of selection program that relies quite a bit on performance tests. The purpose of an assessment center is to obtain multiple measurements of key job dimensions by using a variety of instruments such as role-playing exercises, in-baskets, leaderless group discussions, paper-and-pencil tests, and other written exercises. Judgments about each applicant's behavior are made by assessors who are trained in the scoring of each exercise. Assessment centers are frequently used to select administrators and supervisors, who need skills in such areas as leadership, planning, and decision making. In the public sector, assessment centers are commonly used for the selection of city managers and the promotion of public safety managers.

Biodata. Biodata selection procedures require that applicants complete a questionnaire that asks for biographical information. Questions may include topics such as level of education, demographic profile, work experience, interests and social activities, habits, hobbies, family history, attitudes, values, achievements, and personal characteristics. Individuals are selected based on whether their answers to the questions are related to job success. Biodata is not used extensively in the public sector because the questions often bear no overt relationship to the job, are intrusive, often result in adverse impact, and may be viewed as violating merit principles. A large sample—from four hundred to one thousand incumbents—is needed to develop and validate a biodata questionnaire (Sproule, 1990; Wiesen, Abrams, & McAttee, 1989, p. 44). At the federal level, the ACWA's Individual Achievement Record evaluates and scores biodata information.

Drug testing. Substance abuse is a problem in this country, and drug-dependent employees are 3.9 times as likely as nondependent employees to be involved in workplace accidents (Segal, 1990). Decreased productivity, increased absenteeism, and threats to fellow employees' or clients' safety are some of the problems manifested by substance abusers.

Many organizations have instituted drug testing as part of pre-employment screening. It is important to note that applicants do not have the same rights as employees. Therefore, while applicants for a position may be tested for substance abuse, organizations cannot necessarily test incumbent employees. Drug testing of incumbent employees will be addressed in Chapter Twelve.

Lie-detector exams. The Employee Polygraph Protection Act of 1988 prevents employers involved in or affecting interstate commerce from using lie detectors. The law makes it unlawful for employers to require prospective employees to take lie detector tests or for employers to use test results or a worker's refusal or failure to take a test as grounds for failure to promote, discharge, or discipline. The law does not, however, apply to the federal government, to state or local governments, or to any political subdivision of a state or local government. Other exemptions include individuals or consultants working under contract for federal intelligence agencies; makers and distributors of controlled substances; security companies whose business involves the protection of currency, financial instruments, or vital facilities or materials.

The right of a public employer to require a public employee to take a lie detector test may be limited by state statute. The federal law and most state laws prohibit questions about religion; political, racial, and union activities; and sexual and marital matters. Subjects must be informed of their rights, and written consent must be obtained before administering the test. The test results must remain confidential, and only licensed, bonded examiners may be used. Polygraph exams are used primarily for law enforcement and public safety positions.

Honesty/integrity tests. These tests are lawful under the Employee Polygraph Protection Act of 1988 and most state polygraph laws. There are two kinds of honesty and integrity tests: overt and personality. Overt tests deal with attitudes toward theft and/or admission of theft or other illegal activities. Personality tests do not look at honesty per se but at a variety of counterproductive work behaviors such as impulsiveness, nonconformance, and dislike of authority.

A study in 1990 by the Congressional Office of Technology Assessment (OTA) indicated that the results of honesty testing were inconclusive. OTA neither endorsed them nor called for a ban. Another study on the use of honesty and integrity tests was done by the American Psychological Association Task Force in 1991. The task force criticized the way tests were researched and marketed.

Physical ability tests. Physical ability tests are used when a significant level of physical activity is involved in performing the job. In the public sector, physical ability tests are used most often in the selection of law enforcement and public safety officers, such as police officers, firefighters, corrections officers, and park and conservation safety officials. Physical ability testing has replaced height and weight requirements, which were often used to screen applicants, resulting in adverse impacts on women and Hispanics, and were difficult to defend as being job related. Agencies have turned instead to physical ability tests that were developed to replicate the physical tasks necessary to perform specific jobs (Arvey, Nutting, & Landon, 1992; Hughes, Ratliff, Purswell, & Hadwiger, 1989).

Preemployment Testing Under the ADA

Congress intended the ADA to prevent discrimination against individuals with "hidden" disabilities such as cancer, heart disease, mental illness, diabetes, epilepsy, and HIV infection or AIDS. Employers are permitted to ask applicants about their ability to perform job functions, but they may not ask about disabilities at the preoffer stage. Once a conditional job offer has been made, the employer may require a medical examination and make disability-related inquiries. Employers may ask applicants to describe or demonstrate how they would perform job-related tasks with or without reasonable accommodation. If the examination screens out an individual with a disability as a result of the disability, the employer must demonstrate that the exclusionary criterion is job related and consistent with business necessity. The employer must also show that the criterion cannot be satisfied and the essential job functions cannot be performed with reasonable accommodation.

Medical examinations. Medical examinations are procedures or tests that seek information about the existence, nature, or severity of an individual's physical or mental impairment, or that seek information regarding an individual's physical or psychological health. The following are some of the guidelines established by the EEOC to determine whether a procedure or test is a medical examination:

The procedure or test must be administered by either a health care professional or someone trained by a health care professional.

The results of the procedure or test must be interpreted by either a health care professional or someone trained by a health care professional.

The employer must administer the procedure or test for the purpose of revealing the existence, nature, or severity of an impairment, or to determine the subject's general physical or psychological health.

The procedure or test may be invasive (for example, drawing blood, testing urine, or analyzing breath).

The procedure or test may measure physiological or psychological responses of an individual only if the results determine the individual's ability to perform a task.

The procedure or test must be one that is normally administered in a medical setting (a health care professional's office, a hospital).

Medical diagnostic equipment or devices may be used for administering the procedure or test.

Physical agility/physical fitness tests. Physical agility and physical fitness tests, in which applicants demonstrate their ability to perform actual or simulated job-related tasks, are not medical examinations. These tests measure applicants' ability to perform a particular task; they do not seek information concerning the existence, nature, or severity of a physical or mental impairment, or information regarding applicants' health. They may be administered at the preoffer stage.

Psychological examinations. Aptitude tests, personality tests, honesty tests, and I.Q. tests are all intended to measure applicants' capacity and propensity to successfully perform a job and are not considered to be medical examinations. Psychological tests that result in a clinical diagnosis and require interpretation by health care professionals are considered to be medical examinations and are prohibited at the preoffer stage.

Interviews

Interviews are often the deciding factor in who gets hired for a position. This is unfortunate because interviews are a subjective selection tool. It is easy for interviewers to inject their own prejudices into the selection decision. Another problem with interviews is that job-related questions that can differentiate between successful and unsuccessful employees often are not asked.

Successful interviewing requires planning and structure. The components of a structured oral exam should be incorporated into the interview process. Questions related to the dimensions of the job should be asked. The interviewers should agree in advance what competencies the position requires. The focus should be on the KSAOCs that interviews can assess most effectively, such as interpersonal or oral communication skills and job knowledge.

To minimize the subjectivity, the interview process should be structured. Campion, Pursell, and Brown (1988, p. 25) propose the following steps:

1. Develop questions based on a job analysis.
2. Ask the same questions of each candidate.
3. Anchor the rating scales for scoring answers with examples and illustrations.
4. Have an interview panel record and rate answers.
5. Administer the process to all candidates consistently.
6. Give special attention to job relatedness, fairness, and documentation in accordance with testing guidelines.

Research indicates that team interviews reduce individual interviewer biases about the applicant (Campion, Pursell, & Brown, 1988) and that mixed-race interview panels serve as a check and balance on the evaluation process (Dobbins, Lin, & Farh, 1992).

Interviewers should be trained in how to accurately receive and evaluate information. Even if a structured interview format is not used, interviewers should still document the candidates' responses to the questions.

Interviewers must also comply with the EEOC guidelines concerning preemployment disability-related inquiries. They may not ask about the existence, nature, or severity of a disability, but they may inquire about the ability of an applicant to perform specific job-related functions. Examples of questions prohibited under ADA are

Do you have a disability that would interfere with your ability to perform the job?

How many days were you sick last year?

Have you ever been treated for mental health problems?

Have you ever filed for workers' compensation?

Examples of questions permitted under ADA are

Can you perform the essential functions of this job with or without reasonable accommodation?

Please describe how you would perform these functions?

Can you meet the attendance requirements of this job?

Do you have the required licenses to perform this job?

The interview should be one of many factors considered when selecting applicants. Not all competent people interview well, and not all jobs require competent interpersonal and communication skills. Many positions use a combination of the screening techniques. For example, it is common for applicants for public safety positions to have to pass a written cognitive ability test, a medical examination and drug screen, a polygraph examination, a background investigation, a physical ability test, and an oral interview before the decision to hire is made. Positions that encompass a lot of responsibility, that require time-consuming and expensive training, or in which risk to the organization or public is great typically have more demanding screening procedures.

Testing Issues

Employment tests that measure cognitive ability skills are controversial because they often result in adverse impact on protected-class members. Arvey and Faley (1988) report that African Americans score 1 to 1.5 standards deviations lower than whites. Not only have state, local, and private sector employers found themselves facing litigation, but so has the federal government. In 1979 the Department of Justice signed a consent decree in which it agreed that the Professional and Administrative Career Examination for entry into federal employment would be eliminated. African Americans and Hispanics as groups did not score as high on the exam as white candidates. A class action suit asking for an injunction and a declaratory judgment was filed against the director of the OPM. The plaintiffs alleged that the exam was in violation of Title VII of the Civil Rights Act of 1964 because the test had a disproportionately adverse effect on African Americans and Hispanics and was not validated in accordance with the Uniform Guidelines on Employee Selection (Nelson, 1982, p. 745). An outcome of the consent decree was the establishment of a variety of selection avenues, such as the outstanding-scholar and co-operative education programs used to hire entry-level federal employees.

State and local governments have found themselves mired in controversy over paper-and-pencil tests and adverse impact. Most large urban police and fire departments have found themselves in federal court or having to negotiate consent decrees with the Department of Justice in efforts to remedy the effects of either purposeful discriminatory practices or neutral employment practices such as paper-and-pencil tests, which resulted in adverse impact against protected class members.

Why are tests used? Organizations needing to distinguish among a large pool of applicants must develop formal, objective methods of screening, grouping, and selecting applicants. Testing is a way to do that. Research on testing has established that cognitive ability tests are equally valid for virtually all jobs and that failure to use them in selection would typically result in substantial economic loss to individual organizations (Schmidt, 1988, p. 281). Hunter (1986, pp. 342, 346) found the following evidence in regard to cognitive ability tests:

1. General cognitive ability predicts performance ratings in all lines of work, though validity is higher for complex jobs than for simple jobs.
2. General cognitive ability predicts training success at a uniformly high level for all jobs.
3. Data on job knowledge shows that cognitive ability determines how much and how quickly a person learns.
4. Cognitive ability predicts the ability to react in innovative ways to situations in which knowledge does not specify exactly what to do.

Psychometric Terms and Concepts

Employers need to be familiar with a number of psychometric concepts as they pertain to employment testing.

Reliability

This concept is concerned with the consistency of measurement. An exam's reliability can be determined through a number of different procedures. *Test-retest* reliability occurs when individuals taking the test score about the same on the test in each administration. If a test is reliable, there should be consistency between two sets of scores for the test taken by the same person at different times. *Split-half* reliability is derived by correlating one part of the exam with another part of the exam. If the exam is measuring an aptitude reliably, it should do so throughout the exam. *Odd-even* reliability is when a score is computed for all the even-numbered exam items and then correlated with a score derived from the odd-numbered items. *Internal consistency measure* reliability is when each exam item is correlated with every other exam item. *Equivalent-forms* reliability is when different forms of an exam have been constructed. Each version of the exam is administered to the participants and the two sets of exam scores are correlated.

Validity

Is the test or selection instrument measuring what it is intended to measure? Validity is the most important characteristic of measures used in personnel selection. Why use a particular test or procedure if it is not predicting or evaluating correctly the most qualified candidates? Validity and reliability are often confused. Reliability is necessary for a test to be considered valid, but it cannot stand alone; just because a test gives consistent results does not mean that it is measuring what it is intended to measure.

Three types of validity are recognized by the Uniform Guidelines on Employee Selection: content, criterion, and construct.

Content Validity. Selection instruments and procedures are considered to be content valid if they reflect the KSAOCs considered essential for job performance. If you want to see if at the time of hire an applicant possesses a skill or knowledge necessary to perform a job, then content validity is an appropriate validation strategy. The most common example cited is the typing test. How does an employer know if applicants can type eighty words per minute? By requiring applicants to demonstrate their skills by taking a test.

The procedures that need to be followed to develop a content valid test are as follows: First a job analysis must be conducted. The KSAOCs and responsibilities required for the position must be discovered. Once they have been identified, they need to be rated for their relevancy, frequency, and importance to the job.

It must then be determined whether it is essential for candidates to possess those KSAOCs at the time of hire or whether they can be learned once the person is on the job. Test items must be written or performance measures must be developed to capture the KSAOCs that are essential at the time of hire. Then incumbents and supervisors who are familiar with the job (subject matter experts, or SMEs) must evaluate the test items or performance samples to determine whether the test accurately reflects the competencies required by the job. A majority of SMEs must agree that the items are representative of the types of skills, knowledge, and behaviors required for the job.

Content validity is used very often in the public and nonprofit sectors. Personnel specialists and managers often possess the skills needed to develop content valid exams. One can be trained how to conduct job analyses and how to work with SMEs to develop selection instruments. Large applicant or incumbent populations are not required, and content validation studies do not necessarily require consultants or an extensive background in psychometrics. Content valid exams possess "face validity," that is, candidates understand how the exam relates to the position. Studies have shown that exams with face validity less often lead to litigation.

Criterion Validity. Criterion validity measures whether the test scores (called predictors) are related to performance on some measure (called a criterion), such as supervisory evaluations or success in a training program. Does the test predict subsequent job performance? The most common example is the correlation of test scores with supervisory ratings of job performance.

There are two types of criterion-related validity, *predictive* and *concurrent.* Both methods demonstrate a statistical relationship between the test scores and performance measures. What differs is the sample of test takers and the amount of time between taking the exam and obtaining job performance measures. The meaning of this will become clearer as the procedures are explained.

Predictive validity. The procedure for predictive validity studies is as follows. First, a job analysis is conducted to determine the relevant KSAOCs for the position. Based on the KSAOCs, an exam is developed. Candidates are then tested for the job using the selection instrument developed. Next, candidates are selected using some other standard. For example, decisions may be based on letters of reference, the interview, or previous experience.

After the new employees have been working for the organization for six months to one year, job performance measures are obtained. These could be supervisory ratings or performance in a training program. After these measures have been collected, a statistical analysis is conducted to evaluate the relationship between the test and the job performance measure. If the test is to be considered useful for selection, the high scorers on the test should have higher performance ratings and the low scorers on the test should have lower performance ratings. You are probably wondering why the test is not used to select employees. Why develop an instrument and then ignore it? Good question. The test was not originally used to select candidates because to determine whether the test could predict performance, both high and low test scores are needed. If only people who scored high on the test were selected, it would not be clear whether individuals with low scores on the test could be good employees. If indeed individuals with low test scores turn out to be the best performers, then the test is not measuring what it was intended to measure in order to predict which applicants would be most successful on the job. If it is not yet known whether the test is valid, making selection decisions on its results would be premature.

Concurrent validity. Concurrent validity also statistically demonstrates a relationship between the predictor and criterion measure. However, the procedures are different than in a predictive validity study. Instead of applicants, incumbents take the examination. Because incumbents are already working for the agency, job performance data can be collected immediately. Then the predictor and criterion data can be correlated and a relationship between the selection instrument and job performance can be determined.

There are some factors to consider when doing a concurrent validity study. Because job incumbents are being used, it must be recognized that over time they may have become more proficient in performing the jobs, and hence they might perform better on the exam than applicants. Or they may perform worse. Because they are already employed they may not care about performing well, or they may even resent having to spend the time taking the test.

Concurrent validity studies are conducted more frequently than predictive validity studies because they take less time to administer and are less costly to develop. Also, research shows that their results tend to be comparable to predictive validity studies (Barrett, Phillips, & Alexander, 1981).

Criterion validity studies are used more frequently at the federal or state levels, where large samples can be obtained. At the local level they are conducted for public safety positions (police and fire), for which hundreds or thousands of applicants are available. They may also be used for positions for which large numbers of people are hired and then sent for specific training, such as to the police or fire academy, or to receive specialized training to become Internal Revenue Service agents. The employer is relying on the test to screen in applicants with the cognitive skills likely to be successful in training.

Construct Validity. Construct validity is the most theoretical type of validity. Selection instruments are developed or used that measure hypothesized constructs or traits related to successful job performance. Constructs are intangible or abstract characteristics that vary in individuals—for example, intelligence, motivation, aggressiveness, anxiety, honesty, initiative, and creativity. To validate exams designed to measure constructs requires expertise in psychometrics. The existence of personality or character traits that are often abstract and intangible is difficult to establish through a job analysis. The burden is on the employer to prove empirically that the test is valid for the job for which it is being used. Construct validity exams are not used by most public sector employers. The exception is law enforcement agencies, for which identifying traits such as aggressiveness and hostility might be important (Wiesen, Abrams, & McAttee, 1990).

Organizations that are considering adopting a test to measure constructs should seek advice from a qualified person (not the test vendor). The research is mixed. A study by Cortina and others (1992) revealed that the Minnesota Multiphasic Personality Inventory and the Inwald Personality Inventory did not contribute significantly more validity than the civil service test used to predict the performance of law enforcement trainees. The civil service test was a multiple-choice written examination and an oral board interview. Other research has found a relationship between scores on the California Psychological Inventory and job performance and class standing at a police training academy (Hogan, 1971; Hogan & Kurtines, 1975; Johnson & Hogan, 1981). Day and Silverman (1989) found that scores on a personality inventory test can be valuable predictors of job performance when carefully targeted to a specific job and specific constructs. Most recently, a meta-analysis investigating the relationship of the "Big Five" personality dimensions (extraversion, emotional stability, agreeableness, conscientiousness, and openness to experience) to criteria measures across five occupational groups found personality measures to be predictors for some occupations (Barrick & Mount, 1991).

Executive/Managerial Recruitment and Selection

At the federal and state levels, executives are typically appointed to their positions by the chief elected officials or their designees and are referred to as political executives. They lack permanent status and retain their positions only for as long as the president or governor desires or until the next election. Often these executives have been referred to the respective executive branches by someone they know, such as a legislator, a professional associate, a campaign worker, a university classmate, a Rhodes scholar, or a corporate executive.

At the local level and in nonprofit agencies, the recruitment and selection of city managers or executive directors is usually conducted by search committees. Usually the personnel committees of the city council or board of directors will be responsible for the search. They will identify what qualifications are needed and determine the recruitment strategies that will be used. Often citizens or clients and representative staff persons will be asked to participate in the effort.

Sometimes search committees that lack the time or expertise to recruit executives may choose to delegate much of the responsibility for directing the recruitment and screening efforts to professional recruitment firms or consultants. An advantage of using professional recruitment firms is that they can devote complete attention to the search process. Unlike council or board members, professional recruiters are not part-time volunteers committed to other jobs. Developing recruitment strategies, placing advertisements, screening resumes and applications, responding to correspondence, verifying references, and conducting preliminary interviews are very time-consuming. Professional recruitment firms are knowledgeable about fair employment laws and practices and will document the procedures used should allegations of discrimination arise. Their livelihoods and reputations depend on conducting professional and legal searches.

Another advantage in using a recruitment firm is that they can provide an objective viewpoint if internal candidates apply for the position. Board or council members may place loyalty, politics, or familiarity above proficiency. An example of this occurred after an executive director of the Atlanta Historical Society (AHS) retired after a long tenure. The board selected someone from within AHS to succeed him. Unfortunately, the new executive director was deficient in administrative skills and other abilities required to meet the organizations needs and challenges (Knauft, Berger, & Gray, 1991). Having outsiders direct the process should mitigate much of the subjectivity that is a natural part of the process.

An additional reason to consider a professional firm is that sometimes organizations wish to remain anonymous in the early stages of the recruitment process. Screening applicants through a professional firm retains that anonymity (Ammons & Glass, 1989; Snelling & Kuhnle, 1986).

Even if a professional firm is hired to direct the recruitment and selection process, council and board members should not abrogate their oversight responsibility. They need to work with the firm to identify the professional and personal qualifications that are needed to guide the organization and that are consistent with the organization's mission. They must determine the strategic challenges facing the organization, where it is and where it is going (Albert, 1993; Gilmore, 1993; Stene, 1980). For example, a county health department in fiscal distress might look for an executive with strong financial management skills, or a nonprofit agency having to contend with declining donations due to a former director's scandalous behavior might need to recruit someone known to have integrity and who also possesses successful fundraising experience.

The recruitment and selection process for executive and managerial positions is more complex than for other positions because it is difficult to describe the components of effective job behavior. Taxonomies commonly used to describe executive effectiveness include good planning, organization, communication, leadership, and decision-making skills, as well as industry technical knowledge and management techniques. Competencies more specific to the public sector could include skill in fiscal management and budgeting, council communication, citizen relations, media relations, intergovernmental relations, program development, and the execution of policies and programs (Wheeland, 1994).

Herman and Heimovics (1989) identified twelve other categories of competencies needed to deal with critical events occurring in nonprofit organizations: developing new programs, establishing program decline, collaborating, managing mergers, fundraising, lobbying, relating with government officials, responding to personnel actions, developing human resources, leading accreditation efforts, reorganizing, and interacting with the board. Proficiency in one competency does not necessarily mean proficiency in the others. An individual may have excellent communication skills but lack technical knowledge. Someone may have wonderful fiscal management skills but lack the skills necessary for effective council or board relations. Because of the vast array of skills that are needed for executive positions, organizations should utilize a combination of selection methods. Some of the screening techniques commonly used for executive and managerial selection are in-baskets, leaderless group discussion, assessment centers, performance tests, and structured oral exams (Cascio, 1991b).

Rossheim, Kim, and Ruchelman (1995) investigated the relationship between four managerial roles and organizational survival in urban arts agencies. The managerial roles were defined as follows (pp. 162–164):

Entrepreneur: is active, initiates change by accessing information, seeks opportunities and challenges, and displays a creative style of managing in terms of planning creative programs, capturing funding opportunities, and networking in the community.

Administrator: possesses skills in daily internal and external arts management but is less inclined to engage in creative, experimental, or original programming. Lacks vision for long-range planning.

Artist: has little interest in internal or external arts management. Focuses on short-term tasks, production, and performing.

Caretaker: is a volunteer administrator who depends on a board of directors rather than providing clearly focused leadership.

Rossheim, Kim, and Ruchelman found that if arts organizations are going to survive in this time of declining fiscal resources, viable organizations need to select managers who display a working combination of entrepreneurship and administrative skills. Arts organizations need managers with standard business and accounting skills who also have the skills to find programs that will attract both new and repeat audiences. An arts agency looking to hire an executive director should thus develop such selection procedures as performance tests in which the applicants review the agency's budget and fiscal reports and write a report for distribution to the members of the finance committee explaining the agency's current fiscal standing and recommendations for the future. The applicants might also be asked to evaluate the agency's standard operating procedures. The applicants entre-preneurial skills could be conducted by conducting structured interviews, including inquiring about their past programming experience and assessing their familiarity with programs with which other arts agencies have been successful. The screening techniques developed should enable the search committee to dif-ferentiate among the applicants and to determine whether they possess accounting and general business competencies as well as entrepreneurial skills.

For executive selection to be successful, organizations must invest the time and effort to recognize the interrelationships among individual behaviors, managerial effectiveness, and orga-nizational success, and they must plan the search process accord-ingly (Cascio, 1991b).

Summary

Organizations periodically need to attract applicants for their pre-sent or future staffing needs. Recruitment is the process of locat-ing qualified candidates. Recruitment strategies should be planned in advance of the agency's needs. Strategic job analyses and audits of positions and employee skills should be updated on a regular basis to determine whether incumbent employees are qualified for promotions or newly created positions. For some positions, depending on the qualifications and/or experience needed, agen-cies may prefer to seek applicants from the external labor market.

After applicants submit resumes or employment applications to the organization, the organization must use job-related criteria to screen the applicants' qualifications for the positions. Applicants who do not meet the initial criteria are eliminated from consider-ation. A variety of selection techniques are available for organiza-tions to use to help assess the applicants' present skill levels or potential for success. Cognitive ability tests, personality or interest inventories, performance tests, ratings of experience and training, assessment centers, and structured interviews are examples of some of the techniques that can be used to evaluate applicants. Organi-zations must be vigilant that their recruitment and selection pro-cedures do not violate federal or state equal employment opportunity laws.

The recruitment and selection process should not end with the hiring or promotion of employees. Agencies should record their recruitment and selection procedures so that they can be evaluated later. The evaluation should identify the successes and failures at each step in the recruitment process so that modifications can be made if necessary. Future recruitment and selection strategies should be based on the procedures that attracted the most qualified applicants and on the screening techniques that best predicted successful on-the-job performance.

Chapter Seven

Performance Evaluation

The increasing demands for accountability made by the stake-holders of public and nonprofit organizations have focused greater attention on performance management. As a result, agencies have begun to reevaluate their performance evaluation systems. Because employees are essential to the delivery of quality services, performance evaluation is a critical component of strategic human resources management (SHRM) in public and nonprofit agencies. The information gleaned from an effective evaluation system can be used to assist agencies in accomplishing their missions. The performance appraisal process also provides feedback to the agency about whether the other human resources management (HRM) functions are working in concert to execute the agency's mission.

Performance evaluations provide management with essential information for making strategic decisions about employee advancement, retention, or separation. Evaluation links training and development with career planning and the agency's long-term human resources needs. Used to support job analysis and recruitment efforts, performance evaluations are an important component of evaluating the knowledge, skills, abilities, and other characteristics (KSAOCs) available among the agency's internal supply of labor. Evaluations can be used to assess career advancement opportunities, for succession planning, and to develop compensation and reward systems, as well as to identify deficiencies in incumbent KSAOCs.

Consider the following examples:

• Judith Reynolds, a female paramedic was terminated for attempting to record a conversation between herself and fire captain Steve Schmitt. She claimed that Schmitt, with whom she had had a brief romantic relationship, had started a systematic pattern of harassing her after the relationship ended. Her dismissal was based on accusations that she drank on duty, that on two occasions she was involved in off-duty automobile accidents, and that she had falsified a report involving an ambulance accident. She was never cited with either criminal or departmental charges before her termination. No documentation existed to substantiate the accusations. The city's civil service board recommended by unanimous decision that Reynolds be reinstated and granted back pay (Kuhn, 1993).

• For two years, a nursing assistant at a health care facility was commended by her supervisor for her conscientious performance. After discussing her most recent evaluation, her supervisor recommended that the nursing assistant return to school to become a registered nurse. The supervisor provided her with information about colleges, recommended financial aid strategies, and discussed how the facility could schedule work hours around her classes.

• The state's civil service promotional guidelines stipulate that in order for an employee to be eligible for promotion to the next level in a job classification, a vacancy must exist, the candidate's qualifications must be determined based on a training-and-experience examination, and the candidate must have received at least a satisfactory performance evaluation in his or her present position. Two employees were qualified based on an evaluation of their training-and-experience examination scores. However, one of the candidates had received an unsatisfactory evaluation the previous year. This candidate was not promoted, and he claimed that he was the victim of discrimination because he is disabled. The supervisor reiterated the performance deficiencies identified in the previous year's evaluation and again recommended that the candidate receive training. The employee withdrew his complaint and signed up for training.

Accurate evaluations provide information and feedback to employees. Employees must be informed about the goals and objectives of the agency and about what role the employees play in the agency's success. They must know what standards will be used to judge their effectiveness. Supervisors must communicate to employees the employees' strengths as well as their deficiencies, thus providing the opportunity for employees to correct their weaknesses before serious problems emerge. Through the evaluation process, training and development needs can be identified and addressed.

Performance evaluation systems are indispensable for planning and research. A review of incumbents' competencies and KSAOCs may indicate that they lack critical skills needed by the agency, thus necessitating that external recruitment efforts be undertaken or, if time permits, that incumbents be trained and developed. Performance evaluations are also used to validate selection instruments or techniques. There should be a positive relationship between the methods and criteria used to screen employees and successful performance. If there is not, the recruitment and selection system should be reevaluated and, if necessary, changed.

When used in the context of SHRM, performance evaluation should provide feedback to employees, facilitate personnel decisions, and provide information essential for planning and research. Feedback about the effectiveness of other HRM functions can also be obtained through the evaluation process.

Disappointment in the efficacy of performance evaluation systems has contributed to performance appraisals being one of the most researched and written-about topics in both the academic and professional HRM literature. Employee, or ratee, dissatisfaction with performance evaluation systems has been based on a number of factors. For example, objective performance measures have been lacking; employees have believed that supervisors are often biased in their ratings, and because of this perceived bias, unions have tended to distrust management and to prefer that promotions and pay increases be based on seniority; and employees have recognized that many of their performance outcomes are dependent upon the efforts of other individuals or groups, which typically are ignored in traditional performance evaluation systems.

Rater dissatisfaction with evaluation systems also exists. Supervisors complain that agencies often promote the use of evaluation systems without devoting the necessary time, supervision, and fiscal resources to make the system work. Raters are expected to evaluate employees and provide feedback without first receiving training, which leaves them ill-prepared to coach and counsel their subordinates. Raters also are not held accountable for the accuracy and quality of their ratings, which signals to them that their efforts are better spent elsewhere because upper management is not committed to the process.

Another reason that performance evaluation systems have been heavily researched is that they play an important role in court cases involving promotions, discharges, layoffs, and merit pay increases. Employees who find themselves the victims of adverse personnel decisions, such as terminations or layoffs, seek redress through human rights agencies and the courts. Employers are likely to defuse potential lawsuits or investigations if they can show that performance appraisals are job related and reflect fair and accurate evaluations of performance.

This chapter discusses how to develop an appraisal program, train raters, prepare documentation, and review evaluations, as well as ethical issues in performance appraisal. It also provides examples of performance appraisal techniques and instruments, and concludes with a discussion of alternative evaluation practices. The chapter provides only an introduction to the topic of performance appraisal. For more information, please refer to Bernardin and Kane (1993), Cardy and Dobbins (1994), Mohrman, Resnick-West, and Lawler (1989), and Murphy and Cleveland (1991, 1995), as well as to the many articles found in professional and academic journals.

Developing an Evaluation Program

There is little consistency in performance evaluation systems across federal, state, and local governments and nonprofit organizations. At the federal level, the evaluation system used to evaluate federal employees was developed to tie performance with pay. Yearly evaluations determine pay increases and/or bonuses. This is different than at the local level, where formal performance evaluations systems often do not exist. For example, Roberts (1994) found that one quarter of municipal governments with populations over ten thousand or more do not have formal appraisal systems. Hays and Kearney (1992) note that at the state level personnel directors "are experiencing particular difficulties in evaluating, rewarding and motivating their employees" (p. 385). In many states and local governments, collective bargaining agreements or civil service systems determine promotions and/or pay increases. In this environment, if evaluations exist they are used strictly as communication vehicles.

The performance evaluation systems of nonprofit organizations also vary widely. In many nonprofits, formal appraisal systems do not exist. Health care facilities are known for evaluating direct service providers such as nurses, social workers, and medical assistants on the basis of their individual behaviors and performance, while executive directors receive bonuses or pay increases that are tied to the organization's fiscal performance. A survey conducted by the Mercer Company found that forty-four charities, foundations, and associations provided financial incentives to their senior management in addition to their base salaries (Greene, 1995).

The only commonality found in the performance evaluation systems of public and nonprofit organizations is that both the raters and ratees typically dislike having to participate in the evaluation process. Yet despite the reservations expressed about performance evaluation systems, most organizations do utilize some form of appraisal. Because performance evaluations are used for different and sometimes multiple purposes, it is important for both employees and supervisors to understand why evaluations are being conducted.

The integrity of a performance appraisal system depends on the raters and ratees understanding its objective. The following statement is taken from a state agency evaluation instrument for civil service employees:

> The Employee Performance Evaluation is designed to encourage all civil staff members to grow professionally and to reach full potential in their work. Using actual job performance as a basis for discussion, this review provides supervisors and employees with an opportunity to identify developmental needs on a mutual basis. In addition, it supplies a means of defining goals and objectives and the most appropriate course of action to pursue in order to increase competency and accelerate career progression. Supervisors are urged, in the strongest possible terms, to discuss the completion of this form during as well as after the evaluation process. This review is a tool of that process, not just the result of it.

In this agency evaluation serves one purpose: employee training and development.

Rater Training

Training is essential for both ratees and raters if performance evaluation systems are to be used in the strategic human resources planning process. Ratees who receive training and understand the evaluation system tend to be more committed to its goals. They should understand why the evaluation is being conducted, how it will be used, and what their role is in the evaluation process. Through training they become aware of the difficulty that raters face in evaluating performance. Training also communicates to ratees their expected levels of performance.

For evaluations to be as accurate as possible, raters should receive training in the development of performance standards and objectives, goal setting, observation, and recall and documentation skills; they should also learn how to complete the evaluation instruments, how to give performance feedback, and how to avoid rating errors. Because performance appraisals rely on human judgment, which is subject to error, personal biases need to be removed from the rating process. Employees must be rated on the basis of job-related, nondiscriminatory criteria. The appraisals must accurately reflect job performance. Exhibit 7.1 lists some of the most common rating errors.

Because different organizations evaluate employees for different purposes and use different types of instruments, organizations must provide raters with training relevant to the organization's instruments and objectives. Raters must understand how to use the instruments with which they are provided. In agencies where evaluations are used for training and development purposes, supervisors also need to be trained in how to develop performance objectives and standards, how to motivate employees to achieve the agreed-upon objectives, and how to counsel employees whose performance is unsatisfactory. In agencies where evaluations are used to substantiate personnel decisions such as promotions, terminations, or pay increases, supervisors must understand how the relationship between the evaluation process and the agency's policies and personnel regulations govern those decisions. They must be able to document that their decisions are based on job-related behaviors or performance. Supervisors may not use the evaluation process as a subterfuge for unjust discrimination.

Exhibit 7.1. Common Rating Errors.

Halo effect: Rating an employee excellent in one quality, which in turn influences the rater to give that employee a similar rating or a higher-than-deserved rating on other qualities. A subset of the halo effect is the "logic error." In this situation, a rater confuses one performance dimension with another and then incorrectly rates the dimension because of the misunderstanding. For example, an employee demonstrates a high degree of dependability (is never absent or late) and, from this behavior, a comparable high degree of integrity is inferred (such as, would never use organization property for personal use).

Central tendency: Providing a rating of average or around the midpoint for all qualities. This is the most common and serious kind of error. Since many employees do perform somewhere around an average, it is an easily rationalized escape from making a valid appraisal.

Strict rating: Rating consistently lower than the normal or average; being constantly overly harsh in rating performance qualities.

Lenient rating: Rating consistently higher than the expected norm or average; being overly loose in rating performance qualities.

Latest behavior: Rating influenced by the most recent behavior; failing to recognize the most commonly demonstrated behaviors during the entire appraisal period.

Initial impression: Rating based on first impressions; failing to recognize most consistently demonstrated behaviors during the entire appraisal period.

Spillover effect: Allowing past performance appraisal ratings to unjustly influence current ratings. Past performance ratings, good or bad, result in a similar rating for the current period, although demonstrated behavior does not deserve the rating, good or bad.

Same as me: Giving the ratee a rating higher than deserved because the person has qualities or characteristics similar to those of the rater (or similar to those held in high esteem).

Different from me: Giving the ratee a rating lower than deserved because the person has qualities or characteristics dissimilar to the rater (or similar to those held in low esteem).

Agencies have a responsibility to train their raters because of the sensitive nature of performance evaluations. Training can improve raters' documentation and counseling skills, thereby not only reducing their discomfort but also enabling them to help employees to clearly understand what the employees' strengths are and what areas need improvement. Training can teach raters how to describe job-related behaviors and develop performance standards, how to emphasize the importance of accuracy and consistency in the appraisal process, and how to provide constructive feedback. Training can be provided through a variety of methods: workshops conducted in-house by the HRM department or off-site by trainers from universities or consulting firms or video packages tailored to the performance evaluation process.

Who Should Rate?

In most organizations, the employee's immediate supervisor evaluates the employee's performance. This is because the supervisor is responsible for the employee's performance, for providing oversight, disseminating assignments, and developing the employee. A problem, however, is that supervisors often work in locations apart from their employees and therefore are not able to observe their subordinates' performance. Should supervisors rate employees on performance dimensions they cannot observe? To eliminate this dilemma, more and more organizations are implementing appraisals referred to as 360-degree evaluations. Employees are rated not only by their supervisors but by coworkers, clients or citizens, professionals in other agencies with which they work, and subordinates. The reason for this approach is that often coworkers and clients or citizens have a greater opportunity to observe an employee's performance and are in a better position to evaluate many performance dimensions. Clients or citizens, for example, are a more appropriate source for evaluating such dimensions as the employee's manner of performance, how the employee treated them, or whether the employee answered their questions in an understandable way.

Performance dimensions such as leadership, training and developing employees, communicating agency policies, and delegating and assigning work are responsibilities commonly found in supervisory or management positions. Competency in these dimensions can best be assessed by subordinates who have frequent contact with the supervisor or manager and can observe different aspects of their performance. Region 9 of the Environmental Protection Agency, for example, refers to this practice as "upward evaluations" and has been using subordinate appraisals for many years (U.S. Office of Personnel Management, 1994). The Dade County Public School System implemented a pilot study using subordinates to evaluate central office administrators (Ash, 1994). Bernardin (1986) cautions, however, that some caveats do exist with subordinate evaluations. Like supervisors, subordinates often lack the training necessary to evaluate their managers; ratings may be based on political gains; subordinates may not tell the truth, fearing retaliation from their boss; employees pushed hard may be strict in their ratings; and subordinates may not have a chance to gain an awareness of the larger picture by observing the manager in diverse situations. Despite these difficulties, Bernardin still believes that subordinate appraisals would result in useful feedback to managers, reinforce good management behavior, encourage greater attention to subordinate needs, and facilitate needed group changes.

Research conducted by McEvoy (1990) in five different public sector organizations suggests that managers would accept the use of subordinate appraisals if the following conditions were met: subordinates were made aware of the requirements of the manager's job; subordinates were asked to rate only the people-oriented dimensions of their boss's performance; the accuracy and fairness of subordinate evaluations were monitored; morale issues were discussed in advance; and the ratings were used primarily for developmental purposes.

Aspects of performance such as providing timely and accurate information to other departments or agencies can often best be assessed by asking the individuals who interact with the employees to evaluate their performance. The absence of complaints does not mean that employees are satisfactorily performing their tasks, so supervisors should not rely on such unreliable indicators. Instead, information should come from the sources who are in the best position to evaluate an employee's performance on specific dimensions. The Army Management Engineering College and the

Department of Energy, for example, have successfully adopted automated 360-degree evaluations (U.S. Office of Personnel Management, 1994).

Many organizations require employees to evaluate their own performance independent of other evaluations. This is referred to as self-appraisal. Supervisors and employees complete appraisal instruments and then meet to compare their evaluations. Differences in their perceptions and expectations are clarified, and strategies for improving future performance or developing career goals are discussed. This process is helpful because employees often are aware of performance constraints or have received commendations for their performance that their supervisor does not know about.

Executive Evaluation

The evaluation of city managers and executive directors of nonprofits is typically performed by city councils or board directors, or subcommittees thereof. Again, there is little consistency in evaluation procedures. The International City Managers Association (ICMA) recommends that as part of the employment contract the council should attach a statement of performance standards and evaluation procedures. The simplest approach is to specify an annual review and the evaluation of the manager's performance based on standards agreed upon by the manager and the council. Another recommended approach is to use evaluation forms that are completed by members of the council. Each council member rates the manager on performance dimensions, targeting their critical responsibilities, such as budget management, supervision, personnel management, leadership, execution of policy, and community reputation. The evaluations are sent to the mayor, who compiles the data and determines an overall rating. Other recommendations include having the council and manager meet in executive session to evaluate the manager's performance, or having the manager, council, and mayor set annual work objectives and goals and evaluate the manager's progress toward the goals. ICMA recommends that councils provide yearly evaluations, but leaves the details to be developed by the council and manager in each city (Page, 1984).

In a study seeking information about the methods used to evaluate city managers in Pennsylvania, Wheeland (1994) found that the majority of councils used an "informal, unstructured, haphazard evaluation method" (p. 155). Evaluation forms were used by only 15 percent of the councils, and only 10 percent of the councils received any training on how to evaluate their city manager. Wheeland also found that the evaluations lacked comprehensiveness. Managers were often evaluated on less than a majority of their responsibilities.

Like the ICMA, the National Center for Nonprofit Boards recognizes that there is not one best technique that can be used to evaluate chief executives. Instead, each board must decide which procedures will best serve the agency. Four general methods of assessment have been identified by Nason (1993):

• *Intermittent or continuous observation of the chief executive by board members, especially the chairperson.* This method is used mostly in small organizations in which the board works closely with the chief executive. If problems arise, it is easy to identify the cause and provide remedies. Nason notes, however, that as organizations expand and board members become less involved in the agency's operations, this method may no longer be effective. Should this become the case, the board will have to reanalyze its oversight role and restructure its own performance.

• *Periodic assessment of the chief executive by the board's chairperson or other board members.* This assessment should reflect the chief executive's performance over the previous year. The evaluation should consider the assessments of other board members, especially those of the chairs of standing committees.

Nason believes that the board members should not discuss the chief executive's performance with the staff; he claims that "to do so is to risk good morale within the organization and to distort proper lines of responsibility" (p. 5). That statement needs further consideration. Some aspects of the chief executive's performance—such as communicating agency policies, informing employees about changes, delegating tasks and responsibilities, and leadership characteristics—are best evaluated by subordinates. Should subordinate evaluations be used, it is important that employees first receive training and be asked to evaluate only relevant dimensions.

Information from proximate sources is important because council and board members spend most of their time away from the organization. For evaluating responsibilities such as council and board relations and communication, board members are the most appropriate source. But for other dimensions, such as fiscal management, they may need to rely on an audit prepared by an outside accounting firm or government regulators to verify that the chief executive's fiscal management performance was satisfactory. An audit conducted by the accounting firm of Coopers & Lybrand in July 1995 of the National Association for the Advancement of Colored People found that the two previous executive directors and the board chairman used agency funds for personal expenses (Murawski, 1995b).

In another case in which accountability was missing, Marcus Rodriguez, second in command of the Museum of Natural History of Los Angeles County, was arrested and charged with embezzlement. His secretary and a former chief financial officer for the museum's foundation have been accused of aiding and abetting Rodriguez by receiving the money he stole and placing it into bank accounts. They were caught when the new president of the museum, James L. Powell, suspected that money was being pilfered. The previous president, Craig Black, admitted lax supervision of Rodriguez, who had operated in an environment of complete trust. "While I asked him for reports regularly, I never went and tried to match them up with dollars that came in from the county. . . . I depended on Mr. Rodriguez and others to manage the day-to-day affairs of the organization" (Murawski, 1995b, p. 36). The museum's board could have discovered the looting spree if it had doubled-checked Rodriguez's statements and not relied on what they were told by him. The prosecutor stated, "If someone was checking the books, this wouldn't have happened. . . . There's always a paper trail" (p. 36).

- *Annual board committee review designed to assess the state of the agency and the chief executive's performance.* This is a formal review of the chief executive's goals and accomplishments and is conducted by either the executive committee, the personnel committee, or an ad hoc committee. The standard procedure is for the chief executive to review the accomplishments of the previous year in relation to the goals originally set, and to propose goals for the next year. During the evaluation, the chief executive's strengths and weaknesses are identified and discussed, and the evaluation concludes with an agreement about the next year's goals.

• *Full-dress public assessment of the chief executive, including formal hearings and survey data from an extensive variety of interested parties.* Only a few nonprofit organizations use this approach because it is time-consuming, often requires an outside consultant to administer the process, and can be an emotionally charged procedure.

Regardless of the type of assessment used, chief executives must have advance notice of the board's expectations and of the criteria used for the evaluation. Self-assessments by chief executives are recommended because they permit them to review how they have met the responsibilities, expectations, and objectives of the position. Opportunities are provided for chief executives and boards to resolve any differences they might have in their perspectives about the requirements of the chief executive's position and the role of the board in its governance and management functions.

The strategic purpose of the chief executive's evaluation is to strengthen the agency by improving its management. The board's evaluation of the chief executive should assist in improving his or her performance by identifying the executive's strengths and the areas in which improvement is needed. Boards should also support and encourage executives participation in professional development activities (Nason, 1993).

Documentation

During the evaluation period, raters should document both positive and negative aspects of job performance. One way to do this is by maintaining employee performance logs. Raters note in the logs any critical behaviors (positive as well as negative) exhibited by employees. Information such as when an employee volunteered for difficult assignments or received letters of commendation are examples of positive aspects of performance. Noting that an employee failed to submit an assignment at its deadline or submitted reports that were inaccurate and incomplete are examples of unacceptable performance that should be recorded. By documenting performance throughout the evaluation cycle, raters are able to provide specific feedback as well as to minimize their susceptibility to committing rating errors.

It is important that employees receive feedback throughout the evaluation cycle, not only when it is time to review the formal evaluation. Employees who receive feedback from their raters on a regular basis know how well they are performing their jobs and what improvements might be needed. Poor performers should be receiving feedback on what they can do to improve their performance, and excellent employees should receive positive recognition for performing well. For many employees, positive reinforcement is a powerful motivator that encourages them to sustain excellent performance.

Prior to completing the formal evaluation instrument, raters should retrieve the employee performance logs for inclusion in the evaluation. Raters should be required to justify each rating they give with explicit examples. This corroborates the job-relatedness of the evaluation and diffuses allegations of unfairness, prejudice, favoritism, and so on. For employees whose performance must be improved, supervisors should recommend some potential strategies for employee development. Raters should provide feedback that is clear, descriptive, job related, constructive, frequent, timely, and realistic.

Evaluation Review

It is not enough for raters to complete performance appraisal instruments; they must also review the evaluation with their employees. Employees should play a critical role in the process. They should be given advance notice when the review is scheduled so that they too can prepare. Employees should be encouraged to bring to the review any documentation they feel is relevant, such as letters of commendation or records of accomplished objectives of which their raters are not aware. Some raters ask their employees to complete a self-evaluation (complete with relevant documentation) prior to the scheduled review. This puts employees at ease, making them feel that they are part of the process, not just its victim. By asking employees to complete self-evaluations, raters are able to elicit input from employees about how they rated themselves and why, what accomplishments they are most proud of, and in what areas they believe performance improvement is needed.

In many public and nonprofit organizations supervisors lack the authority to determine the purpose of evaluation. As noted earlier, promotions may be based on competitive examinations and seniority, and pay-for-performance may not exist. In such cases supervisors can, however, use the evaluation process to develop their employees. The evaluation process should open up communication between supervisors and employees. The process should be used to discuss with employees areas for development and the best ways to achieve their goals. A systematic approach to performance appraisal will help employers make sure that they and their employees have the same understanding of the expectations for satisfactory performance.

Ethical Issues in Performance Appraisal

Requiring documentation by raters is critical if employees and supervisors are to believe in the integrity of the process. Longenecker and Ludwig (1990, p. 963) report that supervisors often inflate or deflate performance appraisals. More than 70 percent of supervisors surveyed admitted that they intentionally inflated or deflated subordinates' ratings for a variety of reasons, such as because they believed that accurate ratings would have a damaging effect on the subordinate's motivation and performance, because they wanted to avoid airing the department's dirty laundry, because they wanted to improve an employee's eligibility for merit raises, because they wanted to reward employees for displaying great effort even when results were relatively low, or because they needed to avoid confrontation with certain hard-to-manage employees. Reasons provided by supervisors as to why they often deflate employee ratings included wanting to scare better performance out of an employee, wanting to punish a difficult or rebellious employee, or wanting to encourage a problem employee to leave the organization.

The deliberate distortion of performance evaluations can be discouraged by the organization by not only requiring documentation to substantiate ratings but also by holding supervisors accountable for their ratings. Supervisors should be evaluated on the accuracy and comprehensiveness of the performance appraisals they complete. While inflating performance ratings may be benevolent or discourage conflicts in the short term, the long-term consequences may prove to be deleterious for the agency. Poorly performing employees may not improve. Or an unforseen reduction in force might necessitate the layoff of staff. The courts require documentation for dismissals or layoffs to prove that they were based on performance. And guess what? Inflated evaluations do not demonstrate cause, nor do they differentiate the levels of performance of different employees, thus discrediting the supervisor's and agency's credibility.

Another problem with disingenuous evaluations is that when they are used for SHRM the data they provide are inaccurate. Any decisions made based on the evaluations could prove to be harmful to the future growth and success of the organization by not recognizing liabilities and identifying where the agency needs to acquire talent. Inaccurate evaluations also do not develop individuals (Longenecker & Ludwig, 1990).

Performance Appraisal Techniques

Before specific types of rating instruments are discussed, it should be understood that there are three general approaches to performance appraisals: absolute, comparative, and goal setting.

Absolute methods evaluate the employee without referring directly to other employees. Instead, employees are evaluated against their own standards. For example, John Doe is evaluated in March and then again in September of the same year. John's September evaluation is compared to his March evaluation. The strengths identified in March should have been maintained while any deficiencies or problems identified in March should have been corrected by the September evaluation. Absolute evaluations are used most frequently for developmental purposes.

Comparative methods evaluate the employees in one unit relative to everyone else in the group. In March all of the juvenile probation officers were evaluated on the same performance dimensions and then compared to one another. For example, probation Officer A received the highest ratings in accuracy and timeliness of pre-sentencing investigation reports while Probation Officer C received the lowest rating for that dimension. Probation Officer C, however, received the highest rating for number of clients supervised and number of collateral contacts, while Probation Officer B received the lowest rating on that dimension. Comparative evaluations are used to differentiate levels of performance across employees.

Goal setting evaluates whether the ratee attained predetermined goals. For example, the supervisor and employee agree that the employee will prepare seven more grant applications in the next five months to secure a greater percentage of external funding. After five months have passed the supervisor will evaluate whether or not the employee met his goal.

There are differences not only in the format of evaluation but also in the types of data that are collected and evaluated. Some evaluations rely on *direct indices* or objective data. Direct indices can be quantified, such as the number of errors, the number of clients on caseload, the number of grants that received funding, the number of arrests made, or the number of proposals written. Direct indices are referred to as objective measures because they do not depend on someone's opinion to be verified. Another type of data commonly used are *subjective measures,* which depend on human judgment and should be based on a careful analysis of the behaviors viewed as necessary for effective job performance. Decision-making skills, the ability to solve problems, and oral communication skills are examples of subjective measures.

The types of data and the performance standards used should be based on a current job analysis. Performance standards should be developed based on the critical tasks and responsibilities of each position. The standards should be measurable through quantifiable or observable methods. The following paragraphs provide an overview of some of the most common types of evaluation instruments used in the public and nonprofit sectors.

Trait rating. Raters are provided with a list of personality characteristics, such as cooperation, creativity, attitude, and initiative. Raters then assign a number or adjective, such as average, above average, or superior, to indicate the degree to which employees possess those traits. Trait ratings are difficult to defend in court if challenged. They tend to be subjective, and raters often disagree on their definitions and how they should be measured. Trait ratings also are often not related to job performance or relevant behaviors. Someone may have a poor attitude but still be technically proficient. The scales also do not define what is meant by average or superior. Different raters may apply different standards in evaluating the same behaviors.

Behavioral-anchored rating scales (BARS). Raters evaluate employees based on a set of behavioral descriptions. The descriptions list various degrees of behavior with regard to a specific performance dimension. They identify a range of behaviors from unacceptable performance to outstanding performance. Ratees do not have to actually exhibit the behaviors on the scale; rather, the behaviors serve as a guide to help the rater and ratee understand the level of performance that is required for an assigned rating. Unlike some of the other instruments, BARS rely on employee behaviors—what employees actually do and what is under their direct control.

A problem for many public and nonprofit service providers is that very often, despite their best efforts, unacceptable outcomes result. For example, a psychiatric client may have a psychotic relapse that requires hospitalization, despite the social worker's best efforts to help the client remain in the community (Harkness & Mulinski, 1988). BARS would evaluate the social worker on his behaviors, not on the number of patients needing hospitalization. An advantage to using BARS is that they reduce ambiguity because employees are provided with descriptions of desired levels of performance. They are also accepted by both raters and ratees because both employees and supervisors participate in their development. A disadvantage to BARS is that their development is time-consuming and complex because each dimension requires its own behavioral anchors.

Essay. The rater writes a narrative essay describing the employee's performance. The weakness in this method is that the evaluation may depend on the writing skills of the supervisor or on the amount of time the supervisor takes to complete the evaluation. Another problem is that raters and employees do not necessarily use common criteria.

Productivity data or work standards. Raters evaluate employees on expected levels of output and on the quality of output. If employees are to believe that the standards are fair, they should understand how the standards were set.

Management by objectives (MBO). Raters and employees together determine goals or objectives and a plan of action for achieving them that the employee is to achieve during the upcoming evaluation cycle. At a scheduled time the two participants reconvene and determine whether the goals have been met. The effectiveness of MBOs depends on the skills of supervisors and subordinates in defining appropriate goals and objectives. Often easy objectives are set. Sometimes there is an overemphasis on objectives at the expense of specifying how these objectives are to be obtained. For example, Internal Revenue Service collection agents need to retrieve revenue from delinquent taxpayers but not through illegal or intimidating tactics. Nonprofits must be successful in raising money but not through dishonest fundraising activities.

Critical incidents. Raters record actual incidents of successful or unsuccessful performance or work actions. The rater uses these observations to evaluate employee performance.

Personnel data. Raters tabulate information such as the number of absences or the number of times employees report to work late. The data are used to regulate employees' conformance to organizational policies.

Exhibits 7.2 through 7.5 present examples of various evaluation instruments.

Each of the evaluation instruments has advantages and disadvantages and may be appropriate when used in the correct context. It is important that an appraisal instrument is chosen that is congruent with the objective for the evaluation and suitable for the positions being evaluated. For example, personnel data such as tardiness or absenteeism do not address task proficiency or job-related behaviors. BARS or critical incidents would be more appropriate for capturing such behaviors. Personnel data tend to enforce rules and regulations.

Many agencies also make the mistake of believing that evaluation instruments should be uniform across the organization, regardless of the position being evaluated. That is not the case. The evaluation process is valuable only if it is relevant to the position. There must be a direct link between the requirements of the

Exhibit 7.2. Trait Rating Scale.

Name/rank _____ Section _____ Unit/platoon _____

Outstanding = 1　Very good = 2　Average = 3　Improvement needed = 4　Unsatisfactory = 5

Judgment

Dependability

Work initiative

Quality of work

Appearance

Cooperation

Knowledge of work

Public contacts

Supervisory ability

Overall evaluation

Exhibit 7.3 Sample Critical Incidents.

Positive:

Date　　Employee volunteered for four extra assignments.

Date　　Received phone call from professional X commending the assistance given by employee A.

Date　　Employee submitted progress report B two weeks ahead of deadline. The report was complete and accurate. Employee exercised independent judgment.

Negative:

Date　　Employee failed to submit accurate and complete verification reports. Auditors found deficiencies that warranted a payback.

Date　　Employee refused to return phone calls to client, resulting in loss of client.

Date　　Employee missed the deadline for the grant proposal submission. This resulted in the agency not receiving X amount of funds. Program X had to be eliminated.

Exhibit 7.4 Management by Objectives Rating Scale.

Position Evaluated: Investigator Lieutenant

Dimension:	Maintaining and updating standard operating procedures manual for the investigations section
Objective:	Create a documented review procedure for investigations personnel to review SOP Manual
Type of measure:	Timeliness
Present level:	Manual is reviewed with investigations personnel on a yearly basis but with no formal documented procedure
Desired level:	Manual to be reviewed with investigations personnel once a year, on a scheduled date, with captain present. A review form is signed and initialed by each individual investigator, the supervising lieutenant, and the captain. Review forms are kept on file with the SOP manual.
Time frame:	One month

Method used to achieve objective:

1. Create SOP review form and submit it to the captain for approval.

2. Check with captain and establish a yearly review date in the month of January.

3. Update manual to include file for review forms.

4. Immediately file completed review forms.

Employee signature:

Supervisor signature:

Date completed: Date of review:

Exhibit 7.5 Behavioral-Anchored Rating Scale.

Job: Lieutenant Investigator

Dimension: Assign and review cases to investigators

Superior:	Reviews all cases sent to investigations from records section on a daily basis. Assigns cases to investigators on a daily basis, giving clear, verbal instructions about what is expected of them by supervisor in reference to a particular case. Attaches case assignment log sheet with handwritten instructions. Reviews ongoing cases with investigators at a scheduled time once a week. Keeps a case management log of all cases assigned.
Very good:	Reviews all cases sent to investigations. Assigns cases to investigators. Attaches a case assignment log sheet with written instructions. Reviews cases with investigators when necessary.
Good:	Reviews all cases refereed to investigations from patrol division and records division. Assigns cases to investigators. Reviews cases if requested by investigator.
Needs improvement:	Takes several days before cases are reviewed. Rarely reviews investigators' work. Assignment of cases to investigators takes several days to a week.
Unsatisfactory:	Allows investigators to review all reports given to investigations by records section and to pick their own assignments. No review of investigators' work.

Comments: _____

_____

_____

Rater's Signature: _____

job and the instrument used to evaluate performance. The KSAOCs that some jobs require incumbents to possess will be different from the KSAOCs required in other jobs. For example, nonprofit executive directors or public agency managers need to be evaluated more comprehensively than individuals who perform limited and routine tasks. Performance dimensions such as decision making and oral communication might be very relevant for management positions, but less so for trade positions. Because the responsibilities of different jobs within public and nonprofit agencies vary, different instruments or even different evaluation procedures might be needed. The National Performance Review (1993) has recognized that agencies need the flexibility to develop their own performance management and reward systems that improve the performance of both their employees and the agency. Policymakers, executives, managers, and employees need to understand that to accomplish this evaluation, systems must be updated, revised, and redesigned as job responsibilities and employee abilities change to reflect current organizational performance standards.

Alternative Performance Management Techniques

As agencies move to team-based environments that focus on continuous improvement and total quality management (TQM), traditional performance appraisal techniques are being reexamined and there is a movement away from individual appraisals. The National Commission on the State and Local Public Service (1993), the National Performance Review (1993), and the literature on team building and gainsharing have all suggested that the public sector should move toward team-based pay-for-performance systems in which team members share the savings from higher productivity.

Total Quality Management

TQM is the name given to a variety of management systems designed to improve organizational quality. W. Edwards Deming, an American statistician, is often credited with its invention and his version is influential and widespread (Swiss, 1992). He believed that to improve quality the following steps are necessary:

Create constancy of purpose for the continuous improvement of product and service.

Break down barriers between departments to build teamwork.

Drive fear our of the workplace.

Eliminate quotas on the shop floor.

Create conditions that allow employees to have pride in their workmanship, including abolishing annual performance reviews and merit ratings.

Institute programs of education and self-improvement.

Common practices that he deemed harmful to quality improvements include a lack of constancy of purpose, an emphasis on short-term projects, and individual performance evaluations (Walton, 1986).

To improve performance, Bowman (1994) advocates the elimination of individual appraisals and the adoption of TQM as a way to improve performance. "TQM ensures that planning, organizing, staffing, and directing take place by promoting teamwork, coaching, listening, and leading. Processes are measured instead of people and performance measurements are integrated into daily activities to meet real needs. Everyone is expected to assume responsibility for problem solving to ensure quality and productivity" (p. 134). TQM promotes the continuous improvement of procedures in an agency, from the top to the bottom, so that clients are satisfied with the agency's performance. The organization's culture is changed to focus on establishing and maintaining high performance standards. Unlike traditional management techniques that emphasize control, in TQM quality is achieved by improving process, not by blaming employees.

Performance Targeting

Performance targeting is a technique for improving performance recommended by Halachmi (1993). Unlike performance appraisals, which review what employees have accomplished in the past, performance targeting is oriented toward the future. It is a joint effort by supervisors and employees to determine how to meet the organization's goals, how employees can contribute, and what supervisors can do to assist their employees in meeting the employees' goals. This approach differs a bit from MBO, in which only the employee is responsible for goal accomplishment. In performance targeting a partnership is created. Employees are permitted to provide input about what they do and how it is accomplished. They evolve into "effective followers" (Halachmi, 1993, p. 339), individuals who think for themselves and carry out their duties with energy and with an awareness of the needs of the organization.

Gainsharing

Gainsharing is a group incentive plan that distributes gains from improved performance to employees in a department or organization, based on an established sharing formula. Participative management and teamwork are used to develop performance techniques and standards that control costs or units of output. All members of the team, department, or agency benefit from the increased cost savings. Lawler (1989) refers to gainsharing as a management style, a technology for organizational development, and an incentive system.

A gainsharing program was used by the federal government in its Pacer Share demonstration project stationed at McClellan Air Force Base in California. An evaluation of the program found improvements in attitudes toward the work environment, satisfaction with supervisors and coworkers, trust in management's control of the work, and increased training opportunities and organizational involvement (Siegel, 1994). Gainsharing and increases in compensation will be discussed in greater detail in Chapter Eight.

Can Performance Appraisals and Quality Improvement Processes Coexist?

Many of you reading this probably think, like me, that TQM, performance targeting, gainsharing, and other quality improvement processes rely on many of the same principles as performance evaluation and are not antithetical to the performance evaluation process. If done correctly, quality improvement processes require the development of performance standards and of measures to determine whether the standards have been achieved; they require feedback from multiple sources; and they require the development of an action plan for reaching future goals. What is key to the success of any of these quality improvement and performance assessment systems is not the name of the process used but the personnel policies and rules that support and enhance the total-quality environment of the entire organization. Exhibit 7.6 identifies key questions that management should consider prior to developing a performance evaluation system.

To facilitate change, HRM departments must expand their awareness to insure that all work focuses on the agency's mission and its customers. Continuous improvement must be integrated into its culture. Mutual respect and teamwork between all levels of the organization are necessary. Quality improvement requires that supervisors give workers more autonomy and allow their participation in decision making. Employee training therefore must extend beyond job or technical skills. Since all workers will be expected to function in a group setting, quality improvement and performance evaluation programs must provide training in group dynamics, problem-solving techniques, and the use of quality improvement tools. Quality improvement processes and performance evaluation systems do not have to be at odds with each another. Evaluation systems can be developed that focus on developing individual job skills that support the group's efforts for quality and productivity improvements. The competitive nature of evaluation can be eliminated by comparing employees to standards instead of to one another.

Changing to a quality improvement culture may require the modification of many HRM policies that have become institutionalized throughout the years. Organizations need to analyze their selection, training, development, compensation, and evaluation systems to ensure that they reify the values necessary for quality improvement efforts.

Summary

Performance evaluation is the process that reviews and measures employee performance. Performance evaluations should be objective, job related, and consistent with the organization's mission.

Exhibit 7.6. Questions to Consider When Developing a Performance Evaluation System.

For your consideration:

1. How can your agency effectively involve employees and their representatives in redesigning performance management to promote the credibility and acceptance of the system? Have you identified your mutual interests?

2. Does your performance management system include effective performance planning, goal setting, and communications processes that link to your strategic objectives?

3. Should you be developing measures of customer service and group or team performance outcomes that can be used for planning performance and for distributing rewards based on improved performance?

4. Have you given enough attention to planning, measuring, and rewarding internal customer service for your various staff operations and administrative functions?

5. Have you developed collateral processes for establishing performance goals and monitoring performance, and established how these might be integrated into the formal appraisal and reward process?

6. Do you provide ongoing performance monitoring and feedback to employees about their individual and group performance?

7. Are the people who have the best knowledge of the quality and effectiveness of employee performance providing feedback, either for developmental purposes or as input to a performance appraisal? Should you explore using 360-degree assessment where it is appropriate?

8. Do the elements and standards of your employee performance plans capture the results and accomplishments you expect, or do they merely describe the same tasks and process inputs year after year?

9. Are the distinctions you make among levels of performance credible to internal and external stakeholders? How many distinctions can be made credibly, given your culture and the nature of your work?

Source: U.S. Office of Personnel Management, 1994, p. 51.

When correctly developed and executed they should enhance the organization's effectiveness. The performance evaluation process provides management with important information for making strategic decisions on employee promotions, training and development activities, compensation decisions, and retention or separation. Employees who are performing at high levels in their present positions should be informed as to what career progression paths exist within their organization so that career development activities can be planned. Likewise, employees who fail to meet performance standards should be provided with training or, if necessary, be dismissed. In today's competitive environment nonproductive employees can no longer be tolerated.

Performance evaluations are used to support many HRM functions, but because the appraisal process and/or instruments cannot serve all purposes simultaneously, the organization must first decide on the specific objectives it wishes to achieve, and then develop the appropriate instruments and performance management system. Regardless of the type of instrument used or the purpose of the evaluation, all raters must be trained.

Many researchers have suggested that traditional performance evaluation systems that focus on individual performance should be eliminated and replaced with team or TQM approaches. Other researchers believe that individual assessments compliment TQM because they foster individual accountability and identify individual developmental needs, which in turn benefit the work team (Masterson & Taylor, 1996).

| Compensation

The design, implementation, and maintenance of compensation systems are important parts of strategic human resources management (SHRM). Decisions about salaries, incentives, benefits, and quality-of-life issues are important in attracting, retaining, and motivating employees.

Strategic decisions about pay levels, pay structures, job evaluation, and incentive pay systems influence the ability of an organization to compete in the marketplace to attract the most qualified and competent applicants and to retain its most talented and productive employees. Compensation is a topic that most employees are concerned with, yet most of us do not understand the underlying premises that drive compensation systems. What factors, for example, explain the differences in compensation in the following examples?

• The Forum for Contemporary Art is the primary museum in the St. Louis area that preserves changing exhibitions of contemporary art. Founded in 1979 by a group of civic, cultural, and educational leaders alarmed by the prospect of an artless downtown, the Forum was conceived to bring a fully integrated cultural and educational program to downtown St. Louis and to function as a meeting place for the exchange of ideas. In 1991, the board of directors revised the Forum's mission to concentrate on contemporary arts programming that emphasizes the interaction of urban issues and current trends in the arts. On an annual budget of roughly $300,000, the Forum maintains a yearly schedule of seven exhibits, supplemented by educational programs for adults and children. Friends of the Forum, a membership organization of about five hundred individuals and fifty corporations and foundations supports the Forum with annual membership contributions. The executive director's compensation and benefits are worth $32,365 ("On Board," 1995a).

• Arts in Transit is a community partnership program of the Bi-State Development Agency. It is governed by the Bi-State board of commissioners, guided by an advisory board from the community, and funded by private and public sources. Arts in Transit was formed in 1986 to enhance the community by building partnerships to integrate public transportation with civic goals and activities. With a budget of approximately $282,290, the Arts in Transit educational outreach program has installed twenty-six site-specific public art projects and initiated a public poetry program. The director receives $60,000 in compensation and benefits and the community program coordinator receives $33,100 in compensation and benefits ("On Board," 1995b).

• An administrative specialist working for the federal government in a general salary classification as a GS–6, step 3, makes an annual salary of $19,386. A fellow GS–6, step 8, makes $22,416. They perform the same tasks, but the step 3 administrative specialist is more proficient in his work.

• The starting salary for police officers in municipality A is $26,230 per year, while the starting salary for police officers in municipality B is $23,567 per year. The cities are adjacent to each other.

From a SHRM perspective, employers use compensation to attract, retain, and motivate employees to achieve organizational goals. Employees expect fair renumeration for the services they perform. However, what is often lacking is the understanding that compensation is affected by many factors: the expectations and perception of fairness by employees, competitive labor market wages, the extent of other benefits provided to employees, the organization's ability to pay, and federal and state laws. This chapter introduces the concepts of equity, competitive labor markets, and comparable worth, as well as job evaluation methods, the design of pay structures, and federal laws that influence compensation. Indirect financial compensation, more commonly referred to as employee benefits, are discussed in Chapter Nine.

Equity

Individuals have expectations about what they will be paid. They expect fair compensation. The standards that individuals use to determine whether the compensation they receive is fair are based on perceptions of equity. According to equity theory, employees compare their job inputs and outcomes to the inputs and outputs of other employees performing similar tasks. If they perceive their ratio of inputs to outputs to be equal to those with whom they compare themselves, a state of equity is said to exist. If the ratios are unequal, inequity exists and employees will believe that they are underrewarded.

To develop compensation systems, employers rely on three types of equity: external, internal, and employee.

External Equity

External equity is the standard that compares an employer's wages with the rates prevailing in external markets for the employee's position. What do other organizations pay employees who perform similar tasks and have similar responsibilities? For example, what do other counties pay entry-level budget analysts? What do program directors at nonprofits that provide services to the victims of domestic violence get paid? The federal government and state governments would be interested in the salary range for chemists with Ph.D. degrees working in industry or universities.

To determine external equity, the competitive labor market is surveyed. Labor markets are identified and defined by some combination of the following factors: (1) education and/or technical background requirements, (2) licensing or certification requirements, (3) experience required by the job, (4) occupational membership, and (5) geographical location, such as local, regional, or national labor markets (Wallace & Fay, 1988). The labor market reflects the forces of supply and demand for qualified labor within an area. These forces influence the wages required to recruit or retain qualified employees. If employees do not see their pay as equitable compared to what other organizations pay for similar work, they are likely, if provided with an opportunity, to leave.

Criteria that are typically used by local governments to determine relevant employers for wage comparisons include the size of the government's population, the size of its workforce, its urban/rural mix, and its equalized assessed value (EAV). EAV is the assessed value of real property multiplied by the state equalization factor. (The state equalization factor is a device to provide equity across the state in property tax by equalizing or balancing the property value between jurisdictions. The EAV is divided by the population to understand per capita wealth. Each state has its own ratio.) It is the base against which tax rates are calculated and translates into the government's ability to pay salaries. Using these criteria, small local governments would seek other small local governments with similar features as their reference points, rather than large industrial cities.

Nonprofit agencies should also look for comparable organizations. That may be more difficult because nonprofit services and structures evolve in response to a variety of forces. Programs and services often have been developed by the professional staff and board of directors to be consistent with the agency's mission. Programs also evolve in response to local, state, and federal funding opportunities. Nonprofit staffing patterns and the ability to pay employees are subject to a greater variety of influences than the influences found in the public sector. When looking for comparable employers, agencies must seek organizations that provide similar services and that are similarly situated in terms of size and structure (including number of employees), revenue sources (size of operating budget, and types of grants and contributions received for nonprofit agencies), cash compensation (base and merit pay, increase schedules, and cost-of-living adjustments) and benefits (number of paid holidays, personal days, and sick days; nature and extent of health care coverage, and contributions made to retirement), and position titles and benchmark equivalents (scope of responsibilities, education requirements, years in position, and salaries paid to incumbents). For example, a small community-based social service nonprofit that provides services to the developmentally disabled should compare itself with other organizations of the same size and with similar characteristics that provide comparable services. An agency staffed by fifteen employees should not compare itself with a large metropolitan chapter of the United

Way. These same characteristics (except for grants and contributions as sources of revenue) can be used by local governments to determine comparable employers.

If conducting a survey itself or hiring consultants to do so is not feasible, various government agencies such as the state or federal Department of Labor or commercial firms such as the Bureau of Labor Statistics, the Bureau of National Affairs, and the Commerce Clearing House publish area wage surveys and industry wage surveys as well as professional, administrative, technical, and clerical surveys. Professional associations and consulting firms also publish salary data. For example, the Child Welfare League of America and the National Association of Homes and Services for Children publish the salaries of youth service workers. Abbot, Lager, & Associates publishes a salary survey called *Compensation in Nonprofit Organizations,* the Society of Nonprofit Organizations publishes *Nonprofit World Salary Survey,* and Towers Perrin publishes a study of management salaries in nonprofit organizations.

Internal Equity

Internal equity is the standard that requires employers to set wages for jobs within their organizations that correspond to the relative internal value of each job. Positions that are determined to be more valuable to the organization receive higher wages. Typically, high-level employees receive greater compensation than low-level employees.

The internal value of each position to the organization is determined by a procedure known as job evaluation. Job evaluation determines the worth of one job relative to another. To institute internal equity into its compensation structure, Congress passed the Classification Act of 1923. Prior to the establishment of the classification system, federal employees were paid according to which agency they worked for and wages were determined at the discretion of agency management. The lack of procedures and standardization permitted disparities among employees performing the same type of work. Different positions were often given the same title, and similar positions were often given different titles. Pay was not necessarily related to the work performed. The act created a Personnel Classification Board that mandated that positions be grouped according to similar responsibilities and duties and be compensated accordingly. Employees would be paid according to the value of their work, which would be determined according to the job's *compensable factors,* such as level of education and amount of experience required, the amount of responsibility, the job hazards, and so on. Exhibit 8.1 lists some of the most common compensable factors.

A variety of factor comparison systems are used to determine job value. Compensable factors are identified, weighed, and assigned point values that reflect their weight. Jobs are broken down into their compensable factors and rated along a continuum of points or rank ordered. After the compensable factors have been rated or ranked, they are then summed to derive a total point value for the job. Positions with higher point values are considered more valuable to the agency.

In 1949, Congress passed the Classification Act of 1949, which established the General Schedule (GS) system. The GS system defines the basic compensation system used by nonmanagerial white-collar positions. There are eighteen grade levels, with ranges of pay within each grade. There are approximately 450 categories in the GS, sorted into specialized groups such as finance and accounting, social science, psychology and welfare, engineering and architecture, physical science, and so on. Each grade contains examples of the kind of work performed in jobs that would be assigned to that grade. These examples are referred to as *benchmark positions.* Benchmark positions are jobs with characteristics similar enough to jobs performed in other organizations that can serve as market anchor points. Using a factor comparison system called the Factor Evaluation System, jobs are described and placed in grades on the basis of their duties, responsibilities, and the qualifications required to perform them. The following nine factors with different levels and different point values are used to evaluate jobs: (1) knowledge required by the position, (2) supervisory controls, (3) guidelines, (4) complexity, (5) scope and effect, (6) personal contacts, (7) purpose of contacts, (8) physical demands, and (9) work environment. After all nine factors have been evaluated and levels have been established for the position, the points are summed across each factor until an aggregate total is derived. The total points are then compared to a chart and the position is assigned to a grade.

A problem with this job evaluation system is that the duties and responsibilities of a specific job do not always neatly fit into one grade or job class. The GS has been criticized for its lack of flexibility in supporting individual agency missions, structures, and cultures, and for its inability to respond to rapidly changing external conditions. The National Performance Review (1993) has recommended modifying the GS by reducing the number of occupational categories and permitting agencies to establish broad-banding systems. (Broad banding will be described later in this chapter.)

Employee Equity

Employee equity is the comparison of pay across employees performing the same or similar work. It focuses on the contributions of an individual worker within a job classification. At issue is what coworkers performing the same job get paid. Are differences in levels of proficiency or contribution reflected in compensation?

Most compensation structures include pay ranges. A pay range exists when two or more rates are paid to employees in the same job. The range permits organizations to pay different wages for differences in experience or differences in performance. A pay range reflects the minimum and maximum that the employer will pay for the position.

Table 8.1 presents the General Salary Pay Scale for federal employees. Each grade has ten pay-level increments. New college graduates usually begin at the base pay for the grade, but the Office of Personnel Management may authorize recruitment at rates above the minimum for jobs in which there are shortages, such as engineers, chemists, and architects.

Pay grades and pay ranges for a city-county library district are presented in Table 8.2. Each of the thirteen pay grades in this salary schedule has six pay-level increments. Employees move up to the next highest level on the anniversary of their employment. After six years they have reached the top of the salary grade or "maxed out." Employees at the top of the salary grade can expect to receive only cost-of-living increases.

Exhibit 8.1. Typical Compensable Factors.

Compensable Factors	Questions Addressed in Job Specifications
Experience	Experience is the training and development acquired from previous work that is necessary to qualify for a position, plus the training and development on the job that is necessary for proficiency. The requirement for this factor is usually expressed in terms of the time necessary to acquire the experience. How long should the incumbent have worked in this job or in a closely related job?
Education	Education refers to the basic ability, skill, and intellectual requirements the position demands, normally assumed to have been acquired by attending high school, business school, trade school, college, or graduate school. Referring to periods of formal schooling is convenient when comparing positions; however, the term *"or its equivalent"* should usually form a part of the educational specifications when such reference is made. What does the job require in terms of formal schooling, training, or knowledge of a specialized field?
Complexity of duties	This factor is a measure of the variety and difficulty of the work performed and the degree of skill and judgment necessary in performing it. Complexity is found to some extent in all positions. Does the job require the incumbent to show judgment and initiative and to make independent decisions?

Supervision received   This refers to the degree to which the work is supervised, guided by practice or precedent, and the requirements of the position for problem solving and decision making.

How closely does the incumbent's supervisor check his or her work and outline specific methods or work procedures?

Supervision exercised   This factor measures the responsibility for directing the work of others. Its value is determined by the nature and complexity of the work supervised, the degree of responsibility for attaining desired results, and the number of persons supervised.

How many people does the incumbent supervise directly or indirectly?

Mental demands   This factor appraises the amount and continuity of mental demand required to perform the job.
It is a value factor in positions requiring a degree of concentrated mental effort or constant attention to detail.

What degree of concentration is required by the job?

Physical demands   This factor appraises the amount and continuity of physical effort required to perform the job.
It is a value factor in jobs that require the employee to stand, lift, carry, bend, or walk for extended periods.

Are there special physical demands on this job?

Working conditions   This factor has value in those positions where excessive heat, noise, use of chemicals, poor ventilation, and so forth are elements in the job environment.

Is there anything in the work environment that is unusually hazardous or uncomfortable? If so, what percentage of the time is the incumbent exposed to this?

Table 8.1. General Schedule Pay Scale.

Grade Step	1	2	3	4	5	6	7	8	9	10
GS-1	$10,581	$10,935	$11,286	$11,637	$11,990	$12,197	$12,544	$12,893	$12,910	$13,232
GS-2	11,897	12,180	12,574	12,910	13,053	13,437	13,821	14,205	14,589	14,973
GS-3	12,982	13,415	13,848	14,281	14,714	15,147	15,580	16,013	16,446	16,879
GS-4	14,573	15,059	15,545	16,031	16,517	17,003	17,489	17,975	18,461	18,947
GS-5	16,305	16,849	17,393	17,937	18,481	19,025	19,569	20,113	20,657	21,201
GS-6	18,174	18,780	19,386	19,992	20,598	21,204	21,810	22,416	23,022	23,628
GS-7	20,195	20,868	21,541	22,214	22,887	23,560	24,233	24,906	25,579	26,252
GS-8	22,367	23,113	23,859	24,605	25,351	26,097	26,843	27,589	28,335	29,081
GS-9	24,705	25,529	26,353	27,177	28,001	28,825	29,649	30,473	31,297	32,121
GS-10	27,206	28,113	29,020	29,927	30,834	31,741	32,648	33,555	34,462	35,369
GS-11	29,891	30,887	31,883	32,879	33,875	34,871	35,867	36,863	37,859	38,855
GS-12	35,825	37,019	38,213	39,407	40,601	41,795	42,989	44,183	45,377	46,571
GS-13	42,601	44,021	45,441	46,861	48,281	49,701	51,121	52,541	53,961	55,381
GS-14	50,342	52,020	53,698	55,376	57,054	58,732	60,410	62,088	63,766	65,444
GS-15	59,216	61,190	63,164	65,138	67,112	69,086	71,060	73,034	75,008	76,982
GS-16	69,451	71,766	74,081	76,396	78,190	79,440*	81,710*	83,981*	86,251*	
GS-17	79,762*	82,421*	85,080*	87,739*	90,398*					
GS-18	93,484*									

*Salary limited by Sec. 5308, 5 U.S.C., to Level V of Executive Schedule—$78,200.
Source: Office of Personnel Management, 1994.

Many nonprofits also used a salary grade schedule. For example, the Boy Scouts have 345 local councils across the United States that employ about 2,750 professional staff and an equal number of support staff. For compensation purposes, professionals are ranked as entry-level or classified in grades one through twelve. The average salary for each grade is as follows: entry level, $24,000; Grade 1, $26,000; Grade 2, $27,000; Grade 3, $30,000; Grade 4, $35,000; Grade 5, $38,000; Grade 6, $42,000; Grades 7 through 12, $60,000. Each local council is headed by a Scout Executive, classified in pay grades 51 through 56. Grade 51 salaries begin at $30,800, with the average salary being $40,000. The Boy Scouts do not release information on the salaries for grades 52 through 56 (Vanneman, 1994).

To design pay ranges, the employer needs to establish what the current market rates are for benchmark jobs. After the data have been compiled, organizations then develop salary ranges to fit their structure. Each salary range should have a midpoint, a minimum, and a maximum. The distance separating a grade's minimum and maximum salaries is called the grade's range. The midpoint for each range is usually set to correspond to the external labor market. It specifies the pay objectives for employees performing at satisfactory levels. The minimums and maximums are usually based on a combination of the size of the range identified in survey data and judgments about how the ranges fit the organization. These judgments are based on a variety of factors, such as salaries paid by the organization's competition, the organization's culture, and what is standard across an occupational classification. For example, production and maintenance positions typically have ranges of 20 to 25 percent while professional, administrative, and managerial personnel might have ranges of 40 to 50 percent under certain circumstances. Wider ranges are designed to reflect greater discretion, responsibility, and variations in performance. Pay ranges are useful because they allow an organization to provide a competitive salary and recognize individual differences among employees. Exhibit 8.2 illustrates current market rates and their minimums, maximums, and midpoints for selected benchmark positions in local government.

When establishing pay ranges, employers must look at the degree of overlap in adjacent pay ranges. Overlap is the amount

Table 8.2. City-County Library District Salary/Wage Schedule.

	1	2	3	4	5	6	
A	$593.00	$615.00	$638.00	$662.00	$687.00	$712.50	Payperiod
	$14,232.00	$14,760.00	$15,312.00	$15,888.00	$16,488.00	$17,100.00	Yearly
	$6.82	$7.07	$7.33	$7.61	$7.90	$8.19	Hourly
B	$662.00	$687.00	$712.50	$739.50	$767.00	$796.00	Payperiod
	$15,888.00	$16,488.00	$17,100.00	$17,748.00	$18,408.00	$19,104.00	Yearly
	$7.61	$7.90	$8.19	$8.50	$8.82	$9.15	Hourly
C	$739.50	$767.00	$796.00	$826.00	$857.00	$889.00	Payperiod
	$17,748.00	$18,408.00	$19,104.00	$19,824.00	$20,568.00	$21,336.00	Yearly
	$8.50	$8.82	$9.15	$9.49	$9.85	$10.22	Hourly
D	$826.00	$857.00	$889.00	$922.00	$957.00	$992.50	Payperiod
	$19,824.00	$20,568.00	$21,336.00	$22,128.00	$22,968.00	$23,820.00	Yearly
	$9.49	$9.85	$10.22	$10.60	$11.00	$11.41	Hourly
E	$922.00	$957.00	$992.50	$1,030.00	$1,068.50	$1,108.50	Payperiod
	$22,128.00	$22,968.00	$23,820.00	$24,720.00	$25,644.00	$26,604.00	Yearly
	$10.60	$11.00	$11.41	$11.84	$12.28	$12.74	Hourly
F	$1,030.00	$1,068.50	$1,108.50	$1,150.00	$1,193.50	$1,238.00	Payperiod
	$24,720.00	$25,644.00	$26,604.00	$27,600.00	$28,644.00	$29,712.00	Yearly
	$11.84	$12.28	$12.74	$13.22	$13.72	$14.23	Hourly
G	$1,150.00	$1,193.50	$1,238.00	$1,284.50	$1,332.50	$1,382.50	Payperiod
	$27,600.00	$28,644.00	$29,712.00	$30,828.00	$31,980.00	$33,180.00	Yearly
	$13.22	$13.72	$14.23	$14.76	$15.32	$15.89	Hourly

	Step 1	Step 2	Step 3	Step 4	Step 5	Step 6	
H	$1,284.50	$1,332.50	$1,382.50	$1,434.50	$1,488.50	$1,544.00	Payperiod
	$30,828.00	$31,980.00	$33,180.00	$34,428.00	$35,724.00	$37,056.00	Yearly
	$14.76	$15.32	$15.89	$16.49	$17.11	$17.75	Hourly
I	$1,434.50	$1,488.50	$1,544.00	$1,602.00	$1,662.00	$1,724.50	Payperiod
	$34,428.00	$35,724.00	$37,056.00	$38,448.00	$39,888.00	$41,388.00	Yearly
	$16.49	$17.11	$17.75	$18.41	$19.10	$19.82	Hourly
J	$1,602.00	$1,662.00	$1,724.50	$1,789.00	$1,856.00	$1,926.00	Payperiod
	$38,448.00	$39,888.00	$41,388.00	$42,936.00	$44,544.00	$46,224.00	Yearly
	$18.41	$19.10	$19.82	$20.56	$21.33	$22.14	Hourly
K	$1,789.00	$1,856.00	$1,926.00	$1,998.00	$2,073.00	$2,150.50	Payperiod
	$42,936.00	$44,544.00	$46,224.00	$47,952.00	$49,752.0	$51,612.00	Yearly
	$20.56	$21.33	$22.14	$22.97	$23.83	$24.72	Hourly
L	$1,998.00	$2,073.00	$2,150.50	$2,231.50	$2,315.00	$2,402.00	Payperiod
	$47,952.00	$49,752.00	$51,612.00	$53,556.00	$55,560.00	$56,648.00	Yearly
	$22.97	$23.83	$24.72	$25.65	$26.61	$27.61	Hourly
M	$2,231.50	$2,315.00	$2,402.00	$2,492.00	$2,585.50	$2,682.50	Payperiod
	$53,556.00	$55,560.00	$57,648.00	$59,808.00	$62,052.00	$64,380.00	Yearly
	$25.65	$26.61	$27.61	$28.64	$29.72	$30.83	Hourly
Non-Track 1		$4.61		Hourly	$4.84	Hourly	
Non-Track 2		$5.07		Hourly	$5.33	Hourly	

Note: Salaries are reflected for one full-time-equivalent bimonthly pay period.

of comparability of pay between pay grades. The amount of overlap between pay grades signifies the similarities in the responsibilities, duties, and KSAOCs of the job whose pay ranges overlap. Overlap between pay ranges permits more valuable senior employees in lower-paying jobs to be paid more than new employees in higher-level jobs who have yet begun to make significant contributions to the organization (Henderson, 1988). In both Tables 8.1 and 8.2, GS–1 or Grade A employees at steps 5 and above receive higher compensation than GS–2 or Grade B employees at step 1.

When developing a salary structure you may find that certain jobs in the organization have been underpaid or overpaid. Underpaid positions are referred to as green-circled and overpaid positions are referred to as red-circled. To bring these wages in line with market rates and internal equity standards, underpaid employees should be given pay increases that raise their rates to at least the minimum of the range for their pay grade. The salaries of overpaid employees may need to be frozen until other jobs are brought into line with them. Other options include cutting the wages to the maximum in the pay range for the pay grade, increasing the employees' responsibilities, or transferring or promoting them to positions in which they can be paid their current rate.

Compression

Compression results when the salaries for jobs filled from outside the organization are increasing faster than incumbent wages (that is, when new employees are paid salaries that are comparable to more experienced employees) or the salaries of jobs filled from within the organization. Compression is found in most public and nonprofit organizations. For example, ten years ago the starting salary for county probation officers might have been $15,500. Today, probation officers hired ten years ago might be making $26,000 while new probation officers might start at salaries around $24,500. The pay differential between an employee with ten years of experience and a new employee is compressed because of market wages.

Grade Creep

Grade creep is a form of classification inflation. That is, supervisors and incumbents request that positions be reclassified to the

Exhibit 8.2. Comparable Municipal Market Study for Select Local Government Positions.

Administrative Classifications	City A	City B	City C	City D	City E	Lowest Minimum	Highest Maximum	Mid-Range Index
Personal Property Auditor	20,653.00	32,629.00				20,653.00	32,629.00	25,593.92
Department Secretary Assessor's Office	26,270.40	18,495.00	12,022.40			12,022.40	26,270.40	17,720.96
Finance Director	53,000.00	33,500.00	44,262.40	49,045.00	54,721.00	33,500.00	54,721.00	44,193.26
Deputy Finance Director/ Administrative Assistant	44,923.00	31,000.00	29,899.60	23,490.00	38,629.00	23,490.00	44,923.00	32,610.18
Treasurer	33,904.00	34,819.00	32,510.40	26,979.00	48,065.00	26,979.00	48,065.00	34,070.00
City Clerk	33,904.00	34,819.98	24,481.60	36,649.00	49,851.00	24,481.60	49,851.00	36,632.98
Deputy City Clerk	27,861.00	23,974.16	17,201.60	37,182.00	22,120.00	17,201.60	37,182.00	25,509.85
City Librarian	40,082.00			24,598.00	43,800.00	24,598.00	43,800.00	36,873.40
Assistant Librarian		23,065.00		31,168.00		23,065.00	31,168.00	27,528.50
Museum Curator	26,348.00	15,769.00	31,141.00			15,769.00	31,141.00	22,789.30
Planning Director/ Community Development	53,000.00	33,500.00	31,054.40	26,979.00	39,866.00	26,979.00	53,000.00	38,367.04
Department Secretary Community Development	13,263.00	25,521.60	16,889.60	18,907.00	18,223.00	13,263.00	25,521.60	18,210.40

next highest grade so that the incumbent receives higher compensation despite no change in job tasks or responsibilities. Grade creep typically results when incumbents are at the top of their pay level and no other mechanism exists to increase their pay.

Pay Differentials

Employee equity addresses pay differentials within the same position. It recognizes that employees who possess the same job title and responsibilities often perform at different levels of productivity or proficiency, making different contributions to the agency's mission.

In the public sector, seniority is frequently used to differentiate pay. More senior employees receive higher wages despite their performance. For each year of service, employees' salaries are automatically increased to the next grade step. This is to reward their years of service to the organization. It is why the administrative specialist in step 3 receives a lower salary than his coworker at step 8. The problem with seniority-based differentials is that length of tenure does not necessarily translate into effective performance. If seniority is the only system in place to differentiate pay, organizations may find it hard to attract and retain competent employees. Employees who believe that their pay is low after comparing their inputs and level of pay to other employees in similar positions will become less motivated over time. Dissatisfied employees are prone to file more grievances, to be absent more frequently, and to search for higher paying positions elsewhere. Employers must have in place different strategies to address employee equity concerns. The following paragraphs provide brief descriptions of alternative pay systems that are used to enhance traditional pay systems.

Broad Banding. There has been a movement away from using a system of many pay grades. Instead, salary grades are being collapsed into broader bands with wider ranges. The use of broad bands eliminates having to maintain many narrow salary grades. Broad banding was introduced by the federal government out of frustration with the inflexible federal classification and pay system, and to increase flexibility, managerial control, and accountability (Risher & Schay, 1994). Two naval research and development laboratories found it difficult to recruit and retain scientists and engineers. The laboratories designed a new classification and compensation system that would give their managers the flexibility needed to compete with the private sector.

Broad banding grants managers the discretion to offer a variety of starting salaries and to reward employees with pay increases or different job assignments as needed to fulfill the agency's mission. Advocates of broad banding claim that it simplifies pay administration, helps to facilitate career development, and links compensation with SHRM.

Skill-Based Pay or Pay for Knowledge. In skill-based or pay-for-knowledge pay plans, pay is determined by the number of tasks or jobs or the amount of knowledge an employee masters. It is a compensation system based on paying for what employees can do, for the knowledge or skills they possess. Under skill-based pay, employees can be expected to perform a broad range of duties. Benefits attributed to skill-based pay from an organizational standpoint include developing a cross-trained and more flexible workforce, improving the flow of information throughout the organization, placing an emphasis on the work to be done rather than on the job itself, encouraging the acquisition of skills needed to perform a variety of jobs, and increasing employees' interest in and commitment to their work. Benefits from the employees' perspective include higher motivation, increased job satisfaction, and greater opportunities for increased pay (Feuer, 1987; Gupta, Jenkins, and Curington, 1986; Shareef, 1994; Towers Perrin, 1992).

The city of Englewood, Colorado, developed a skill-based pay-for-performance plan called Creating Opportunities to Excel. New salary schedules were developed by determining the skill base for jobs and then assigning monetary values to each skill category. Skills were divided into two categories: skills essential to the job and skills of excellence such as certification, licensing, or the performance of duties beyond one's job description. In addition to modifying the salary schedule, a career development program was developed for employees. The program was divided into three parts: updated job descriptions, job outlines that showed different skill levels and corresponding compensation, and individualized career development plans.

The last part of the process was to develop a cafeteria-style reward and incentive plan. The employees were given the opportunity to discuss and decide which compensation packages were most attractive to them. The program has allowed Englewood to get a better inventory of its staff's skills. Many employees have skills not included in their job descriptions. The city has been able to benefit by capitalizing on incumbents' previously hidden talents. For example, one employee who was skilled in desktop publishing and layout created a brochure that saved the city $10,000. The city was also able to save $250,000 when employees in one division accepted responsibility for projects that the city normally contracted out (Leonard, 1995a).

Organizations that implement skill-based pay need to be aware that wages and salaries will increase as employees learn new skills. And despite the strategic focus of skill-based training, many employees unfortunately will resist its implementation (Shareef, 1994).

Merit Pay or Pay for Performance. Merit pay or pay-for-performance systems are grounded in the belief that individuals should be paid according to their contributions; increases are rewarded on the basis of performance rather than seniority, equality, or need (Heneman, 1992). As logical as that may sound, research over the years has indicated that merit pay systems have not achieved the expected and desired results (Heneman, 1992; Kellough & Lu, 1993; Perry, 1991, 1995).

Pay-for-performance systems fall victim to much of the same criticism made about performance evaluations noted in Chapter Seven, as well as additional criticism. Critics claim that the pay-for-performance evaluation process is subjective, that employees are rated by instruments that do not reflect their actual job competencies, that supervisors lack skills to develop performance standards and provide feedback, and that comparing individuals to one another sets up a competitive environment that can be destructive. An additional criticism is that adequate financial resources are not always allocated. For example, at the Social Security Administration (SSA) only employees rated as outstanding received performance awards in 1995. This was because Congress restricted the amount that SSA could spend on performance awards to one percent of its payroll. The American Federation of Government Employees (AFGE) has alleged that the decision to limit awards to so-called outstanding employees discriminates against employees in the lowest grades. The union alleged that managers and non-field workers received the most outstanding ratings and that the hardest workers in the lowest grades were punished (Harris, 1995). Even when pay rewards are not restricted, the small percentage of difference between high and low performers typically found in merit systems does not encourage improved performance or reward outstanding employees (Heneman, 1992).

Merit pay systems have been condemned for focusing on compensation rather than on improved performance. Research has found that when pay and performance are discussed, employees fail to address the developmental issues and instead focus on not receiving a pay increase or on receiving an increase lower than expected. When provided with constructive feedback in a training-and-development context, employees are likely to accept the information. When feedback is tied to pay increases, however, employees process the information differently. They tend to get defensive, believing that the rater is taking something away from them by not granting a pay increase. Other research indicates that when performance appraisal results determine pay, employees often set lower goals so that they can achieve them (Cascio, 1991b; Lawler, 1989).

The concepts of procedural justice and distributive justice must be considered when developing and administering pay-for-performance systems. *Procedural justice* focuses on the perceived fairness of the evaluation procedures used to determine performance ratings and/or merit increases. For example, what procedures and/or instruments are used to guarantee a link between pay and performance? *Distributive justice* focuses on the perceived fairness of the rating and/or increase received relative to the work performed (Greenberg, 1986). For example, is the rating and/or increase congruent to the performance inputs? Merit systems that are not developed with these principles in mind will lack the integrity and credibility necessary for employees to perceive that the system can discern and will reward differences in performance.

Research by Heneman (1992) indicates that for employees to perceive the process as just, five components must exist: performance must be clearly defined, rewards must be communicated to employees, rewards must be made contingent upon desired performance, opportunities to improve performance must exist, and the perceived relationship between rewards and performance should be viewed as important as the actual relationship.

To be successful, pay-for-performance must be linked to the strategic mission of the organization and upper-level management must support the plan. Employees should participate in the development of the plan. This increases their understanding, commitment, and trust in the plan. Organizations must provide training to the raters and hold them accountable for the accuracy of their ratings (Heneman, 1992; Newlin & Meng, 1991; Perry, 1995, Healy & Southard, 1994).

Aurora, Colorado, failed in its attempt to introduce a merit pay plan. The city's supervisors were not trained in making evaluations, they were not sure what the standards were, and they did not know how to give performance feedback. The system produced uneven results and therefore lacked credibility among the employees. City manager Jim Griesemer acknowledged, "We hadn't made the investment in our supervisors that was necessary to give them the tools to do this as well as they were capable" (Witt, 1989, p. 33).

The less-than-favorable endorsement of merit pay programs has not discouraged the public sector from attempting to institute them, and there have been some successes. Siegel (1994) reports that federal government demonstration projects at Navy research laboratories—the Naval Ocean Systems Center in San Diego and the Naval Weapons Center in China Lake, California—and at the National Institute of Standards and Technology (NIST) appear to be successful. Evaluation of the Navy programs found that money was a motivator, performance was rewarded and the rewards were considered fair, and employees believed that good and bad performance was distinguished and that the process was fair. The NIST program had not yet been evaluated on its pay-for-performance, but preliminary comments by employees indicated that employees who do a better job are rewarded, relationships between supervisors and subordinates have improved, and the system forces poor performers to leave the organization.

Gainsharing. Gainsharing is a team bonus program that measures controllable costs, such as improved safety records or decreases in waste or units of output. Teamwork is encouraged and all team members are rewarded for controlling costs or improving productivity. Formulas are used to measure costs that are controllable, and these costs are then compared to the costs of a historical base period. When performance improves relative to the base period, a bonus pool is funded. When performance falls short, no bonus pool is created. Employees keep a percentage of the bonus pool, while the organization keeps the rest.

The State of Michigan and the Service Employees International Union, which represents the state's prison guards, are using a gainsharing plan to determine pay increases. The plan was a compromise resulting from contract negotiations between the governor and the prison guards. The guards were looking at another year with no pay increases. To break the impasse, union representative Fred R. Parks proposed a plan relating increases in compensation to benefit cost savings. If the guards saved money on health care costs, he recommended, the money saved could be used for raises. The Governor agreed that if health care costs were kept below certain percentages, the guards' compensation would increase in some proportion to those savings (Walters, 1994b).

Another form of gainsharing plan has been adopted by Zebulon, North Carolina. The town distributes a small percentage of any overall end-of-the year budget surplus equally among its forty-eight employees. Not only do the employees receive bonuses, but the real benefit of the plan, according to the town manager, is that it eliminates barriers between departments and creates a culture in which everyone is helping everyone else become more productive. The sanitation department employees have become the eyes and ears of law enforcement, and the police department alerts public works employees about potholes or missing signs (Walters, 1995).

As these examples demonstrate, not all gainsharing plans are the same. The formulas and participative management features need to fit each other as well as the organization. Different situations require different designs. However, some common critical elements are necessary for any plan to succeed: (1) There must be a credible and trusted development process. (2) Employees must believe that improved performance and decreased costs will lead to bonuses; the bonuses must be understandable and large enough to influence performance; and employees must recognize how their behavior can influence the size of the bonus. (3) Employees need to be involved in the process; they must have influence over the measures used to calculate the bonus. (4) There must be appropriate measures and they must focus on all of the controllable costs. Measures such as units of output, materials, and supplies must all be addressed, otherwise employees may focus on one cost, leading to its reduction but also to increases in other costs. For example, data processing clerks may produce a greater number of records, but if the number of errors on the records has increased, the effort has been counterproductive. Or public works employees may be able to maintain and landscape more of the city's property in less time, but if the increased productivity results in equipment breakdowns and expensive repairs, then that is counterproductive. (5) The program must be maintained; because missions and environments change, gainsharing formulas and programs must change as well to stay relevant (Lawler, 1989).

Closing Thoughts on Equity

Despite an organization's best efforts to ensure equity, there are a number of factors outside of an agency's control that affect compensation. For example, as positions demand higher skill requirements, organizations can expect to pay more for those skills. If skills are in abundance, then employers can offer less even if those skills are critical to the organization. For instance, school teachers are often paid less than electricians, despite the greater value of teachers to the school, because unions may restrict the number of qualified electricians, thus driving up their salaries, while there are plenty of applicants wishing to be teachers. Or jobs with unpleasant or hazardous working conditions, such as sanitation or public works, might demand higher salaries because they are necessary to attract individuals to those positions.

Developing a compensation system that meets employee and organizational goals will require fine tuning. Not all employees have the same priorities. Today, quality-of-life issues are also considered important by applicants and employees. To attract and retain employees, organizations need to offer either competitive wages or other benefits deemed important to employees and applicants, such as flexible work schedules, career mobility, a sense of purpose and the opportunity to use their skills, and child care or educational reimbursement programs.

An example of an organization that has made use of the many available options is Sheltering Arms, a nonprofit social service and welfare agency that provides assistance to abused and battered women. Sheltering Arms developed a compensation structure with three components to attract and retain employees. First, it compares its wage levels with industry standards and maintains parity with other voluntary agencies. Second, it provides greater emphasis on personal time off and other nonfinancial benefits. And third, it provides an incentive-based payment plan in which a U.S. savings bond is given to employees who contribute to agency goals (Kraten, 1995).

Executive Compensation and Benefits

The compensation and benefits provided to executives in public and nonprofit organizations are often different from the compensation and benefits other employees receive. In the public sector, executives are exempt from civil service protection and serve at the discretion of elected officials. In the nonprofit sector, executives serve at the discretion of the board of directors. Because in both sectors the positions lack security, executives are likely to have negotiated employment contracts that specify the level of compensation and benefits they will receive. Some common benefits found in executive employment contracts include severance protection; moving expenses; health, retirement, and disability insurance; professional association memberships and dues; and paid conference registration and associated expenses such as travel and accommodations.

Executives are hired for their professional experience and expertise. They must often make hard choices and unpopular decisions that run counter to the wishes of the policymaking and governing body. Severance protection allows executives to be free to make those decisions without having to worrying about their financial situation if they are terminated. Severance protection usually includes a fixed amount of salary and the continuance of insurance benefits for a predetermined period of time.

Executives are typically recruited from the national labor market and often relocate to accept a position. Organizations that pay for moving expenses and in some cases provide a housing allowance in jurisdictions where housing is expensive make it easier to attract key executives. Executives will be less likely to relocate if they will continue to lose equity in their homes or if the costs associated with moving are prohibitive.

Because it is the responsibility of executives to guide as well as manage the organization, it is imperative that they have access to training and development activities such as attending conferences and belonging to professional associations. Organizations benefit when their executives are aware of the external forces affecting their agencies and changes in industry standards and practices. Agencies that maintain their competitive posture are led by proactive executives.

In both the public and nonprofit sectors, salaries are determined by surveying what relevant organizations in the external labor market pay for executive positions (Albert, 1993; Stene, 1980). Albert recommends that nonprofit executive salaries should be at the median or above the median of comparable organizations in the area. Board members should assess the agency's resources and offer the best salary and benefit package they can afford.

A survey of seventy-two nonprofit organizations conducted by William M. Mercer Company found that in setting salaries forty of the agencies considered the pay offered at other nonprofit groups as a benchmark, and eighteen used the salaries offered for like positions at nonprofit and for-profit groups to develop their own. Six organizations based their salaries on for-profit agencies (Greene, 1995).

At a meeting sponsored by the Conference Board on the topic of improving the way nonprofits handle executive compensation it was recommended that agencies develop formal incentive programs that link the agency's performance with cash bonuses in order to attract and retain the best executives and make them more productive. James E. Thomas III, vice president for human resources at the American Red Cross, acknowledged that "it's almost an oxymoron to say 'not-for-profit' and then say 'incentive plans' all in the same breadth, and I think many of our C.E.O.'s and board chairs are wrestling with that today for that very reason" (Greene, 1995, p. 39). Thomas believes that just as there is concern about gainsharing in the public sector, in which employees receive bonuses for saving money, "the press, donors, and people served by the organizations are skeptical of plans that provide special financial rewards for a job well done" (Greene, 1995, p. 39).

Despite these reservations, a salary-and-benefit guide published by Ernst & Young and titled *1994 Survey of Not-for-Profit Organizations' Compensation and Benefits* (cited in Rocque, 1995) indicates that one in five New York City nonprofits rewarded chief executives with bonuses. The average bonus received was $14,600, or 10.6 per cent of that person's average base salary. The report was based on data supplied by two hundred charities and foundations in the New York City metropolitan area. The budgets of the organizations surveyed ranged from less than $300,000 to $16 million or more in assets (Rocque, 1995).

Nonprofit organizations must be careful that their executive salaries do not come at the expense of lower-level employees. Skip Parham, associate director of human resources at the Young Men's Christian Association (YMCA) national headquarters in Chicago, believes that low beginning salaries in agencies like the YMCA limit the number of college graduates who will enter the field of working with youth. YMCAs are willing to pay competitive salaries for executives while junior staff are underpaid. Some YMCAs in the Midwest pay beginning salaries of $14,000 or $15,000. After two or three years the employees leave and the agencies need to recruit and train new staff (Vanneman, 1994).

According to Ellen Prior, director of not-for-profit consulting at the Hay Group, an HRM consulting firm, "Execs tend to have the old nonprofit mindset: you're here to do good, so you shouldn't be asking for a top salary. But that went along with another old idea: because you're doing good, you don't have to face a rigorous evaluation. Now nonprofits are expected to show explicit results. If you're going to demand performance, then you should pay for it" (Vanneman, 1994, p. 4).

Federal Laws Governing Compensation

All public and nonprofit employers are required to comply with two federal laws, the Fair Labor Standards Act (FLSA) and the Equal Pay Act.

The Fair Labor Standards Act

The FLSA was enacted in 1938. Minimum wage, overtime pay, equal pay, and child labor rules are its major provisions. The FLSA requires that employers keep records of the hours that employees have worked. Its overtime provision requires that employers pay one and one-half the regular rate of hourly pay for each hour worked that exceeds forty hours per week.

The FSLA divides employees into "exempt" and "nonexempt" workers. Exempt employees are not covered by the overtime provisions. They can be expected to work more than forty hours per week without additional compensation. Title 29, Part 541 of the Code of Federal Regulations (1993) defines exempt employees as those who spend 80 percent of their work time performing administrative, executive, or professional duties.

> *Administrative* employees' primary responsibilities consist of performing office-based duties related to the implementation of management policies or general business operations. They customarily and regularly exercise discretion and independent judgment.
>
> *Executive* employees exercise discretionary decision-making powers and supervise two or more employees. They have the authority to hire or fire employees or make recommendations as to the advancement and promotion or any other change of status of the employees they supervise.
>
> *Professional* employees perform duties requiring advanced knowledge acquired through specialized intellectual instruction. Their work is predominantly intellectual and varied in character and is of such character that the output produced or the result accomplished cannot be standardized in relation to a given time period [§541.1, §541.2, §541.3].

Employees are considered to be paid on a salary basis within the meaning of the FLSA if each pay period they receive a predetermined amount that constitutes all or part of their compensation and is not subject to reduction because of quality or quantity of the work performed. This means that employers are prohibited from making hourly deductions of pay from exempt employees.

Agencies with restricted budgets should not be tempted to classify employees as exempt as a way to avoid paying overtime. The Immigration and Naturalization Service (INS) has settled a lawsuit with criminal investigators who worked for the agency between 1985 and 1994. The INS claimed that the investigators were managerial employees, not covered by the FLSA overtime provisions, and therefore not entitled to be compensated for any overtime they worked. The AFGE, the union representing the criminal investigators, maintained that the employees had no role in setting policy and were therefore entitled to overtime compensation. In 1994, the INS lost in court and faced lengthy litigation over back pay, prompting them to settle. Individual settlements ranged from $6,000 to $86,000, with an average settlement of $46,000 (Rivenbark, 1995b).

In 1985, the Supreme Court ruled in *Garcia v. San Antonio Metropolitan Transit Authority* that the FLSA could be applied to state, county, and municipal employees. This meant that public employers could no longer use compensatory time in lieu of dollars and would have to pay overtime. Because of the financial burden this would cause, public agencies petitioned Congress for relief. Congress reacted by amending the FLSA with the Fair Labor Standards Amendments of 1985 (Pub. L. 99–150). Section 7(o) of the FLSA authorizes compensatory time off as a form of overtime. It applies only to public sector agencies. To be legal under the FLSA, compensatory time must be 1.5 hours for each hour worked; nonsworn personnel (public employees other than sworn officers such as police, fire, and corrections) may have no more than 240 hours of compensatory time on the books at any one time; and sworn personnel can accrue no more than 480 hours of compensatory time at any one time. Nonsworn and sworn personnel who reach the limits of 240 and 480 hours respectively must either receive cash for additional hours of overtime worked or use some compensatory time off before accruing further overtime compensation in the form of compensatory time off.

The 1985 amendment also has special provisions for hospital employees and for police and fire officials who typically work nontraditional shifts. Section 7(j) permits the use of a fourteen-day work period (instead of the usual seven-day work week) in the computation of overtime provisions. Overtime is considered only if an employee works more than eighty hours during the fourteen-day period.

Section 7(k) provides for work periods of up to twenty-eight days for public safety officials. They do not have to be paid overtime until they work more than 212 hours.

Nonprofit employers must comply with the FLSA overtime provision of one and one-half times an employee's normal hourly rate of pay for each hour that exceeds forty hours per week. Employees may elect compensatory time in lieu of overtime, but it must be their choice and not imposed by the employer.

In 1996, Senator John Ashcroft (R-MO) has introduced to Congress the Work and Family Integration Act (S. 1129), which would eliminate the current 40-hour-week threshold for overtime pay. Instead, employees would have to work in excess of 160 hours over a four-week period before receiving overtime pay. Supporters of the bill claim that it would encourage flexible work schedules, enabling employees to better balance their family and work lives. The legislation requires that any flexible work schedule must be agreed upon by both the employee and the employer. For unionized work environments, the establishment or termination of a flexible work schedule would be subject to collective bargaining.

Equal Pay Act of 1963

In 1963 the FLSA was amended by the Equal Pay Act, which prohibits unequal pay differences for men and women who are performing equal work on jobs requiring equal skill, effort, and responsibility and performed in the same establishment under similar working conditions. Pay differences between equal jobs can, however, be justified when that differential is based on (1) a seniority system, (2) a merit system, (3) a piece-rate payment system that measures earnings by quality or quantity of production, or (4) any factor other than gender (for example, different experience or different work shifts).

Comparable Worth

Should sign painters and tree trimmers receive higher wages than emergency room nurses? What about state grain inspectors who are at the same job evaluation level as administrative secretaries? Should they be paid more than the secretaries? If you think yes, then you are probably not surprised that the ratio of women's 1994 median weekly earnings to men's was 76.4. Even in traditionally female occupations, such as elementary school teachers, registered nurses, and general office clerks, where women outnumber men, they still earn less than men (U.S. Department of Labor, Women's Bureau, 1995a). If you think no, then you are likely to favor *comparable worth* as an element to be considered in the development of compensation systems.

Comparable worth is the idea that each job has an inherent value or worth that can be compared to different types of positions across the organization. Jobs of greater inherent value to the organization should be paid more. Comparable worth has been defined as "equitable compensation relationships for jobs that, while not the same, have been evaluated as equivalent based on the composite skill, effort, responsibility and working conditions required" (Dellion & Pearson, 1991). Comparable worth tries to eradicate the pay disparity between jobs that are traditionally female versus jobs that are traditionally male. Comparable worth argues that jobs associated with women tend to be undervalued and discriminated against in the marketplace—for example, when nurses are paid less than tree trimmers, or when clerical employees are paid less than male-dominated physical plant employees (*Christensen v. State of Iowa*, 1977; *Lemons v. City and County of Denver*, 1980).

Opponents of comparable worth claim that pay disparities are the result of supply and demand, that market rates provide impartial values of labor (Taylor, 1989). In 1985, the Court of Appeals for the Ninth Circuit upheld that belief, ruling that salaries resulting from the market system do not amount to deliberate discrimination based on sex (*American Federation of State, County, and Municipal Employees v. State of Washington*, 1985; Graham, 1992; Gaston, 1986).

Advocates for comparable worth believe that labor market rates are not entirely objective. There is no going rate for any job. The determination of what wages to pay involves making value judgments and decisions. For example, to determine external equity, the agency decides which organizations should be compared; whether the data should be collected directly, purchased, or taken from government sources; and whether it wants to be a wage leader. It is also responsible for considering other forms of compensation. These decisions are rarely assessed for their discriminatory impact (Elliott, 1985; Taylor, 1989).

It has also been suggested that the compensable factors used during the job evaluation procedure to assign points or rankings often devalue women's work. Treiman and Hartman (1981), Elliott (1985), and Wittig and Lowe (1989) propose that sexual stereotypes and perceptions of gender differences combined with the expectations and experiences of work could influence the nature of job evaluation procedures and outcomes. Historically, female work was devalued, subject to the perception that a woman's income was secondary to her husband's. Blumrosen (1979, p. 435) states that "value systems and perceptions of the job analyst influence what information is collected and therefore what is available in later stages in the process."

Arvey (1986) and Elliott (1985) observe that subjectivity can play a major part in the evaluation process in determining the job factors that are considered to be important and in deciding their weights or points. For example, supervision is a compensable factor beneficial to men, while responsibilities such as planning, coordination, and scheduling (typically female tasks) are usually ignored. Physical strength (required for typically male tasks) is valued while dexterity or handling multiple tasks simultaneously (required for typically female tasks) are not. Other characteristics and responsibilities, such as counseling and teaching, that are common in occupations heavily populated by women are often neglected as compensable factors. To eliminate these biases, compensable factors must be reevaluated, otherwise organizations risk incorporating these inequities into future job evaluation procedures.

The federal courts have not recognized comparable worth as a statutory requirement under the Equal Pay Act or Title VII of the Civil Rights Act of 1964. However, various legislative bodies have acted to remedy pay disparities across jobs of similar value to the organization. In 1984, Congress enacted the Pay Equity and Management Act, reflecting the federal government's interest in comparable worth. In 1987, the U.S. Federal Employee Compensation Study Commission Act examined and attempted to promote equitable pay practices within the federal workforce. This legislation was followed by the Federal Equitable Pay Practices Act of 1988, which directed a study to determine the extent to which wages are affected across the board by gender, and to determine the role this influence may play in the formation of wage differentials between male- and female-dominated jobs (Kovach & Millspaugh, 1990, p. 94).

Several states and local governments have passed legislation requiring that public jobs are to be paid according to their worth to the organization. An investigation by the state of Minnesota found that grain inspectors for the state were at the same job evaluation level as administrative secretaries, but they were paid $300 more per month. Each state job was evaluated using skill, effort, responsibility, and working conditions as the compensable factors. Despite similar internal value scores, men were paid more throughout state positions. To correct the disparity, in 1982 the Minnesota legislature passed a comparable worth law for state employees. The law required equitable compensation relationships between comparable male-dominated and female-dominated jobs.

In 1984, the Minnesota legislature enacted another law, which required other public employers such as city and county governments, public utilities, libraries, hospitals, and school districts to develop plans to institute pay equity and to implement those plans by 1987 (Aho, 1989; Watkins, 1992). Rhode Island followed in 1990, when it amended its classification and pay plan to authorize classification and pay increases for seventy job categories that were traditionally held by females. A study by the National Committee on Pay Equity revealed that more than fifteen hundred local governments, school districts, and community colleges have taken steps to identify and eliminate sex bias in public positions (Horrigan & Harriman, 1988, p. 704). As of 1993, approximately twenty states had passed some form of comparable worth legislation to raise the pay of employees in jobs filled predominately by women (Bernardin & Lee, 1993).

While no federal legislation presently exists that mandates equal pay for comparable worth, in 1995 Washington D.C.'s nonvoting delegate to the House of Representatives, Eleanor Holmes

Norton, and twenty-one members of Congress introduced the Fair Pay Act (H.R. 1507), which aims to reduce differences in wages that are based on sex, race, or national origin. The bill is designed to ensure equal pay for comparable work. It would provide that no employer could discriminate between employees based on sex, race, or national origin by paying wages at a lower rate for work of equal value, except where the payment is made based on a seniority system, a merit system, or a system in which earnings are measured by quantity or quality of production. H.R. 1507 has been referred to the Committee on Economic and Educational Opportunities.

Summary

Compensation systems should be designed with the intent to attract, motivate, and retain proficient employees. A number of factors determine the salaries paid to public and nonprofit employees: the salaries paid in the external labor market, federal laws such as the FLSA and the Equal Pay Act, and the responsibilities and KSAOCs required to perform the job, as well as an agency's ability to pay competitive wages.

Equity refers to the perception by employees that they are being paid fairly. External, internal, and employee equity influence compensation systems. Market factors influence external equity, job evaluation or job worth influences internal equity, and employee equity is said to exist when employees performing similar jobs are compensated based on their individual contributions. Broad banding, skill-based pay or pay for knowledge, merit pay, and gainsharing are examples of some of the innovations beginning to be seen in public and nonprofit sector compensation systems.

Public and nonprofit executives are hired for their professional experience and expertise. They lack job security and serve at the discretion of elected officials or board members. Because of this unique aspect of their employment, executives typically negotiate employment contracts that specify the level of compensation and benefits they will receive. Executives of some nonprofits also receive bonuses based on their agency's performance.

Chapter Nine

Benefits

The previous chapter on compensation provided an overview of salaries and wages, the direct financial compensation provided to employees for their contributions to the organization. But wages constitute only part of the compensation system. This chapter addresses indirect compensation, more commonly referred to as benefits.

The emphasis in compensating employees should be on the total compensation package, not just on direct wages or salary (Rosenbloom & Hallman, 1991). Benefits are a critical ingredient in creating an accurate compensation picture. The importance of benefits should not be underestimated. An attractive benefits package can assist in the recruitment and retention of qualified employees. Traditional benefits such as health insurance, retirement pensions, and paid time away from work combined with less traditional benefits such as child and elder care, flexible scheduling, and educational assistance are critical for attracting quality applicants, encouraging loyalty and long-term employment, and motivating and rewarding incumbent employees.

Consider the following examples:

• A homeless shelter in New York City experienced employee turnover at approximately 60 percent for several years. Three senior managers were hired from outside the agency and instituted change. Employee turnover was reduced the following year to 38 percent. The reasons cited for the reduced turnover were increased training opportunities, the implementation of a pension plan, improved medical benefits, and better recruitment procedures (Jerrick & Berger, 1994).

- Colorado College, located in Colorado Springs, offers an on-site day care facility for employees and students. It provides services to forty children ranging from infant care to kindergarten. The center is supported by the college's board of directors and the college subsidizes its expenses. The center has been mentioned by employees as a reason for accepting employment at the college (Hand & Zawacki, 1994).

- More than 86,000 federal employees used the services provided by employee assistance programs in 1993. Seventy-nine percent of the people who sought help did so on their own, not because they were referred by management. Employees sought help for emotional and psychiatric illness; for family, financial, and other personal problems, including substance abuse; to avert workplace violence; and for AIDS training (Walker, 1994).

- The U.S. Department of Labor has launched the Working Women Count Honor Roll as a new initiative to improve the lives of working Americans. The Honor Roll encourages employers to improve pay and benefits, build family-friendly workplaces, and provide training and advancement opportunities. The Honor Roll has received one hundred pledges from businesses, community organizations, state and local governments, and labor unions around the country. Personal leave time, flexible work schedules, on-site child care, and training for higher paying jobs are examples of some of the pledges (U.S. Department of Labor, Women's Bureau, 1995b).

Recent surveys indicate that benefits often reach 40 percent of total compensation costs (Bureau of National Affairs, 1995b). However, employees often think of benefits as entitlements and not as compensation. In reality, the only entitlements are those benefits that are required by federal or state laws, such as employer contributions to Social Security or state pension plans, unemployment compensation, and workman's compensation. Aside from the legally required ones, employers have tremendous discretion in deciding what types of benefits to provide. This chapter discusses the variety of benefits that organizations may choose to offer, as well as the quality-of-life and quality-of-work issues that are becoming more prevalent in today's workplaces.

Required Benefits

All employers are required to contribute to Social Security, unemployment compensation, and workers' compensation benefits. Public employers may be required by federal or state statutes to offer additional benefits, such as retirement or disability. The benefits provided by nonprofits are determined or approved by the board of directors.

Social Security

Social Security provides retirement, disability, death, survivor, and Medicare benefits for those beyond age sixty-five. The Social Security system was established in 1935; however, public and nonprofit employers and employees could decline to pay Social Security taxes and earn no credit toward Social Security benefits. The Social Security Amendments of 1983 made Social Security coverage mandatory for all employees of nonprofit organizations as of January 1, 1984. Coverage was extended to nonprofit employees working for organizations that had previously terminated coverage, as well as to employees who had never been covered by Social Security. The 1983 amendments included a special section that provided for nonprofit employees fifty-five years and older to be considered fully insured for benefits after acquiring at least twenty quarters of coverage (Commerce Clearing House, 1989, p. 3250).

The Social Security Act originally excluded state and local governments from coverage because of the concern that taxation of state and local governments by the federal government might be unconstitutional (McGill, 1992, pp. 533–534). The act was subsequently amended in the 1950s to permit state and local governments to choose coverage for employees not already covered under a retirement system. After five years of participating in the Social Security system, state and local governments could choose to repeal their action and terminate coverage of their employees. This was changed in 1983 by the Social Security Amendments Act, which eliminated the right of state and local government employers to withdraw from the system. Another change came in 1986. The Budget Reconciliation Act amended the Social Security Act and required all individuals hired by a state or local government to be covered by the Medicare segment of the program and subject to employer and employee payroll taxes. As of July 2, 1991, all state and local government employees (except police officers) not covered by a retirement program are required to participate in the full Social Security program (McGill, 1992). Federal employees hired on or after January 1, 1984, are covered by Social Security and are subject to full Social Security taxation.

Social Security provides four kinds of benefits: (1) old-age or disability benefits, (2) benefits for the dependents of retired or disabled workers, (3) benefits for the survivors of a worker who dies, (4) and the lump-sum death benefit.

Unemployment Compensation

Unemployment compensation was established as part of the Social Security Act of 1935. It was designed to provide a portion of wages to employees who have been laid off until they obtain another job. The employer pays into the unemployment compensation fund at a rate based on the average number of former employees who have drawn benefits from the fund. The fund is primarily financed through a payroll tax paid to the state and federal governments based on employees' wages. Each state determines its own waiting period for eligibility, level of benefits provided, and the length of time that benefits are paid.

Workers' Compensation

Workers' compensation is an employer-financed insurance program that provides compensation to employees who are unable to work because of job-related injuries or illness. Most states have their own workers' compensation laws and are responsible for administering their own programs. For this reason the levels of protection and the costs of administering the programs vary from state to state. Some features that all of the programs have in common are the following (CCH Business Law Editors, 1992, p. 8):

Workers receive benefits for accidental injury; wage-loss, medical, and death benefits are provided.

Fault is not an issue; if the employee was somewhat or entirely at fault in the injury, the employee still has the right to receive workers' compensation benefits.

In exchange for the assurance of benefits, the employee (and the employee's dependent family members) gives up the right to sue the employer for damages for any injury covered by a workers' compensation law.

The responsibility for administering the system usually resides with a state board or commission.

Employers are generally required to insure their workers' compensation liability through private insurance, state insurance funds, or self-insurance.

Independent contractors are not considered to be employees and do not have to be covered under the workers' compensation policy of the organization that hired them. Most state workers' compensation agencies apply the same test as the Internal Revenue Service (IRS) for determining whether a contractor is truly independent and not just called so by an employer who does not want to match the contractor's Social Security contributions or deduct and withhold income taxes (Joel, 1993, p. 237). To decide whether a contractor is "independent," the IRS uses common law factors to determine whether the contractor controls what she or he does and how she or he does it:

Can the contractor be fired or quit without any contractual liability?

Is the contractor reimbursed for business and travel expenses? Does the contractor perform the task in person, on company property, and during set hours?

Is the contractor paid by the hour, week, or month rather than by the job?

Does the organization provide the contractor with tools or equipment?

If the answer to most of these questions is yes, the contractor should probably be covered under the organization's workers' compensation policy. The state's workers' compensation agency should be contacted for verification (Joel, 1993, p. 237).

The IRS's test for determining independent contractor status is not, however, the only test used by the courts and other administrative agencies. O'Meara (1994) identifies additional criteria. The National Labor Relations Board, for example, uses the common law right-to-control factors but also scrutinizes the degree of investment by the worker and the opportunity for entrepreneurial profit or loss. The Department of Labor uses an "economic reality" test, which focuses not exclusively on the right to control but on whether the worker is economically dependent upon the employer to whom he or she renders service.

In most states, unpaid volunteers are not considered to be employees and are typically not covered by workers' compensation. But in some states there are exceptions for police and fire volunteers, and other volunteers may be covered under special circumstances.

Optional Benefits

In addition to the employer-provided benefits required by law, employers often provide a variety of benefits that are optional.

Pensions

Pensions provide retired or permanently disabled employees with income throughout the remainder of their lives. In the public sector, different classes of employees are often covered by different pension plans. For example, teachers, police, and firefighters have pension plans separate from those of other general employees. Some states have separate pension plans for judges and legislatures. Police and firefighters may retire with full benefits at a younger age and with fewer years of service than other employees.

Prior to 1984, the retirement plan covering most civilian federal employees was the Civil Service Retirement System (CSRS); employees covered by CSRS were excluded from paying Social Security taxes. The Social Security Amendments of 1983, however, required that federal employees hired after December 31, 1983, be covered by Social Security. A new retirement plan, the Federal

Employees Retirement System (FERS), was established by Congress on June 6, 1986, and went into effect on January 1, 1987. Most federal employees hired after January 1, 1987, are covered by FERS, and employees covered under CSRS were given the opportunity to join FERS.

Like state and local government retirement systems, the federal government also has different age and years-of-service criteria that permit select groups of employees to retire early and with full benefits. Law enforcement officials, firefighters, air traffic controllers, military reserve technicians, and defense intelligence Senior Executive Service (SES) and senior cryptologic SES are examples of some of the positions eligible for early retirement.

Defined-Benefit and Defined-Contribution Pension Plans

Two types of pension plans are commonly found in the public and nonprofit sectors: defined-benefit and defined-contribution plans.

A *defined-benefit plan* is a pension plan that specifies the benefits or the methods of determining the benefits at the time of retirement but not the level or rate of contribution. The benefit amounts to be paid are determined by a formula that weighs the retiree's years of service, age, and salary history. An advantage of the defined-benefit plan is that employees and employers can estimate the probable size of their pension benefits by assuming retirement dates and salary histories.

In *defined-contribution* plans, the employer guarantees that specified contributions, usually a percentage of annual salary, will be deposited to employees' accounts every year that they work. These accounts are invested. Employees are provided with a variety of investment options from which to choose. When employees retire, they receive lifetime payments or annuities, the size of which are determined by the amount on deposit, the interest rate earned on funds in the account, and the length of time during which the annuity is expected to be paid. The employee, the employer, or both may contribute to the pension plan.

Defined-contribution pension plans are becoming more popular as more employers have realized the expense and long-term liabilities associated with funding defined-benefit plans. The state of West Virginia, for example, provides new teachers with a defined-contribution plan to provide for retirement, the California state retirement system is investigating defined-contribution alternatives, and the governor of Michigan has proposed that new state employees be covered by a defined-contribution plan with a 5 percent employer match (Zolkos, 1994). An advantage of defined-contribution plans is that the money is usually portable if employees change jobs because there are no vesting requirements. A disadvantage is that employees tend to be more conservative in selecting their investment options than professional investors. Conservative investment plans will lead to lower interest rates and fewer funds for retirement. Employers who offer defined-contribution plans need to provide training and assist their employees with information on how to invest their money and plan for retirement.

Cost-of-Living Adjustments

Cost-of-living adjustments (COLAs) are supplements made to retirees' initial pension benefits to offset some of the purchasing loss caused by inflation. COLAs are often based on changes in the consumer price index.

Vesting

Vesting is when contributions made to a retirement plan belong to the employee. For most defined-benefit pension plans, if you leave the organization you retain the nonforfeitable right to those benefits when you retire. However, you may be required to wait until you actually retire before receiving the benefits. Most defined-contribution pension plans allow you to take the accrued amount when you depart in a lump sum payment that is taxable.

Vesting standards for nonprofit and private organizations were amended as part of the Tax Reform Act of 1986. New minimum standards went into effect in 1989 that enable employees to become fully vested in their pension plans after five years of service, or they may be 20 percent vested after three years of service, 20 percent for each year thereafter, and 100 percent vested after seven years of service.

In the public sector, wide variations exist as to when employees are entitled to vested benefits. In some plans, employees are required to work five years before benefits are guaranteed. Other plans require ten years of plan participation before vesting occurs. Employees considering employment in another organization covered by a different retirement system would want to find out whether they meet the minimum requirement for vesting.

As noted earlier, retirement systems at the federal, state, and local levels have special provisions for public safety officers. They can retire at an earlier age with full benefits after shortened working careers.

The Employee Retirement Income Security Act of 1974 (ERISA) safeguards the pensions of nonprofit and private sector employees. ERISA sets minimum standards to ensure that employee benefit plans are financially sound so that employees receive the benefits promised by their employers. ERISA does not cover plans established or maintained by government entities or churches.

Deferred Compensation Benefits

A wide variety of employer-assisted savings plans are available to employees. One of the most common plans is the deferred compensation plan, such as the 401(k) plan, which permits employees to postpone paying income taxes on a portion of their salary if that portion is contributed to a qualified plan. Some employers will match an employee's contribution to a plan at a limited rate, such as twenty-five to fifty cents per dollar, or with matching stock options. The federal government provides a thrift savings plan for employees enrolled in the FERS retirement system. The government will match up to 5 percent of the employees' contributions. Unfortunately, while most state and local governments have deferred compensation plans, they typically do not match the employee's contribution.

Nonprofit organizations that are exempt under Section 501(c)(3) of the Internal Revenue Code and public schools and colleges may also provide voluntary supplemental retirement plans for employees through the Section 403(b) tax-sheltered annuity plan (Bartlett & Lichtenstein, 1992). Public schools, colleges, and charitable nonprofits that offer 403(b) plans to their employees must oversee the plans even if they are administered by third parties such as insurance companies or investment firms. The IRS has found that many nonprofits and their employees are not complying with the requirements of 403(b) plans. Many have set aside more money than is legally permissible; some nonprofits have not been offering comparable 403(b) benefits to all of their employees but only to executives, which is illegal; some agencies have not offered 403(b) benefits to consultants, part-time employees, or contractors who qualify; employees are changing the amount of their contributions in the middle of the tax year, which is prohibited; and in some cases trade associations, advocacy groups, and other nonprofits not allowed to offer 403(b) plans have done so. When violations have been found, the charities have paid the back taxes owed by the employees. In one case, the employer paid $18,000 in back taxes. The IRS is advising all employers to examine their annuity systems and report any violations (Murawski, 1995a; Rowland, 1994).

Insurance

Health insurance, life insurance, and long-term sickness and accident/disability insurance are some of the benefits provided to employees. Health insurance is the most frequently provided benefit and the benefit over which employees most commonly are willing to strike (Fisher, 1990). Benefits have become so important that union members have occasionally given up wage increases in order to maintain their health care benefits (Ray, 1993). The types of insurance programs and the amount that employees and employers contribute to the plans vary.

The Consolidated Omnibus Budget Reconciliation Act of 1986 (COBRA) requires employers to offer laid-off or terminated employees the opportunity to continue their health insurance coverage. COBRA covers employers of twenty or more employees, except for federal government and religious organizations. Many states have their own versions of COBRA to cover small employers. COBRA enables former employees, spouses, and dependents to purchase insurance coverage for a limited amount of time after leaving the organization. COBRA also applies to divorced, separated, or widowed spouses. COBRA also extends Medicare coverage to state and local government employees.

More insurance programs are also beginning to offer dental, optical, and prescription drugs benefits in addition to traditional medical coverage.

Disability Benefits

Disability benefits are paid to employees who becomes disabled before qualifying for regular or early retirement benefits. Generally, disability benefit insurance provides a monthly benefit to employees who due to injury or illness cannot work for an extended period of time. According to the U.S. Department of Labor (1994), 28 percent of full-time state and local government employees are covered by long-term disability insurance. Some employees, however, are not insured for long-term disability but are eligible for an immediate disability pension through their retirement plans. In most instances, long-term disability payments are a fixed percentage of predisability earnings. Most plans distinguish between disability attributed to an accident on the job, which pays higher benefits and has fewer requirements with respect to years of service, and disability that is not job related.

Paid Time Away from Work

Most employers grant employees paid sick leave, vacation days, holidays, and personal days. Employers are not obligated to grant these benefits, and they vary across organizations. Moore (1991) reports that state and local employees receive an average of twelve days of vacation after one year of service, 21 days of vacation after twenty years of service, 11 paid holidays, and 2.7 personal leave days, which is more than the amount of paid leave received by private employees.

In many public organizations, employees who accumulate their sick and vacation days are able to cash them in for cash compensation at a reduced rate when they retire. This policy is meant to discourage capricious time away from work and to reward employees for their commitment to the organization. However, many organizations are rethinking this policy because accrued time becomes an unfunded liability for the agency.

Reed and Swain (1990) cite an example of a midwestern community that provided this benefit but never costed it out. A city manager retired after twenty years of service and received $20,000 in sick-leave benefits. After further examination, the city realized that it had one million dollars in unfunded liability. In 1995, the East St. Louis School District, which is a district managed by the state because of its fiscal distress due to mismanagement, paid more than $2 million dollars to retiring teachers and administrators. Under the school district's contract, employees receive twelve sick days each year. They are allowed to accumulate up to 180 sick days and cash them in at the employee's latest daily pay rate. For many administrators, the latest daily rate ranged from $222 to $305 a day. Many school districts permit employees to cash in unused sick days, but usually at a lower rate of pay or fewer numbers of days. In Illinois, for example, the Edwardsville School District limits the cash-out rate to $50 per day for up to two hundred days, and the Belleville School District permits employees to receive compensation for ninety sick days at pay rates lower than their daily salaries (McDermott & Gillerman, 1995). Organizations that provide this benefit need to understand and plan for its fiscal implications.

Education Programs

Many organizations provide tuition reimbursement to employees for additional education if the employee receives a B or better grade for the course. The Congress of National Black Churches in Washington, D.C., offers employees in their national office a training allowance of $750 to $1,500 per person per year. The money can be used for job-related education and for training services and materials. Education assistance is often combined with career and development programs.

A type of education benefit that is attractive to employees with children is the college savings plan. The employer establishes a payroll deduction plan designed to help employees save for their children's college education. The money that has been deducted is placed into an investment fund. Some employers match up to 25 percent of the employees' savings (Leonard, 1995b).

Quality-of-Work and Quality-of-Life Issues

Changes in family structures and employee priorities have encouraged the evolution of a variety of employer-provided benefits.

Employers wishing to compete for highly skilled employees are finding that quality-of-work and quality-of-life issues can give them a competitive edge.

Flexible Benefits

As early as the 1970s, private sector organizations recognized that different family structures necessitate different employee benefits (Johnson, 1988; Wallace & Fay, 1988). Conventional employee benefit plans were designed to serve the needs of the family structure that was dominant during the 1940s and 1950s: a working father and his dependents (namely, a wife who stayed at home with small children). Today, families have changed and so have their needs. Current family structures often include a single parent, multiple generations, and domestic partnerships. Continuing increases in dual-career and single-parent families will likely result in a continued demand for a variety of elder- and child-care services.

Two recent studies by federal agencies have recognized this phenomena. The U.S. Merit Systems Protection Board's (1991) report titled *Balancing Work Responsibilities and Family Needs: The Federal Civil Service Response* and the U.S. General Accounting Office's (1992) report titled *The Changing Workforce: Comparison of Federal and Nonfederal Work/Family Programs and Approaches* acknowledge the changing structure of American families and the need for evolving and flexible benefits. Employees with small children may need child care, employees with elderly or infirm parents may prefer elder care, and employees without any dependents might opt for a variety of other benefits such as dental care. Some solutions have been employer-sponsored group insurance plans that provide lower premiums, or flexible spending accounts that enable greater flexibility in the types of services that benefits will pay for (Kossek, DeMarr, Backman, & Kolar, 1993).

In the past, wives often took care of elderly parents or in-laws and children, but today there are more single-parent families or families in which both spouses work full-time, and they are unable to care for their children and/or parents. Thus many benefit plans now have provisions for elder and child care.

The American Business Collaboration for Quality Dependent Care launched a dependent care initiative in 1991 that aimed to improve the quality and availability of child and elder care. Today approximately 137 U.S. employers, including 21 government and nonprofit organizations, are members. In 1995, the same group pledged $100 million to finance the creation and enhancement of programs for elder care and programs for child care for school-aged children nationwide. The commitment will be used to support a variety of innovative programs, such as a voice-technology program that will allow parents to become more involved in their children's education; after-school and summer plans for school-age children; training for child-care providers; and science and technology camps.

Child- and elder-care responsibilities have an impact on job performance. Research has found that caregiver responsibilities result in the excessive use of the phone at work, lateness, and unscheduled time off. Employee time spent on caregiver responsibilities affects productivity, absenteeism, turnover, and morale (Nelson-Horchler, 1989).

Two employers who qualified for the Working Women Count Honor Roll because of their family-friendly policies are the city of Kansas City, Missouri, and Little Hoop Community College in Fort Totten, North Dakota. Kansas City grants city employees four hours of paid leave annually to participate in their children's school activities. Mayor Emanuel Cleaver has challenged area businesses to follow suit. Little Hoop Community College has created a day care center for the college and is working in partnership with local businesses to raise money for a major community child-care center (U.S. Department of Labor, Women's Bureau, 1995b).

The concern about child care of parents who work nonstandard hours is increasing. In 1991, nearly 14.3 million America workers worked nontraditional hours. It has been estimated that one thousand different work schedules are in use today (U.S. Department of Labor, Women's Bureau, 1995c, p. 5). Many twenty-four-hour jobs in the public and nonprofit sector, such as those in public safety and health services, have always existed, but an increasing number of other employers have begun to provide services in the early mornings and the evenings, and on nights and weekends, making it difficult in some communities to arrange for quality child care.

To address this problem, the Women's Bureau of the U.S. Department of Labor has published *Care Around the Clock: Develop-*

ing Child Care Resources Before Nine and After Five (1995c) as a resource guide for parents, child-care providers, employers, and community care organizations. Included in the report are examples of three general models for providing nonstandard child care. The first model is the *single employer model,* in which one employer designs a child-care program to fit the agency's work schedule. For example, the Massachusetts Bay Transportation Authority (MBTA), located in Boston, fits this profile. MBTA owns and operates the public transportation system that serves the greater Boston area. It employs approximately 6,966 employees. Most of the employees are transit operators whose schedules may change every three months. Operators may work a mixture of morning, evening, weekday, and weekend shifts. MBTA developed a two-pronged approach to assist employees in meeting their child-care needs. First, they contracted with a local child-care resource and referral agency to provide information and education. Second, they developed the Reserved Slot Child Care Program for employees' children aged two months to twelve years. This program contracts with thirty-two licensed child-care centers in twenty-three Boston area communities. An employee handbook describes the program's eligibility requirements, registration procedures, payment system, waiting list, and procedures for program withdrawal. The child-care resource and referral service is completely subsidized by MBTA. Tuition subsidies in the form of a sliding scale provide financial assistance to employees who participate in the Reserved Slot Child Care Program (U.S. Department of Labor, Women's Bureau, 1995c).

The second model is the *employer consortium model.* In this approach, a group of employers come together on an industry or geographic basis to share knowledge, pool resources, and conduct joint child-care projects. Central Atlanta Hospitality Childcare, Inc. (CAHCI) is an example of an industry-based employer consortium. Several of the major hotels in Atlanta, Georgia, joined together to address the unique child-care difficulties facing hospitality industry employees. CAHCI was founded as a nonprofit organization to oversee the development of a child-care center and to provide services and resources to parents who are hotel workers. The childcare center is called Children's Inn; it is open twenty-four hours a day, seven days a week, and offers educational programs focusing on child development (U.S. Department of Labor, Women's Bureau, 1995c).

In the third model, the *community partnership model,* a variety of stakeholders such as employers, parents, providers, unions, resource organizations, and local governments join together to identify community child-care needs and solutions, and to pool resources and share skills and expertise. Palcare is a nonprofit organization that was formed to meet the child-care needs of employees based at the San Francisco International Airport and in the surrounding Bay Area communities. Labor unions, the San Francisco Airport Commission, both large and small employers, including local and county governments, Mills Peninsula Hospital, United Airlines, and the Child Care Coordinating Council, and community members are all partners. It took ten years of effort to open the Palcare Child Care Center in May 1993. The child-care center is licensed to serve 150 children between the ages of three months and five years at any one time. It is open twenty-four hours per day, seven days per week. Parents who are asked to work overtime or who have last-minute schedule changes can request additional care.

An emerging issue in the public, nonprofit, and private sectors is the provision of domestic partnership benefits to employees. Such benefits extend workplace benefit coverage to unmarried heterosexual or gay couples. One way to support employees and make them feel part of the organization is to recognize and respect alternative families. Health insurance, sick leave, bereavement leave, pension plans, life insurance benefits, and access to EAPs are some of the benefits that have been extended to domestic partners. Typically, couples qualify if they are living together and are jointly responsible for their financial well-being. As of 1994, there were approximately forty-two government entities, sixty-three colleges and universities, and ninety-six nonprofit and private employers providing some form of domestic partnership benefits.

Employee Assistance Programs

EAPs are another important type of employer-provided benefit. Marital conflicts, alcohol and substance abuse, family stresses, AIDS, and other health-related concerns are some of the problems that come to work with employees. These problems often result in lower employee productivity and morale, and may also lead to legal liabilities and high financial costs for the employer (Johnson & O'Neill, 1989; Perry & Cayer, 1992).

EAPs provide counseling services for employees and their families. In the past, the focus of EAPs was on alcoholism and drug-related problems. The services of EAPs have since expanded to include counseling for marital problems, drug abuse, mental illness, financial stress, and the improvement of employer-employee communications (Ramakrishnan & Balgopal, 1992, p. 490).

EAPs also address such issues as prevention, health and wellness, employee advocacy, and the dysfunctional workplace (Ramanathan, 1992). Employees with stressful lives are absent more often, resulting in lost productivity. Wellness programs are designed to improve employees' overall health, thus decreasing the occurrence and severity of medical problems and lowering the costs and number of medical claims (Hyland, 1990). Accident prevention classes, smoking cessation seminars, weight control programs, stress management workshops, and on-site exercise programs are also an outgrowth of EAPs. The largest use of EAPs however, is still for drug or alcohol addictions.

Alcohol and Drug Testing

A pervasive problem in the American workforce is employees with substance abuse problems. Alcohol and drug abuse are cited for decreases in productivity and increases in work-related accidents. To combat substance abuse in the workplace, legislators, judges, and regulatory agencies have passed laws or rendered decisions that regulate substance abuse testing in the workplace.

In 1986, President Reagan signed Executive Order 12564, which required federal agencies to set up programs to test workers in sensitive positions for illegal drug use and to establish a voluntary drug testing program for all other employees. In 1988, the Drug-Free Workplace Act was passed by Congress. The act required federal contractors and grantees who receive more than $25,000 in government business to certify that they would maintain drug-free workplaces. Organizations that did not comply with the requirements of the act could have their payments suspended and lose governments contracts for up to five years.

Nonprofit organizations that are the recipients of federal funds in excess of $25,000 are required to comply with the Drug-Free

Workplace Act. State and local governments may also require government contractors to comply with drug abuse prevention efforts. In addition, nonprofits receiving state and/or local funds are expected to comply with state regulations.

Nonprofit employees employed under a collective bargaining agreement may be subject to an employer-imposed drug and alcohol testing policy. In 1989, the National Labor Relations Board (NLRB) ruled that the drug testing of current employees was a mandatory subject of collective bargaining but the drug testing of applicants was not (Johnson-Bateman Company, 1989). This decision was reversed by the Seventh Circuit Court in the case of *Chicago Tribune v. National Labor Relations Board* (1992). The court held that the newspaper could rely on its broad management rights clause to implement a drug testing program on a unilateral basis. The management rights clause gave the employer the exclusive right "to establish and enforce reasonable rules and regulations relating to the operation of the facilities and employee conduct."

Public employees have been insulated by the U.S. Constitution from the capricious use of drug testing. They have challenged drug testing on grounds that it violates the Fourth Amendment's prohibition against reasonable search and seizure. The Supreme Court rendered two decisions on this issue in 1989. In *Skinner v. Railway Labor Executives Association* (1989) and *National Treasury Employees Union v. Von Raab* (1989), the Court ruled that public employers may require drug testing when a compelling government interest exists that overrides the employee's right to privacy. The court upheld drug testing when the public's health and safety is at risk or for law enforcement occupations that are involved in drug interdiction activities.

The Fourth Amendment is not applicable to nonprofit and private organizations, which may be restricted by state constitutional provisions, state and local laws regulating drug testing, collective bargaining obligations under the National Labor Relations Act, and federal and state laws prohibiting employment discrimination on the basis of disability. It is important that employers review these laws and regulations before instituting drug testing policies.

In 1991, the Omnibus Transportation Employee Testing Act (OTETA) was passed by Congress. OTETA requires the alcohol and controlled substances testing of employees in safety-sensitive jobs in transportation, regardless of which sector they work in. Any employee required to hold a commercial driver's license or who performs other covered safety-sensitive functions is subject to testing. The law requires postaccident and random testing, as well as testing when there is a reasonable suspicion that employees are under the influence of controlled substances.

All organizations should establish alcohol and substance abuse policies, and supervisors should be trained to identify warning signs and instructed to refer employees to EAPs for further evaluation. Some of the common signs of alcohol and substance abuse are mood swings, slurred speech, memory loss, and drowsiness. There may be a decrease in productivity, or increased absenteeism, tardiness, and workplace accidents. Supervisors should be educated in substance abuse issues; they should know how to identify problems, and what assistance programs are available to employees.

Alcohol and drug testing policies should provide for written notice to employees that testing will be conducted; explain the procedures that will be used in the testing; employ a chain of custody so that samples are not lost, switched, or lost; confirm positive tests with more sensitive tests; and ensure confidentiality of test results. After an employee has completed rehabilitation and is ready to return to work, the organization should require written documentation from a health care professional that the employee is in recovery and is no longer using drugs or alcohol.

Quality-of-Work Issues

Changing family structures have focused attention not only on the need for variety in employer-provided benefits but also on the need for more flexible workplace policies. Employers must acknowledge that family life and work have changed. As early as 1986, 51 percent of mothers with children under six were in the workforce (Kahn & Kamerman, 1987). By 1988, in 63 percent of married couples both the husband and wife worked outside the home, and the number of single-parent households had risen to 23 percent (Hyland, 1990). These factors have led to increased stress on employees as they strive to balance the demands of both work and family life. Employees who cannot manage these conflicting demands are often less productive and, as noted earlier, are absent more often and have lower morale.

To better meet the needs of their employees, many organizations have developed flexible work structures. Flextime, voluntary shifts to part-time work, job sharing, flexible leaves, compressed work weeks, and work-at-home or telecommuting opportunities are some of the strategies that are used to alleviate work and family conflicts.

Another issue affecting morale and motivation at work is career plateauing. As public and nonprofit agencies are confronted with fewer promotional opportunities, more employees have reached career plateaus. Career plateauing is the inability to move upward in the organization. To keep employees motivated, organizations must institute HRM policies that focus on the contributions employees can make to the organization without being promoted. Techniques such as job rotation, job enlargement, skill-based pay, and midcareer breaks have been used to maintain employee motivation.

Job rotation allows workers to diversify their activities. Employees perform a variety of tasks by moving to a new activity when their current tasks are no longer challenging or when the work schedule dictates it. They are thus provided with a range of experience that broadens their skills, provides them with a greater understanding of other activities within the agency, and prepares them to assume more responsibility. *Job enlargement* increases the scope of a job by increasing the number of different operations required in it. The job becomes more diverse and challenging because more tasks must be completed. *Knowledge-* or *skill-based pay* can be used to keep employees motivated by keeping them engaged in learning new skills. Employees are not promoted to a higher-level position but they are still able to perform new skills and assume new responsibilities.

Typically, *midcareer breaks* or *sabbaticals* have been considered to be one of the benefits of academia. However, many organizations have begun to realize the benefits of time spent away from work. Apple Computer, for example, offers employees six weeks of paid time off after every five years of work. This approach is designed to help Apple employees "de-stress." It is not a reward for past service but an opportunity to recharge for the future. Apple has found that returning employees are more committed and productive. It has also found that this option gives Apple a competitive edge when recruiting new employees (Barciela, 1995).

Not all organizations can afford to give paid leaves to employees, so some have developed alternatives, such as unpaid leave with a guarantee of a job upon return, or unpaid leave but with tuition reimbursement to defray the costs of school.

Quality-of-life and quality-of-work benefits have become very important in organizations' ability to attract and motivate employees in this period of economic hardship. Sheltering Arms, the nonprofit social service and welfare agency mentioned in Chapter Eight that provides assistance to abused and battered women, is able to motivate it's employees, in an environment in which stress and job burnout are high, through the use of personal time off and other nonfinancial benefits (Kraten, 1995).

Preston (1990) found that the opportunity to perform a variety of work and to enhance one's skill development has been instrumental in attracting women to nonprofit organizations. Many women choose to work in nonprofits despite the often lower pay they provide in order to take advantage of the opportunities they offer. Organizations should not overlook the importance of quality-of-work and quality-of-life enhancements in motivating employees.

Summary

A study by the U.S. Chamber of Commerce revealed that in 1993 employer spending on benefits rose to 41.3 percent of payroll costs. Health benefits constitute 26.7 percent of benefit costs, followed by paid leave at 25.2 percent; Social Security, unemployment, and workers' compensation at 21.1 percent; retirement and savings plans at 16 percent; paid rest periods at 5.6 percent; life insurance at 1.5 percent; and miscellaneous benefits such as tuition aid, severance pay, and child care at 3.9 percent (Bureau of National Affairs, 1994a).

Employer-provided benefits play an important role in strategic human resources management. Most organizations offer a variety of benefits, ranging from those mandated by law, such as Social Security, Unemployment Compensation, and Workers' Compensation, to those that are optional, such as pensions, health insurance, paid time away from work, educational programs, and a variety of quality-of-life and quality-of-work programs.

The types of benefits provided by employers are key to attracting quality applicants, to encouraging loyalty and long-term employment, and to motivating and rewarding incumbent employees. The literature on organizational culture and employee retention indicates that different human resources strategies result in different psychological climates that foster varying levels of commitment and retention among employees (Kerr & Slocum, 1987; Sheridan, 1992). Flexible benefits that are sensitive to employee needs have the advantage of creating a work climate that is conducive to high levels of employee commitment, satisfaction, and morale (Barber, Dunham, & Formisano, 1992; Crooker & Grover, 1993).

Chapter Ten

Training and Development

The demands placed on public and nonprofit organizations keep changing. Agencies are threatened with budget cuts and reductions in staff while citizens and clients are requesting increases in the level of services or new services. Changes in technology are requiring new skills. Carnevale and Carnevale (1993) note that technology has taken on much of the workplace's mentally and physically repetitive tasks, so jobs today are requiring employees to assume more challenging responsibilities. For example, the downsizing of managerial staff in many organizations has required that first-level supervisors possess conceptual and communication skills in addition to their technical and applied skills. Higher-level managers must develop skills that will enable them to scan the external environment and develop organizational strategies. Training and development are used by organizations to improve the skills of employees and enhance their capacity to cope with the constantly changing demands of the work environment.

Agencies that wish to be viable must develop strategies to maximize their human resources. Training and development are intrinsic components of strategic human resources management (SHRM). Consider the following examples:

• The Rhode Island Municipal Police Training Academy in collaboration with personnel from the Criminal Justice Services of the American Association of Retired Persons has developed a training program to help police officers communicate better and be more effective when working with older citizens (Shibley, 1995).

• The General Services Administration is developing strategies to change its culture in the areas of organizational productivity, performance management, and training (U.S. Office of Personnel Management, 1994).

• Direct care workers employed in a State Division for Youth Facilities attend training sessions on multicultural awareness. Supervisors participate in a three-day program designed to improve their communication and documentation skills. The Division for Youth went from no formal training in 1983 to five weeks for line staff in 1995.

• The National Academy for Voluntarism, the training arm of the United Way of America, has developed a training program focusing on broad management topics such as the development of management skills, managerial leadership and team excellence, organizational change, and strategic planning (Cosier & Dalton, 1993).

• Kentucky's Social Services Department is using videoconferencing to train foster parents and to conduct caseworker conferences (Richter, 1994).

• The Department of the Interior's Fish and Wildlife Service has developed ecosystem teams that will function across traditional program and regional boundaries. It has identified an assessment tool to help determine team effectiveness and training needs; developed training modules that offer an array of team development and team work training; and created tools to evaluate the effectiveness of training (U.S. Office of Personnel Management, 1994).

Change has become an inevitable part of organizational life and to remain viable, organizations must learn how to manage change. The preceding examples are just a few of the training programs currently under way in public and nonprofit agencies to help employees manage deal with change. Such training and development activities are critical if agencies are going to survive.

Technology is being used to communicate with many people across large geographic areas, eliminating the need to be nearby for personal interactions. Demographics are changing; for example, senior citizens are now a significant percentage of the population, and there has been an increase in the number of racial and ethnic minorities employed in public and nonprofit agencies. Jobs have become less specialized, forcing employees to work in teams to deliver services; and productivity needs to be improved despite declining personnel and fiscal resources. Changes in goals, the purchase of new equipment, the enactment of new laws or regulations, fluctuations in the economy, increased pressures from stakeholders, and the actions of competitors are some of the other variables that influence change. As the demands placed on public and nonprofit organizations keep changing, organizations must implement training and development activities to ensure that their staffs have the requisite knowledge, skills, abilities, and other characteristics (KSAOCs) to confront these new challenges. Training can be targeted to help employees learn new job-specific skills, improve their performance, or change their attitudes. Changes need to be anticipated; training and development needs should be identified, planned for, and budgeted. Developing a comprehensive long-range training program requires an SHRM plan and a recognition that employees are a most valuable resource. Agencies wishing to be viable must develop strategies to maximize their human capabilities. Training and development must be integrated into the core human resources management (HRM) functions.

Training and development has been defined by Wexley and Latham (1991, p. 3) as "a planned effort by an organization to facilitate the learning of job-related behavior on the part of its employees." Training and development programs seek to change the skills, knowledge, and/or attitudes of employees. Programs may be focused on improving an individual's level of self-awareness, increasing an individual's competence in one or more areas of expertise, or increasing an individual's motivation to perform his or her job well.

It is important to note the word "planned" in Wexley and Latham's definition. Training and development efforts need to be thought out and the following questions need to be answered:

1. How can you develop a comprehensive training plan to address the needs of managers, elected officials, support staff, direct service providers, volunteers, and board members?
2. What methods can you use to assess your agency's training needs?
3. How can you design and implement the training program?

4. What training delivery methods will you use?
5. How will you demonstrate that the training budget was well spent?

This chapter first presents the fundamental steps in training: assessing needs; developing objectives; developing the curriculum, including determining which methodologies and techniques to use; delivering the training, including a discussion of learning styles; and finally, evaluating training. Next, career development is defined, managerial and executive development are discussed, and examples of training and development efforts that have been implemented in public and nonprofit organizations are presented.

Needs Assessment

The first step in the training process is to determine the specific training needs. A need can be defined simply as the difference between what is currently being done and what needs to be done. This difference can be determined by conducting a needs assessment of the skills and knowledge currently required by the position and those anticipated as necessary for the future. A needs assessment is critical to discerning whether performance deficiencies can be eliminated by training. Without a needs assessment, it is possible to design and implement a training program as the solution to a problem that is not related to a training deficiency.

For example, it comes to the attention of higher management that one supervisor rates women and minorities lower than he rates white males, and the ratings are not based on job-related performance criteria. The supervisor is sent to performance evaluation training, where he is exposed to common rating errors and the need for unambiguous performance standards, timely feedback, and so. Despite the training, the supervisor refuses to use job-related performance criteria when he evaluates his female and minority staff. Performance evaluation training did not resolve the problem; the ratings were deliberately lowered because of prejudice and not because the supervisor lacked knowledge of performance evaluation techniques.

A true needs assessment would have discovered that the problem was different than originally thought, and that the solution may involve a different kind of training. In this case, the supervisor was not deficient in skills; rather, it was his attitude that needed to be modified. Multicultural diversity training or training on employment discrimination would have been more appropriate. It is very important for a needs assessment to be accurate if training is to be successful.

Organizations can determine training needs through a variety of techniques. A strategic job analysis performed prior to the needs assessment is useful. The job analysis should identify the KSAOCs that incumbents need to effectively perform their jobs. Surveys and interviews with incumbents and supervisors; performance evaluations that identify performance deficiencies; criticisms or complaints from clients, staff, or personnel in agencies working with your employees; changes in regulations or operating procedures; and requests for additional training by incumbents can all provide clues as to what training is needed.

The training required to provide the needed KSAOCs should be divided into training that can be learned on the job and training that requires formal instruction. For example, some jobs require certification or licenses mandated by state or federal regulations. More and more states are requiring, for instance, that substance abuse counselors be state certified. In Missouri, paramedics are required to pass a state written exam and attend refresher courses every three years. In New York State, nonprofit residential facilities for delinquent or status offender youths, such as Berkshire Farms, are required to comply with a regulation that new employees must receive training on the HIV virus and AIDS within fifteen days of being hired. In these examples, training is provided by experts outside the agency. Training to acquire other KSAOCs can be provided on the job. Having supervisors explain new policies and procedures or train employees on how to use new equipment can be part of any training plan.

Developing Training Objectives

Training objectives are statements that specify the desired KSAOCs that employees will possess at the end of training. The objectives provide the standard for measuring what has been accomplished and for determining the level of accomplishment. For training objectives to be useful, they should be stated as specifically as possible. For example:

Recreation assistants will be able to apply basic first aid to injured participants such as cleaning and bandaging scraped knees and elbows.

Supervisors will be able to explain the agency's sexual harassment policy to employees.

Receptionists will be able to transfer and route calls on the new telephone communication system without disconnecting callers.

The development of training objectives should be a collaborative process incorporating input from management, supervisors, workers, and trainers, to ensure that the objectives are reasonable and realistic.

Developing the Curriculum

After assessing the training needs and developing objectives, a training curriculum must be developed. Before developing the content and the manner of presenting the information, an analysis of the trainees must first be done. This step is critical because the trainees often prescribe the kind of training that is likely to be effective. Some of the relevant issues to examine include the following:

What are the participants' levels of education? For example, classroom instruction may be intimidating for employees with limited formal education.

What are participants' expectations? Will all participants come to training with the same concerns?

What are participants' knowledge levels, attitudes, and relationships with one another?

Are participants prepared to receive technical instruction?

Is the training voluntary or imposed from above?

If the training is mandatory, will the participants be threatened by it?

The answers to these questions will provide some guidance to the trainers when developing the curriculum. The curriculum should provide the necessary information and be developed to maximize the imparting of KSAOCs.

One of the first decisions that needs to be made is whether to provide on-the-job instruction or off-the-job classroom instruction, or a combination of the two. On-the-job instruction takes place while the employee is actually working at the job site. It is usually provided by supervisors, who instruct subordinates in the correct way to perform a task, such as filling out new purchase order requisitions. Or a representative from the management information systems (MIS) department could demonstrate how to load and set up a new software package. On-the-job training is useful when employees are expected to become proficient in performing certain tasks or using equipment found at their work stations. Because the training is directly related to the requirements of the job, transferring skills is easier. Employees learn by actually doing the job, and they get immediate feedback as to their proficiency. Other examples of on-the-job training include job rotation, in which employees move from job to job at planned intervals, either within their departments or across the organization. For example, many organizations train managers by placing them in different positions across the agency so that they are provided with a comprehensive perspective of its operation.

Some KSAOCs are difficult to teach at the work site, so off-site training will be necessary. For example, training probation officers in counseling and listening skills would be difficult to do at their desks because other employees not involved in the training would be distracted by the instruction. Off-site training provides an alternative to on-the-job training. Employees receive training away from their work stations. In addition to avoiding disruptions to the normal routine at the job site, off-site training also permits the use of a greater variety of training techniques. Discussion of some other common training techniques follows.

Lecture. In a lecture format, a trainer presents material to a group of trainees. Lectures have been criticized because the information in them flows in only one direction—from trainer to trainees. The trainees tend to be passive participants. Differences in the trainees experiences, interests, expertise, and personalities are ignored. Lectures are limited to the transfer of cognitive material. Wexley and Latham (1991) report that lectures are beneficial when they are used to introduce new information, or provide oral directions for learning tasks that eventually will be developed through other techniques. Lectures are readily adaptable for use with other training techniques.

Experiential exercises. Experiential exercises attempt to simulate actual job or work experiences. Learning can be facilitated without the cost and risks of making mistakes while actually on the job. For example, law enforcement agencies use experiential exercises to train officers in emergency and disaster planning.

Role-playing. Role-playing gives trainees the opportunity to practice interpersonal and communication skills by applying them to lifelike situations. Participants are expected to act out the roles they would play in responding to specific problems that they may encounter in their jobs. Role-playing can be used in a variety of contexts. Law enforcement academies use it when training officers how to interview crime victims, such as sexually abused children, or witnesses to a crime. Role-playing is frequently used in supervisory training in which participants are asked to counsel a problem subordinate who is suspected of having a substance abuse problem.

Case studies. The use of case studies in training involves having participants analyze situations, identify problems, and offer solutions. Trainees are presented with a written description of a problem. After reading the case, they diagnose the underlying issues and decide what should be done. Then, as a group the trainees discuss their interpretations and understanding of the issues and the proposed solutions.

Audiovisual methods. Videos are often used for training in a variety of contexts. There are videos to educate employees on legal topics such as sexual harassment, hiring disabled applicants, and using progressive discipline; videos that focus on interpersonal and communication skills; and videos that simulate a grievance arbitration hearing, permitting trainees to view the process, hear witnesses testify, see the behavior of management and union representatives, and learn how arbitrators conduct proceedings. Videos can be used to demonstrate particular tasks, such as the procedures to follow when apprehending a suspect or extinguishing a chemical fire. Videos are often used in orientation sessions to present background information on the agency—its history, purpose, and goals. This use eliminates the need for trainers or supervisors to repeat themselves for all new employees and ensures that the same information is always presented.

Trainees may also be videotaped. They may be asked to make a presentation or to provide performance feedback to colleagues. They may then view the videotape to identify their strengths and weaknesses related to the topic.

An advantage of video is that it provides the opportunity to slow down, speed up, or stop the video to review specific activities and enable questions to be asked and answered. A disadvantage to the use of videos is that they can be expensive to purchase or make.

Programmed instruction and computer-based training. Programmed and computer-based instruction are self-teaching methods designed to enable trainees to learn at their own pace. Training materials are developed about a specific content area, such as grant writing. Learning objectives and instructional goals are specified. Information and training materials are assembled for the employees to read and use for practice. At their own pace the employees read the materials or practice the competencies required by the training objectives. The employees are then asked to demonstrate what they have learned.

An example of programmed instruction is *The Practice of Local Government Planning,* developed by the International City Managers Association (1994). The course provides a comprehensive introduction to the principles of urban planning. Students are assigned readings, then asked to complete written assignments covering the material learned in the lessons, to review questions based on the material, and to carry out a series of activities that apply what they have read.

Computer-based training uses interactive exercises with computers to impart job skills. Training materials are on diskettes or compact disks. Employees read information, instructions, and diagrams or other graphics on the computer screen and then respond accordingly.

Equipment simulators. Anybody who has taken a driver's education course probably remembers the driving simulator that replicated a car's dashboard and gas and brake pedals. Simulators are used to bring realism to training situations. For many jobs, like law enforcement, on-the-job training can be too dangerous, such as training police officers when to discharge firearms. So equipment and scenarios that replicate the shadows and noises of alleys are used to train police officers not to overreact. Fire departments use burn buildings, which are designed to withstand repeated fires, to give firefighters opportunities to practice rescue attempts while battling heat and smoke. It would be too expensive or dangerous to burn vacant or decayed buildings. With the use of simulators, new procedures can be attempted without the risk of endangering human lives.

Videoconferencing. Improvements in technology have made videoconferencing less expensive and more accessible to an increasing number of public and nonprofit organizations. Two-way video cameras and high-speed networks are able to transport interactive live images across large geographic distances. For example, when training dollars became tight and it could not afford to send individual employees for training, the city of Phoenix contracted for a satellite and videotape service to train employees in its MIS department. New York City's information technology and personnel departments worked together to establish a video training network using a channel of the city's subscriber cable system coupled with fiber-optic links to provide closed-circuit audio and video service to city agencies. A pilot program was designed to teach fire academy drills at fifty fire department locations (Cranford, 1995).

The nonprofit sector has also begun to offer videoconferencing. The National Center for Nonprofit Boards and Civic Network Television are offering two video workshops focused on nonprofit boards: "A Working Asset: Creating Effective Boards" and "Who Does What: Balancing the Board and Staff." The workshops will be broadcast into more than two hundred communities across the country.

The advantages of video training include more flexibility in meeting training needs, a reduction in time lost in travel to training sites, and increased uniformity of training.

Community resources. Nonprofit and public agencies should be aware of the many community resources that are often available to provide training for nominal costs or even for free. Many health care facilities offer workshops on topics that are targeted to specific clientele groups, such as adolescent or elderly depression, sexual abuse, or substance abuse. Chapters of Planned Parenthood offer seminars on boosting self-esteem and preventing teenage pregnancies. Hospice associations offer training on the issues associated with death and dying, and various professional associations also sponsor training classes. Managers and HRM departments need to be on the lookout for relevant community-based training opportunities. Each technique has its advantages and disadvantages, which need to be weighed in relation to time constraints, staff resources, finances, and desired outcomes.

Delivering Training

Other issues must be addressed in addition to curriculum. Should the training take place for short periods of time spread over many days, or should it encompass long periods over fewer days? What time of day should the training take place? What size group should be involved? No one right answer exists. It depends on the information being presented or the skills that need to be taught, as well as the aptitudes of the participants and the techniques that are used. Failing to consider any of these factors can negatively influence the results of training efforts. Most public sector and nonprofit employers cannot afford such waste.

The delivery of the training program is the stage where the trainers and the participants converge. At a well-organized work site the employees selected for training understand what the objectives of the training are and what they can expect. Patricia Murray, a trainer with the New York State Division for Youth, notes that one of the most common training errors is not to recognize that the participants are adults with life and work experiences. Murray recommends providing an agenda with training objectives so that participants will know where the training is headed and what methods and techniques will be used. She also recommends incorporating the group members' experience into the training, and recognizing that many adults have had "bad" public school experiences and may be struggling with literacy issues. It is up to the trainers to create a climate in which individual learning styles are recognized and considered in the delivery of the content. This is especially important for employees who resist training or perceive it as a punishment and not as an opportunity.

Sims, Veres, and Heninger (1989) suggest that if public sector trainers understood how individuals learn, they might be able to design programs that enhance learning and that therefore are more effective. Sims (1993a) and Sims and Sims (1991) acknowledge that training programs must address not only substantive content or material but also how people learn, and therefore incorporate different learning strategies.

As the workforce becomes more diverse there will be more variation in employees' ability to learn, in their learning styles, in their basic literacy skills, and in their functional life skills (Cohen, 1991, p. 33). It will be even more important for training to take into account individual backgrounds and needs. Organizations and trainers will also need to recognize that adult employees learn differently than children. Adult learners see themselves as self-directed and expect to be able to answer part of their questions on the basis of their own experiences (Laird, 1985). Instruction tailored to adult learners allows the trainees the opportunity to participate in the process. The role of the training instructors is to facilitate learning; they use lots of questions, guide the trainees, and encourage two-way communication between the instructor and the class, as well as communication among the class's participants.

Evaluating Training

An evaluation of the training program is necessary to determine whether the training accomplished its objectives. Unfortunately this is often the most neglected aspect of training, especially in the public sector (Sims, 1993b). Evaluation improves training programs by providing feedback to the trainers, participants, and managers, and it assesses employee skill levels (Swierczek & Carmichael, 1985).

Researchers such as Kirkpatrick (1994), Gordon (1991), and Martin, Harrison, and Ingram (1991) suggest that there are four primary levels at which training programs can be evaluated. The first level is measuring the participants' reactions to the training program. Kirkpatrick (1994) refers to this step as a measure of customer satisfaction. Participants are asked to answer questions such as Was the trainer knowledgeable? Was the material/information relevant? Will the information they learned assist them in performing their jobs? Data are gathered through the use of surveys distributed at the conclusion of the training session. Asking these questions provides data on the training program's content and the trainer's skill. (Trainers refer to this step as a smile meter.)

According to Kirkpatrick (1994, p. 22), learning has taken place when one or more of the following occurs: attitudes are changed, knowledge is increased, and skills are improved. The second level of evaluation measures whether learning has occurred as a result of attending the training. Did the participants acquire the skills or knowledge that were embodied in the objectives? Did the training impart the KSAOCs that were deemed important? To determine whether learning took place, participants can be tested on the information presented, follow-up interviews can be conducted, skill demonstrations can be required, or as recommended by Erickson (1990), case studies can be developed that test the competencies that were intended to be taught. Three to six months after training, the participants can be asked how they would handle situations provided in the case studies if they arose as part of the job. Supervisors can evaluate the participants on their use of the learned competencies to solve the work-related problems. It is important to note that the methods used should be selected on the basis of the level of mastery desired.

The third level of evaluation attempts to measure the extent to which on-the-job behavioral change has occurred because the participants attended the training program. Evaluation activities are aimed at determining whether the participants have been able to transfer to their jobs the KSAOCs they learned in training. Measurement at this stage is more difficult; it requires supervisors to collect work samples or observe employees' performance. Another technique would be to utilize performance evaluations designed to measure the new competencies.

Kirkpatrick (1994, p. 23) acknowledges that for change to occur, four conditions are necessary: (1) the employee must have a desire to change, (2) the employee must know what to do and how to do it, (3) the employee must work in the right climate, and (4) the employee must be rewarded for changing. Kirkpatrick notes that a training program can accomplish the first two requirements, but the right climate is dependent upon the employee's immediate supervisor. Some supervisors may prevent their employees from doing what was taught in the training program; others may not model the behaviors taught in the training program, which discourages the employees from changing; some supervisors may ignore the fact that employees have attended the training program, and thereby not support employees' efforts to change; others may encourage employees to learn and apply their learning on the job; and finally some supervisors may know what the employees learned in the training and make sure that the learning transfers to the job.

The fourth condition, that the employee must be rewarded for changing, can include the feelings of satisfaction, achievement, proficiency, and pride that can occur with change. Extrinsic rewards such as praise from the supervisor, recognition from others, and possible merit rewards or promotions can also result.

Carolyn Balling (cited in Joinson, 1995, p. 56) recommends that if the training did not accomplish what it was intended to, HRM departments should assess the conditions the trainee returns to by trying to determine what the problem was and working with the line managers to make the necessary changes. Such an assessment could begin with the following questions: What gets in the way? Does the employee who just received training on a new computer system have to go back to the same old equipment? Does the employee reenter a crisis situation and have to revert to the way things were always done? Often so-called training problems are not training problems at all—they are environmental problems. For training to be most effective, the organization's culture must support training and hold its supervisors accountable for providing a climate in which employees can transfer what they have learned to their jobs.

The fourth level of evaluation attempts to measure the final results that occurred because employees attended the training. Ideally, training is linked to improved organizational performance. At this level, evaluation is concerned with determining what impact the training has had on the agency. Satisfactory final results can include such things as fewer grievances filed against supervisors, greater employee productivity, a reduction in the number of client complaints, a decrease in workplace accidents, increased dollars raised through fundraising, improved board relations, and less discrimination in the workplace. Some final results will be easier to measure than other. For example, the dollars raised from fundraising activities, the number of workplace accidents, or the number of grievances filed can be easily quantified and compared to times before the training. Other final results, like eliminating discrimination, changing attitudes, and improving leadership and communication are less tangible and more difficult to measure. Such results will have to be measured in terms of improved morale and attitudes.

As a final step, organizations must determine whether the benefits of the training outweigh its direct and indirect costs. Examples of direct costs include expenses for instructor fees, facilities, printed materials, and meals. Indirect costs include the salaries of participants who are away from their regular jobs. Has there been a reasonable return on this investment? Basically, was the training worth its costs? Did it accomplish what it was designed to accomplish?

The potential benefits from evaluating training programs include improved accountability and cost-effectiveness for training programs; improved program effectiveness (Are programs producing the intended results?); improved efficiency (Are they producing the intended results with a minimum waste of resources?); and information on how to redesign current or future programs (Sims, 1993b).

Career Development

Fitzgerald (1992, p. 81) defines training as "the acquisition of knowledge and skills for present tasks, which help individuals contribute to the organization in their current positions. . . . To be successful, training must result in a change in behavior, such as the use of new knowledge and skills on the job." Career development, however, provides the employee with knowledge and skills that are intended to be used in the future. The purpose of career development is to prepare employees to meet future agency needs, thereby ensuring the organization's survival (Fitzgerald, 1992).

Career development is used to improve the skill levels of and provide long-term opportunities for the organization's present workforce. Career development programs provide incumbents with advancement opportunities within the organization so that they will not have to look elsewhere. Taking the time and spending resources to develop employees signals to them that they are valued by the agency. As a result, they become motivated and assume responsibility for developing their career paths (Fitz-enz, 1990).

The focus of career development plans is on where the agency is headed and where in the agency incumbents can find future job opportunities. Employees and supervisors should produce a development plan that focuses on employee growth and development. The plan should have measurable development objectives and an action plan. For example, supervisors should review their employees' skills with the job descriptions of higher-level positions within the same job family or of positions within the organization to which the employee might be able to cross over. By comparing employees' skills with the skill requirements of other positions, the employees and supervisors can determine what experience and training might still be needed for advancement or lateral movement. Supervisors should direct employees to relevant training opportunities and, when possible, delegate additional tasks and responsibilities to employees so that they may develop new competencies.

A number of career development programs can be found in the public and nonprofit sectors. Some of them focus on moving employees from clerical or paraprofessional positions into higher-paying administrative jobs. Others focus on developing supervisory and management skills. Examples of some of the programs follow.

- The *Service Employees International Union* has established a joint training program with Cape Cod Hospital called the Career Ladder Program. The program is aimed at expanding upward-mobility opportunities. The collective bargaining agreement establishes policies with the hospital to ensure that job vacancies are filled by upgrading current employees. Participants in the program receive a range of training opportunities, from on-the-job and in-house training programs to educational courses outside of the hospital (Roberts & Wozniak, 1994).

- The American Federation of State, County, and Municipal Employees (AFSCME) has negotiated training provisions into a number of contracts. District Council 37 negotiated an education fund with New York City government agencies that provides for high school equivalency classes, clerical skills programs, and civil service preparatory classes, and includes financial assistance and counseling for higher education. District 37 also negotiated training and upgrading programs between the union and the New York City Health and Hospitals Corp. The programs provide training for employees to move into health care professions such as registered nursing or respiratory therapy (Roberts & Wozniak, 1994).

- The state of Illinois instituted a career development program called The Upward Mobility Program as part of a master agreement between AFSCME and the state. Employees can work toward advancement in five career paths: data processing, office services, accounting, human services, and medical occupations. Employees receive individual counseling to inform them of the career opportunities available and to guide them in developing their career plans. Participants take proficiency exams and/or complete required education and training programs designed to provide the skills and knowledge needed for advancement. The program covers all tuition costs and most mandatory registration fees for classes taken at public institutions. Partial tuition and fees are paid by the program for private schools. When all necessary training and education has been completed, employees are given special consideration when bidding on targeted titles.

Two career tracks are available: credential and certificate. The credential track is for positions that require specific degrees and licenses, such as social worker, licensed practical nurse, or child protective associate investigator. Employees meet with Upward Mobility Program counselors to discuss the education required for the chosen position. When the employees obtain the necessary degree and/or license, they are issued a credential.

The certificate track is for positions that require employees to pass written proficiency exams before they can enroll in specific courses. The exam identifies which classes, if any, are required. Employees are required to take courses related to the sections of the exam in which they did not demonstrate proficiency. After completing the required course work, employees are retested. When they demonstrate proficiency in all segments of the exam, they are issued a certificate. The certificate gives an employee priority for the next vacancy in that title in any agency, even if the title is in another bargaining unit job. Seniority prevails should two or more employees with certificates apply for the same position. Two-thirds of the participants are women and one-third are minorities.

Upward Mobility's 1994 contract calls for expanding services to laid-off state employees by enabling them to reenter the workforce through the priority promotions list. The program is financially stable, with an annual budget between $3 and $3.5 million (Roberts & Wozniak, 1994).

Managerial and Executive Development

Problem-solving skills, initiative, the ability to function as a team player, interpersonal skills, the creativity to seize opportunities, fundraising skills, and the possession of a customer orientation have been identified by John Garrison of the American Lung Association, Carol Tweedy of Asphalt Green, and David Jones of the Community Service Society of New York as some of the critical skills managers and executives of nonprofit agencies will need to guide their agencies into the twenty-first century (Wheeler, 1995). Technical experience and competence is no longer enough; nonprofits need leaders with the vision to direct and guide their agencies as city, state, and federal funding are cut.

To assist in the development of these skills, the National Academy for Voluntarism has developed a training program consisting of four one-week modules that emphasize the development of the human, conceptual, and coordination skills needed to effectively manage nonprofits (Cosier & Dalton, 1993). Programs also exist in the public sector that emphasize managerial and executive development. The Arkansas Public Administration Consortium offers a public management training program leading to the designation of Arkansas Certified Government Manager (Vanagunas & Webb, 1994). Unlike the Illinois Upward Mobility Program, in which career progression is the objective, the participants in the Arkansas program are already middle- or upper-level managers. The emphasis of this program is to improve innovation in administration. To receive the certification, the participants must complete six seminars and a capstone requirement: a "Project Plan" aimed at improving the efficiency and effectiveness of their agencies.

On March 30, 1994, President Clinton signed into law H.R. 3345, the Federal Workforce Restructuring Act of 1994 (Public Law 103–226). The act includes amendments to the Government

Employees Training Act of 1958. The amendments expand the definition of training from being directly related to the performance of "official duties" to any training that is "mission related." The expanded definition allows agency managers greater flexibility to provide training that will assist in achieving the agency's mission and performance goals. The amendments also eliminate the distinction between government and nongovernment training, thereby allowing managers to take full advantage of available resources. The amendments broaden the purpose of training and target it to strategic business plans, thus making training more responsive to the current and future needs of agencies; and they emphasize leadership development, retraining, and cross-training, along with continuing professional education and technical training.

The U.S. Office of Personnel Management's Human Resources Development Group has developed the Leadership Effectiveness Framework (LEF). The LEF provides a model of twenty-two competencies identified by incumbent supervisors, managers, and executives as necessary for effective performance in their positions. The model is used for planning succession and development efforts. Some of the competencies addressed include managing a diverse workforce, technology and quality management, and creative thinking. Figure 10.1 presents a diagram of the competencies.

The Human Resources Development Group provides a variety of programs designed to strengthen individual leadership and agency management. A brief summary of each program follows.

Senior Executive Service Candidate Development Program. Designed for SES candidates, SES members, and high-potential GS/GM 15 employees, this program provides all formal training needed to meet the requirements of the Office of Personnel Management's (OPM) Qualification Review Board for SES candidates.

Executive Potential Program. Designed for occupational specialists who are moving into management, this program provides training and development experiences for individuals in the GS/GM 13–14 classifications to prepare them for managerial and executive positions in the federal government.

Women's Executive Leadership Program. This program is designed for nonsupervisory women and men and new supervisors with less than one year of supervisory experience who are at the GS–11 or

Figure 10.1. Leadership Effectiveness Framework.

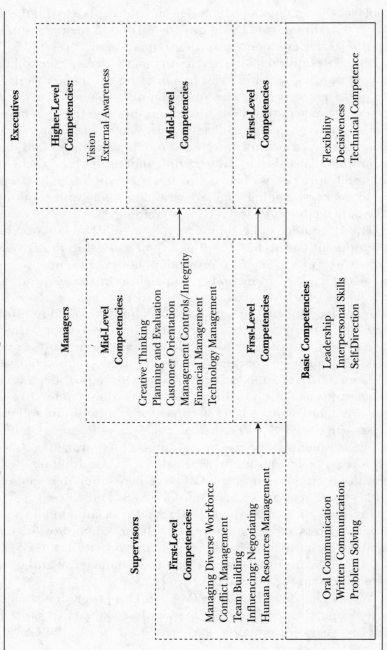

Source: U.S. Office of Personnel Management, 1995, p. 34.

GS–12 level. It is a developmental program that provides supervisory and managerial training, preparing the candidates for future positions as supervisors and managers.

Presidential Management Program. This is an entry-level career development and training program designed to attract to the federal government outstanding graduate students with a commitment to a career in public service. Applicants must be nominated by their chairperson, dean, or graduate school dean. The Presidential Management Internship is a two-year program by which interns participate in training conferences, seminars, and Congressional briefings. They rotate to federal agencies while developing management and leadership skills.

In addition to these programs, the OPM provides a number of training sessions that federal employees as well as state and local government employees are eligible to attend. The training sessions are provided at the regional training centers located in Atlanta, Chicago, Dallas, Philadelphia, San Francisco, and Washington, D.C. The general topics include administration, clerical, and secretarial courses; budgeting, finance, bookkeeping, and accounting courses; equal employment opportunity and other special-emphasis-program courses; supervisory and management courses; personnel/human resources development/labor-management relations courses; management analysis and statistical courses; and miscellaneous general interest courses on such topics as AIDS in the workplace or career development for the hearing impaired.

OPM's National Independent Study Center provides independent study training courses and services to federal, state, and local government employees nationwide and overseas. More than thirty self-study courses are offered on a variety of topics. Individuals can complete these courses (programmed instruction) at their own pace. The courses cover topics in financial management, computer skills, personnel management, supervision and management, written communication, and general interest.

Summary

Training is typically associated with improving the performance, knowledge, and/or skill of employees in their present positions. Career development is viewed as a continuous process consisting of evaluating abilities and interests, establishing career goals, and planning developmental activities that relate to the employees' and organization's future needs. Organizations must recognize the importance of both training and career development planning and provide career enhancement and developmental opportunities.

It is important that, once their career development programs have been developed, organizations maintain their programs and revive them with new initiatives. According to Gutteridge, Leibowitz, and Shore (1993), career development should be linked with other HRM strategies, such as succession planning, performance evaluations, Total Quality Management, and new-employee orientation. Managers should be held accountable for developing their individual employees. Providing feedback and coaching to their staff should be one of their main responsibilities.

Agencies that are serious about training and career development should continue to monitor, evaluate, and revise their training and career development programs. To be successful, training and career development programs need to be fully integrated with the SHRM system. Increased skill acquisition will be effective only if agencies accurately identify and predict the types of KSAOCs and positions that will be required. If career paths are identified, then training and development programs must be used to move employees along the path. New approaches to training need to be considered, and organizational reward structures should encourage individual growth and development that benefits both the employee and the organization.

Chapter Eleven

Collective Bargaining in the Public and Nonprofit Sectors

The economic, technological, social, cultural, and legal changes affecting the workplace have also provoked changes in labor-management relations. Public concern about waste and inefficiency has generated support for redesigning government. The threat of downsizing and privatization requires that unions and employers reexamine their structure and systems to see how they can make government more vibrant. To remain competitive, management and unions must adopt new approaches and attitudes for resolving conflicts. Together, management and unions must creatively resolve problems and develop solutions advantageous to both sides.

Improving the relationship between labor and management in nonprofit organizations is also important. Poor employee-management relationships have provoked employees to seek the aid of unions. Consider the following four situations:

- In Indianapolis, American Federation of State, County, and Municipal Employees (AFSCME) Council 62, representing employees in the transportation department, agreed to compete with private sector companies for construction and maintenance contracts if the mayor would eliminate some of the administrative overhead, such as the thirty-eight supervisors for ninety truck drivers. Mayor Goldsmith agreed to cut midlevel managers, and the union has been winning contracts ever since (Walkers, 1994).
- Labor-management cooperation and partnership is the heart of Hoover Dam's Total Quality Management effort. In 1992, union and management leaders participated in a Department of

Labor training course called Partners in Change. The American Federation of Government Employees (AFGE) was made a full member of the team for the dam's total quality project. Most grievances are now settled by work teams, saving thousands of dollars in legal fees as well as employee time and energy. Unions and management now take a mission-based approach to bargaining (U.S. Office of Personnel Management, 1994).

• On October 1, 1994, staff attorneys for the nonprofit Legal Aid Society in New York went on strike to protest the 4.5 percent raise that management gave to itself while giving staff nothing and cutting their benefits and at the same time agreeing to the Society's absorbing 30 percent more of the city's criminal cases with no increase in funds ("Legal Aid Lawyers," 1994).

• At DePaul Health Center, nurses have voted to determine whether they should unionize. The nurses say they are fighting for their professional lives. They are getting part-time status, back-to-back shifts, and jobs for which they are ill-trained. To curb costs, many hospitals have hired fewer highly skilled nurses and have instead assigned many basic bedside nursing duties to lower-salaried aides. The nurses say that the quality of care is declining and that patient safety has become a serious concern. Administrators say they must cut staff to compete for discounted insurance plans and health maintenance organizations. They argue that unions would ruin the hospital's teamwork and bank account and create "an us against them mentality."

Collective bargaining has been defined as a process that obligates management and union representatives to negotiate in good faith in an attempt to reach an agreement concerning issues that affect employees. While many employers dislike having to recognize and negotiate with employee unions, other employers appreciate the continuity and stability that collective bargaining can bring to an organization. Issues that have been negotiated and that are part of a collective bargaining agreement are often resolved for the length of the contract. Collective bargaining includes the execution, interpretation, and enforcement of the negotiated contract.

This chapter presents the legal framework of collective bargaining, beginning with the history of private sector collective bargaining because the laws permitting public employee unionism are often patterned after the laws granting private sector employees the right to bargain; furthermore, nonprofit collective bargaining is governed by the same laws and rulings as collective bargaining in the private sector. This history is followed by an overview of the laws relevant to collective bargaining in the nonprofit and public sectors, then by discussion of the concepts and practices that constitute the collective bargaining process, including bargaining unit determination, the selection of a bargaining representative, unfair labor practices, the obligation to negotiate, union security devices, the scope of collective bargaining, management rights, impasse resolution, striking, and grievance arbitration. Distinctions between public and nonprofit labor relations are noted, and the chapter concludes with a discussion of the future of collective bargaining.

The History of Private Sector Collective Bargaining

Private sector labor-management relations were initially governed by the National Labor Relations Act of 1935 (NLRA). The NLRA permitted employees to organize and join unions for the purposes of collective bargaining. It addressed the rights of employees in the areas of union security agreements, picketing, and striking. Employer unfair labor practices were defined, as were the criteria for an appropriate bargaining unit, the selection of a bargaining representative, and the enforcement of the act. Under this law, employers were required to bargain in good faith with employee unions and could be cited for unfair labor practices if they attempted to interfere with the establishment of such unions. The NLRA established the National Labor Relations Board (NLRB) to be the administrative agency responsible for enforcing the provisions of the act.

In 1947, Congress amended the NLRA with the passage of the Labor-Management Relations Act (LMRA). This act articulated union unfair labor practices. In 1959, the Labor-Management Reporting and Disclosure Act was passed by Congress. This act established a bill of rights for union members, specifying internal union election procedures and financial reporting disclosure requirements for unions and union officers. It also added restrictions on picketing, prohibiting "hot cargo" clauses, and closed certain loopholes in the LMRA. ("Hot cargo" agreements are contract provisions in which the employer promises not to handle products that the union finds objectionable, because they have been produced by nonunion labor or at a plant on strike.) These three acts have been consolidated and are presently referred to as the Labor-Management Relations Act, 1947, as amended (Feldacker, 1990, p. 4). Federal and state governments are excluded from coverage by the act. Nonprofits became covered in the 1970s.

The NLRB can direct elections and certify results only in the case of employers whose operations affect commerce. The LMRA applies to any employer or unfair labor practice affecting commerce. Therefore, the statute has a broad scope covering most employers (Feldacker, 1990, p. 13).

Because the courts have broadly interpreted "affect commerce," the NLRB could theoretically exercise its powers to enforce the act for all employers whose operations affect commerce. However, the board has chosen not to act in all cases. In 1950, the board decided to distinguish between businesses that interrupt the flow of interstate commerce and those that are so small that a dispute would probably have no impact on the flow of commerce. It set monetary cutoff points, or standards, that limit the exercise of its power to cases involving employers whose effect on commerce is substantial. The board's requirements for exercising its power or jurisdiction are called "jurisdictional standards" or "jurisdictional yardsticks." These standards are based on the yearly amount of business done by the employer, or on the yearly amount of its sales or purchases. The standards are stated in terms of total volume of business and are different for different kinds of enterprises (Commerce Clearing House, 1990, pp. 710–712; Feldacker, 1990; National Labor Relations Board, 1991). Exhibit 11.1 provides the board's current jurisdictional standards.

Collective Bargaining in Nonprofit Organizations

Until the 1970s, the NLRB excluded nonprofit employers from the NLRA's coverage. However, in the 1970s the board asserted jurisdiction over nonprofits that had a "massive impact on interstate commerce," or those that met certain financial criteria—such as nursing homes with revenue over $100,000, visiting nurses' associations, and

Exhibit 11.1. National Labor Relations Board Jurisdictional Standards in Effect July 1, 1990.

Nonretail businesses	$50,000 total annual revenues
Office buildings	$100,000 total annual revenues
Retail enterprises	$500,000 total annual volume of business
Public utilities	$250,000 total annual volume of business or $50,000 direct or indirect outflow or inflow
Newspapers	$200,000 total annual volume of business
Radio, telegraph, television, and telephone enterprises	$100,000 total annual volume of business
Hotels, motels, and residential apartment houses	$500,000 total annual volume of business
Transportation enterprises, links and channels of interstate commerce	$50,000 total annual income
Transit systems	$250,000 total annual volume of business
Taxicab companies	$500,000 total annual volume of business
Private universities and colleges	$1,000,000 gross annual revenues
Symphony orchestras	$1,000,000 gross annual revenues
Law firms and legal assistance programs	$250,000 gross annual revenues
Employers that provide social services	$250,000 gross annual revenues
Privately operated health care institutions; defined as hospitals, convalescent hospitals, health maintenance organizations, health clinics, nursing homes, extended care facilities or other institutions devoted to the care of the sick, infirm, or aged	$250,000 total annual volume of business
Nursing homes, visiting nurses' associations, and related facilities	$100,000 total annual volume of business
associations	Regarded as single employer in that annual business of all association members is totaled to determine whether any of the standards apply.
Enterprises in the Territories and the District of Columbia	Jurisdictional standards apply in the Territories; all businesses in the District of Columbia come under NLRB jurisdiction.
National defense	Jurisdiction is asserted over all enterprises affecting commerce when their operations have a substantial impact on national defense, whether or not the enterprises satisfy any other standard.

similar facilities as applied to profit-making nursing homes (Drexel Homes, Inc., 1970).

In August 1974, Congress amended the LMRA to bring non-profit health care institutions under the law's coverage. At that time, Congress added Section 2(14), which defines "health care institutions" as including hospitals, nursing homes, and other health care facilities without regard to whether they are operated for profit. The health care amendments indicated that Congress had no objection to bringing nonprofit employers under federal labor law. Two years later, in 1976, the NLRB began to treat non-profit and charitable institutions the same way it treated businesses operated for profit. If a nonprofit employer was sufficiently involved in the interstate flow of money or goods that a labor dispute might disrupt the flow of commerce, the board would take jurisdiction. The board has established a jurisdictional standard of $250,000 annual revenue for all social service agencies other than those for which there is another specific standard applicable for the type of activity in which the organization is engaged. For example, the specific $100,000 standard would still apply for a nursing home (Feldacker, 1990, p. 14).

The NLRB asserts jurisdiction over nonprofit service organizations that provide services to or for an exempt governmental agency such as Head Start, child-care services, and medical clinics that are supported by state and/or federal funds (Feldacker, 1990, pp. 10–11). Some of these agencies have argued that they are excluded by the NLRA by the exemption for government agencies. The board holds that such agencies are covered by the act, even though government funded, if they retain independence in labor-management matters, such as establishing the wages, hours, and working conditions of their employees. The sole standard for taking jurisdiction is whether the contractor has "sufficient control over the employment conditions of its employees to enable it to bargain with labor organization as its representative." The board looks closely at the nature of the relationship between the government institution and the contractor (Bureau of National Affairs, 1992; Commerce Clearing House, 1990, pp. 736–739).

An interesting issue of jurisdiction surfaced in *National Labor Relations Board v. Catholic Bishop of Chicago* (1979). The Supreme

Court held that the NLRB cannot assert jurisdiction over church-operated schools, because such jurisdiction would violate the First Amendment establishment of freedom of religion and the separation of church and state. The Court held that the religious and secular purposes of church-sponsored schools are so intertwined that the board's jurisdiction would unconstitutionally introduce the board into the operations and policies of the church. The board does, however, assert jurisdiction over church-operated, nonprofit social agencies such as nursing homes, hospitals, and child-care centers because they function essentially the same as their secular counterparts: they receive government financial support, they are regulated by the state along with other nonprofit social agencies, and their activities only tangentially relate to the sponsoring organization's religious mission (Feldacker, 1990, p. 12).

Collective Bargaining in the Federal Government

The Civil Service Reform Act of 1978 (CSRA) and Executive Order 12871 issued on October 1, 1993, govern labor relations in the federal sector. The CSRA covers most employees of the executive agencies of the United States, including the Library of Congress and the Government Printing Office. The exclusions include federal employees working for the Government Accounting Office (GAO), Federal Bureau of Investigation (FBI), National Security Agency (NSA), Central Intelligence Agency (CIA), Federal Labor Relations Authority, Federal Service Impasses Panel, Tennessee Valley Authority (TVA), and the U.S. Postal Service. TVA employees and postal employees are covered by other statutes. TVA employees are covered by the Employment Relationship Policy Act of the New Deal and have been covered since 1935. The Postal Recognition Act of 1970 granted collective bargaining rights to postal employees under the NLRA. However, unlike private sector employees, postal employees are denied the right to strike. Employees working for the GAO, FBI, NSA, and CIA have no statutory authority to engage in collective bargaining.

Title VII of the CSRA enacted the provision known as the Federal Service Labor-Management Relations Statute (LMRS). This statute created the Federal Labor Relations Authority (FLRA) to administer and enforce the CSRA. The FLRA is governed by three bipartisan members who are appointed by the president with the advice and consent of the Senate. The members are appointed for staggered five-year terms.

Dissatisfied parties may appeal rulings made by the FLRA to the U.S. Court of Appeals. The authority of the FLRA is similar to the NLRB. The FLRA determines appropriate bargaining units, supervises and conducts union elections, conducts hearings and resolves allegations of unfair labor practices, prescribes criteria and resolves issues relating to determining compelling need for agency rules or regulations, resolves exceptions to arbitrators' awards, and takes such other actions as are necessary and appropriate to effectively administer the provisions of Title VII of the CSRA.

Federal employees may not bargain over wages and benefits or prohibited political activities. Executive Order 12871 modified the scope of bargaining requiring agencies to negotiate "the numbers, types and grades of employees or positions assigned to any organizational subdivision, work project, or tour of duty, and the technology, methods and means of performing work" (5 USC7106). Despite this change, the scope of negotiable issues is still more restrictive for federal employees than for employees at other levels of government, for nonprofits, and for the private sector. For example, federal employees may not strike. You may recall that in 1980 President Reagan fired striking air traffic controllers.

Collective Bargaining in State and Local Governments

Many states have passed legislation that grants state and local government employees the right to participate in collective bargaining with their employers. Other states, however, only permit public employees the right to "meet and confer" with a public employer. In Alabama, Georgia, and Nebraska, teachers' collectives may meet and confer, but all other employees may bargain; in California, local employees may meet and confer while all other employees may use collective bargaining; in Texas, teachers may meet and confer, but there is no coverage for state employees; and all public employees in Missouri may meet and confer. Still other states lack statutes that permit or recognize the right of public employees to join unions or bargain with public employers. The duty to meet and confer provides unions with the right to discuss with the public employer proposals establishing the terms and conditions of employment. However, employers are free to ignore the views of the unions and make unilateral decisions as to the terms and conditions of employment.

Many state statutes are very complete and are referred to as *comprehensive statutes*. These statutes are modeled after the Labor-Management Relations Act, 1947, as amended. Like the LMRS, they guarantee public employees the right to join or form labor unions or to refrain from joining unions; they also establish procedures for the selection of employee representatives, define the scope of bargaining and unfair labor practices, address union security provisions, permit or prohibit strikes, prescribe remedies to resolve contract negotiation impasses, provide mechanisms for contract grievance resolution, and establish an administrative agency to oversee the law. These statutes are referred to as public employee relations acts, or PERAs.

Concepts and Practices of Collective Bargaining

What follows are explanations of the issues introduced in the preceding overview, along with specific examples to illustrate the concepts of collective bargaining as they are applied in the federal, state, and local governments and in the nonprofit sector. For purposed of this discussion, all of the labor-management collective bargaining acts—private/nonprofit (LMRA), federal (LMRS), and state (PERAs)—will be referred to generically as labor-management relations acts.

Labor-management relation acts designate or create agencies to provide oversight of the acts and to administer relations among employers, employees, and unions. The NLRB governs private and nonprofit labor relations, the FLRA provides oversight for the federal government, and although the names of these administrative agencies tend to vary across the states (New Jersey's version is the Public Employment Relations Commission, the Illinois version is known as the Illinois State Labor Relations Board, and Florida calls its board the Public Employee Relations Commission), they are often referred to as public employee relations boards, or PERBs.

Unit Determination

The labor-management relations acts generally define the procedures for designating the employees' representative or union. Before a union can represent a group of employees, the constituency of the group must be determined. The group of employees that can potentially be represented by one representative at the bargaining table is called the *appropriate bargaining unit*. The acts contain both guidelines for the determination of the appropriate unit and procedures for determination.

The labor-management relations acts exclude some general categories of employees from a bargaining unit. For example, managerial and confidential employees are excluded as a matter of policy because their interests are more closely aligned with management than with the bargaining unit. Managerial employees are individuals employed by an agency in positions that require or authorize them to formulate, determine, or influence the policies of the agency. Confidential employees are those who assist the individuals who formulate, determine, or execute labor policy. Included in this category are employees who have access to information about labor relations or who participate in deliberations of a labor relations nature and are required to keep that information confidential from the labor organization representing a bargaining unit.

Professional and technical employees, and in some cases supervisors, may also be excluded from an overall bargaining unit, but they are still entitled to representation as their own units. Professional employees perform work of a predominantly intellectual, nonstandardized nature. The work must require the use of discretion and independent judgment, and knowledge that is customarily acquired through college or university attendance. Technical employees perform work of a technical nature that requires the use of independent discretion and special training. They may have acquired their training in college, in technical schools, or through on-the-job training. A supervisor is an individual who has the authority to, in the interests of the agency, hire, direct, assign, promote, reward, transfer, furlough, lay off, recall, suspend, discipline, or remove employees, and to adjust their grievances or effectively recommend such action.

Public safety officers often receive special treatment. Some states have separate statutes for police officers and firefighters, while others include them in municipal or general statutes. Fourteen states have statutes that require police officers to be in units composed only of police officers, and twelve states require the same for firefighters. This special treatment is meant to ensure the community's safety. The state of Delaware has separate police and firefighter units "to protect the public by assuring the orderly and uninterrupted operations and functions of public safety services" (Police Officers' and Firefighters' Employment Relations Act, 1986).

Selection of a Bargaining Representative

The labor-management relations acts also contain specific procedures for the selection of an exclusive bargaining representative. *Exclusive recognition* is the term applied when one union has the right and responsibility to speak on behalf of all employees in the bargaining unit. Voluntary recognition by the employer is the easiest way of designating a union. It is available only if the union can demonstrate support by a majority of employees in the unit. This is usually achieved by having employees sign recognition cards authorizing the union to represent them in collective bargaining.

If voluntary recognition is not achieved, or if it is challenged by a claim of majority representation by another representative organization, a secret ballot election may be held to select the exclusive bargaining representative. The administrative agencies have the authority to regulate these representation elections, which are also subject to judicial review. Some states, such as Delaware, Hawaii, Iowa, Rhode Island, and Wisconsin, insist that a secret ballot election be held to determine employee representation. A union that has been voluntarily recognized by the employer as the exclusive representative possesses the same rights as a union that has been certified through a formal certification election.

The procedures for a certification election are similar across the nonprofit, federal, and state sectors. Unions must request that employees in the proposed unit sign recognition cards authorizing the union to represent them. The union must obtain a "show of interest" by the unit members. The required show of interest is not less than 30 percent for nonprofits, the federal government, and the majority of states. However, if the employer chooses not to voluntarily recognize a union, an election will be held. If the union receives 51 percent of the votes, it will be recognized as the exclusive representative.

Union Security

Labor-management relations acts contain provisions for union security devices. Union security provisions address the degree to which unions can compel union membership or mandate the payment of dues to support their activities. Most contracts in the nonprofit and private sectors contain some kind of union security provision, and union security provisions are articulated in each state's public employee relations act. Neither the LMRS nor the Postal Reorganization Act of 1970 permit any form of required membership as a condition of employment. Federal employees are free not to join unions. The different types of union security provisions are explained in the following paragraphs.

Closed shop. Under a closed shop agreement, an employer was not permitted to hire anyone who was not already a member of the union. Closed shop arrangements became illegal in the private sector under Section 8(a)(3) of the Labor-Management Relations Act, 1947, as amended. Closed shop arrangements have always been prohibited in the public sector because they infringe upon the employer's prerogative in determining employment standards, as well as restricting the selection of new employees.

Union shop. Under a union shop provision, all unit employees are required to join the exclusive bargaining representative after being hired. An employer operating under a union shop agreement may hire employees who are not members of the union. However, the nonunion employees must join the union within the period specified in the agreement, which is usually thirty days, and remain a member of the union as a condition of continued employment. Compulsory membership by a certain date after employment prevents "free riders," employees who are not union members but who benefit from union negotiations without paying their share of the union's operating expenses. Free riders are a particular problem in the federal government, where union shops are prohibited.

Agency shop. Under an agency shop agreement, all of the unit employees are required to pay a service fee to the exclusive bargaining representative, whether or not they are union members. The service fee is designed to make nonmembers pay their share of the expense of representing all of the unit employees.

Fair share. The fair share provision resembles the agency shop provision in that employees must pay a proportion of regular union dues to cover the exclusive representative's costs for collective bargaining. However, unlike agency shops, nonbargaining activities are not funded by nonunion members.

Maintenance of membership. Under maintenance of membership provisions, employees are not required to become union members. However, employees who join a union must remain members and pay membership dues to the union until the contract expires.

Dues checkoff. Because unions depend on the fees collected from employees for their support, they must have a reliable and continuous system for collecting membership dues. A dues checkoff mechanism permits unions to collect fees from employers, who withhold the union dues from the employees' paychecks and forward the funds to the union. This is a more efficient process than collecting fees from individual members. Dues checkoff is typically combined with one of the other union security provisions.

Right-to-work states. Many states are known as "right-to-work" states (Alabama, Arizona, Arkansas, Florida, Georgia, Idaho, Iowa, Kansas, Louisiana, Mississippi, Nebraska, North and South Carolina, North and South Dakota, Tennessee, Texas, Utah, Virginia, and Wyoming). According to right-to-work laws, individuals cannot be forced to join or pay dues to a labor union. Furthermore, no worker need be a union member to acquire or retain employment. In the nonprofit and private sectors, section 14(b) of the LMRA permits states to outlaw various forms of union security provisions: "Nothing in this Act shall be construed as authorizing the execution or application of agreements requiring membership in a labor organization as a condition of employment in any State or Territory in which such execution or application is prohibited by State or Territorial law." This provision means that an employer can reject a union's demands for the recognition of union security arrangements that are illegal under state law.

Unfair Labor Practices

Labor-management relations acts enumerate specific unfair labor practices that may be committed by the employer, union, or both. Unfair labor practices are actions by either the employer or the union that interfere with the employees' exercise of statutory rights. The administrative agencies generally have exclusive jurisdiction to hear unfair labor practice suits filed by an employee, the employer, or the union, which is subject to limited judicial review.

Unfair labor practice provisions are intended to protect the rights of employees, unions, and employers by prohibiting discrimination, interference, and coercion by both employers and unions. For unions, unlawful activities would constitute interference with the employer's management duties and rights. Charges of employer discrimination, interference, and coercion often pertain to the rights of employees to engage in union activity and the rights of unions to represent their members.

The Scope of Collective Bargaining

The scope of collective bargaining constitutes which subjects are negotiable. Specific topics have generally been classified on a case-by-case basis into three types: mandatory, permissive, and illegal.

Mandatory topics of bargaining are topics that the laws (whether private, nonprofit, federal, or state) require management and labor to bargain over. Either side can bargain to impasse on a mandatory topic if they can demonstrate that they made a good faith effort to reach agreement on it. Mandatory topics in both the nonprofit and for-profit sectors typically include wages, salaries, fringe benefits, and working conditions. Mandatory topics for federal employers and employees are restricted to conditions of employment that affect working conditions, including personnel policies, practices, and matters, whether established by rule, regulation, or otherwise. Federal employees may not bargain over wages or fringe benefits.

The statutes that permit collective bargaining by public employees vary in what they consider to be mandatory topics of bargaining. For example, Massachusetts has a requirement that "the employer and the exclusive representative shall meet at reasonable times, including meetings in advance of the employer's budget-making process, and shall negotiate in good faith with respect to wages, hours, standards or productivity and performance, and any other terms and conditions of employment, including without limitation, in the case of teaching personnel employed by a school committee, class size and workload" (Massachusetts General Laws Annotated, Chapter 150E, Section 6, amended in 1986). Notice that this law requires negotiation over standards of performance and productivity, and class size and workload for teachers, as well as the more standard issues. Some states, such as Nevada, are even more explicit in defining and articulating mandatory subjects.

A *permissive topic* is a matter related to optional policy that may be bargained over if there is mutual agreement between labor and management, but neither side may unilaterally insist on such bargaining. Neither management nor labor has to bargain over permissive topics. In many states permissive topics of bargaining include insurance benefits, retirement benefits, productivity bargaining, and grievance and discipline procedures. Permissive topics in the federal sector under Section 7106 include, at the election of the agency, work projects, tour of duty, or the technology, methods, and means of performing work. Education benefits could be considered a permissive topic. Because they are not wages, hours, or working conditions, they would not be considered mandatory topics. However, the employer and union could elect to negotiate them.

Deciding whether an issue is mandatory or permissive has generally been accomplished on a case-by-case basis. Administrative agencies and the courts have devised varying and flexible tests rather than establishing fixed rules. The decision is difficult because many issues affect both the terms and conditions of employment and management policymaking. Examples of this dilemma surface frequently in teaching and social work. Teachers want to negotiate issues such as class size, curriculum, teaching loads, and nonteaching duties and responsibilities. Social workers want to bargain over caseload, treatment alternatives, or the process of deciding what services are appropriate for clients. These issues address working conditions, but they are also dimensions of management policy.

Illegal topics cannot be bargained and any agreement to bargain with respect to illegal topics will be void and unenforceable. Instead, illegal topics typically must be resolved through the legislative process. Examples of illegal or prohibited subjects of bargaining at the federal and state levels include the negotiation of the organization's objectives, how the objectives should be implemented, the agency's organizational structure, and employment standards. Issues regarding retirement, job qualifications, selection, placement, promotion criteria, and the functions of the civil service commission or merit system are often excluded from bargaining in the public sector. The Iowa Public Employee Relations Act specifically excludes the public retirement system from the scope of mandatory bargaining. Other states exclude the merit system. Illegal topics for nonprofit and private organizations could include a closed shop union security provision or contract terms in violation of state or federal laws. For example, contract clauses that permit unions to discriminate against persons of color or against members of certain religious groups would be illegal because they violate Title VII of the 1964 Civil Rights Act and many state fair employment practice acts.

Employer/Management Rights

The missions of public sector organizations are decided by legislative bodies. The managers responsible for the performance of these functions are accountable to those legislative bodies and ultimately to the people. Major decisions made in bargaining with public employees are inescapably political because they involve critical policy choices. The matters debated at the bargaining table are not simply questions of wages, hours, and vacations. Directly at issue are questions of the size and allocation of the budget, the tax rates, the level of public services, and the long-term obligation of the government. These decisions are political in the sense that they are to be made by elected officials who are politically responsible to the voters. They are generally considered legislative decisions and not subject to delegation (Edwards, Clark, & Craver, 1979). Therefore, public sector employers tend to have more discretion than nonprofit or private sector employers in exercising their management rights.

Impasse Resolution

When management and labor are unable to agree to contract terms, an impasse occurs. Third-party intervention often becomes necessary to help resolve their differences. Three procedures are commonly used to resolve impasses: mediation, fact-finding, and arbitration.

Mediation

When a bargaining impasse occurs, either one or both of the parties may request mediation. Mediation involves the introduction of a neutral third party into the negotiation process to assist the bargaining parties in resolving their differences. Mediators often meet with the parties individually at first to discover the conflict. They then encourage the parties to resume bargaining. Mediators may suggest compromise positions that bridge the gap in negotiations, or they may act as intermediaries to persuade the parties that their proposals are unrealistic. Mediators serve only an advisory role. They have no power to compel the settlement of disputes. Mediation findings are not binding unless approved by both parties in the dispute.

Fact-Finding

Fact-finding involves holding an adversarial hearing, at which each side presents its position on the issues involved in the dispute. The fact-finding body studies the evidence that was presented at the hearing, then makes recommendations for a final settlement.

Fact-finder recommendations are not binding on the parties. However, fact-finder recommendations are often made public, and the threat of unfavorable publicity often makes both sides more willing to reach a negotiated settlement. Fact-finding is grounded in the belief that public opinion will encourage the parties to accept the fact-finder's report so as not to appear unreasonable.

Interest Arbitration

Interest arbitration is the procedure used when mediation and/or fact-finding have not resolved bargaining impasses. An arbitrator will hold an adversarial hearing and, based on the evidence presented, determine the terms of the final agreement. Arbitration resolves conflicts without the use of a strike. State and local governments typically use arbitration as a substitute for permitting the right to strike. Only statutes may compel the use of arbitration to conciliate contract disputes. The courts lack jurisdiction to compel arbitration in the absence of statutory authority. To discourage routine reliance on arbitration many statutes impose the cost of arbitration on the parties.

Interest arbitration has been criticized for intruding upon local government sovereignty. The third party is unaccountable to the voters or elected officials, yet makes decisions that affect the employer-employee relationship. To avoid this concern, many statutes require that arbitration decisions be approved by a majority of the appropriate legislative body.

Public sector arbitration varies across the states, and there are several forms. *Compulsory binding arbitration* requires that any dispute not settled during negotiations must end in arbitration. Arbitrators are free to make awards based on the evidence presented. The arbitrator is free to take any reasonable position, and is usually inclined to make a decision that accommodates the positions of both parties in order to create a realistic and effective agreement.

Final-offer arbitration permits each party to submit proposals, or final offers, to arbitration. There are two types of final-offer arbitration: final offer by issue and final offer by package. In final-offer-by-package arbitration, the arbitrator must select either the union's or the employer's final offer on all of the disputed issues. The arbitrator may not modify the proposals or compromise on the two offers. This procedure assumes that each side will make reasonable offers to prevent the arbitrator from selecting the other party's final package. In final-offer-by-issue arbitration, the arbitrator selects either side's final offer on an issue-by-issue basis. The arbitrator is free to select the most reasonable position on each issue. The arbitrator's decision may reflect a combination of employer and union offers. Arbitration by issues gives the arbitrator more flexibility in developing an agreement, because the award may incorporate proposals from both sides. This method has been criticized for possibly producing compromise awards that eliminate some of the risk by going to arbitration.

An arbitrator's decision tends to be final and is limited to issues within the permissible scope of collective bargaining. The determination of an issue outside the scope of bargaining will be viewed as a decision made beyond the jurisdiction of the arbitrator and will therefore be reversed. All mandatory topics of bargaining are considered to be within the scope of compulsory arbitration. Non-mandatory topics of bargaining generally are not considered to be within the scope of arbitration unless both parties agree to submit the topic. Most arbitration statutes contain specific criteria that arbitrators must consider in making their decisions. In addition to guiding arbitrators, these criteria facilitate judicial review.

Strikes

It is illegal for federal employees to go on strike, nonprofit employees are permitted to strike, and presently ten states—Alaska, Hawaii, Illinois, Minnesota, Montana, Ohio, Oregon, Pennsylvania, Vermont, and Wisconsin—have laws that permit some public employees the right to strike. However, there is little consistency across the states in which employees are covered and in the conditions that permit them to strike.

Among states that permit strikes by public employees, a clear delineation is made between those employees who are permitted to strike and those who are prohibited from striking. Most states limit permission to employees who are not responsible for the public's welfare. The state of Alaska, for example, divides its employees into two groups; those who do essential services, such as police and fire protection, and employees who provide services that will not seriously affect the public, such as sanitation. Police and firefighters are prohibited from striking due to the threat to the public's safety that their absence would impose. Sanitation, public utility, and snow removal employees, however, may engage in strikes if there has first been an attempt at mediation with the employer and if a majority of employees in the unit vote by secret ballot to authorize the strike.

For most states that permit public employee strikes, a set of stipulations must be adhered to before a strike is considered allowable. For example, Hawaii state statutes permit strikes for nonessential employees in a bargaining unit if the unit has no process for binding arbitration. Before these employees may strike, they must first comply with impasse procedures; sixty days must be allowed to elapse after the fact-finding board publishes its recommendations;

and the unit must give a ten-day notice of intent to strike. Still, the Hawaii Labor Relations Board retains the right to set requirements to avoid danger to public health or safety.

In Montana, nurses in public health care facilities are permitted to strike only if a written notice is given thirty days in advance and no other health care facility within a 150-mile radius intends to strike or is engaged in a strike. These limitations to strike allowance permit the public employer to take action to prevent the strike or to prepare for the absence of public workers. If the restrictions concerning strikes are not adhered to, public employers have the right to certain disciplinary actions toward the union and the striking employees.

Even where strikes are permitted, many state statutes grant the courts the authority to issue injunctions or restraining orders if the strike presents a danger to public health or safety. If a strike is enjoined by the courts, violation of the court order could result in civil contempt penalties for the union and employees.

Grievance Arbitration

Grievance arbitration occurs when labor believes that management has violated the terms of a labor contract and files a grievance. In grievance arbitration, a neutral third party is asked to resolve the disagreement that could not be settled by the involved parties. A hearing is held that enables the parties to present evidence and testimony that support their respective positions on the case. After reviewing all of the evidence presented, the arbitrator then renders a decision based on the merits of the case. The arbitrator's decision tends to be final and legally binding upon both parties.

The scope of an arbitrator's authority is usually negotiated and stated in the collective bargaining agreement. A commonly negotiated clause authorizes the arbitrator to resolve all disputes concerning the application or interpretation of the contract, but it prohibits the arbitrator from adding to or subtracting from the express terms of the agreement in formulating an award.

Grievance arbitration is undertaken as the last resort in settling disputes because it is an expensive process. Direct costs involve the expenses associated with preparing the case and the arbitrator's fee. Indirect costs involve all the time spent away from work by the grievant, supervisor, union representative, witnesses, and other associated employees. The contract usually specifies which party will be responsible for paying the arbitrator's fee. It is common for labor and management to equally share the cost of an arbitration proceeding. Because sharing the costs makes it less expensive for the union to extend the grievance and appeal process until arbitration, some agreements require that the losing party pay all of the fees associated with arbitration. Holding the losing party responsible for all of the costs should provide the party whose grievance is weak with an incentive to settle at a lower level in the proceedings, and it should encourage the union to more carefully screen cases.

Grievance arbitration is expressly authorized by statute for the nonprofit and private sectors. The LMRA requires that all contracts contain a grievance resolution procedure. This requirement is also found in Section 7121 of the Federal Service Labor-Management Relations Statute and in most state statutes.

Public Sector Distinctions

Public sector collective bargaining has been influenced by underlying beliefs and organizational structures not found in the private sector. The principle of government sovereignty and the doctrine of illegal separation of powers are two examples of such beliefs. The *sovereignty doctrine* holds that employees have only the rights that government permits them to have. The *doctrine of illegal separation of powers* forbids a government to share its powers with others. It has been used most frequently to limit the scope of mandatory topics of bargaining. Opponents of public sector collective bargaining have noted that there is a fundamental conflict between collective bargaining and these doctrines because government has a responsibility to act on behalf of all citizens, not just union members, and the public interest should not be subjugated to the political struggles between unions and government.

Another belief unique to public sector collective bargaining is that public employees have no right to withhold services from their fellow citizens. For many public sector jobs, such as police and firefighting, no competitive market exists. Machines cannot provide those services and consumers cannot turn to other suppliers of the service.

Public sector contract negotiations tend to be more difficult due to the diffusion of authority that exists in the public sector. The executive branch of government is responsible for the day-to-day administration of public organizations and for contract negotiations. It is the legislative branch that has responsibility for the budget and the final authority to legitimize a settlement. Because members of public unions are also voters, they often attempt to influence the collective bargaining process by lobbying the people who are dependent upon them for reelection.

For these ideological and structural reasons, and because many people did not see the need for unionization, the legal framework for public sector collective bargaining lagged behind that of the private sector. Job protection was granted to public employees through civil service systems. Selection, retention, and promotion were based on merit qualifications. Over the years, civil service systems expanded to include job classification, salary administration, and the administration of grievance procedures, training, and safety. Public sector employees had protections usually not found in the private sector. The impetus for change surfaced when proponents for bargaining contended that civil service systems were often inflexible, that they were unable or unwilling to respond to demands for wage and fringe benefit adjustments and changes in working conditions that typically required legislative adjustment (Kearney, 1992).

Changes in the legal framework. In 1959, the state of Wisconsin enacted the first state statute permitting municipal employees the right to form, join, and be represented by labor organizations. Three years later, President Kennedy issued Executive Order 10988, which granted federal employees the right to join and form unions and to bargain collectively. The order established a framework for collective bargaining and encouraged the expansion of collective bargaining rights to state and local government employees. Kearney (1992) outlined the demise of the sovereignty doctrine: beginning in 1976, the federal courts have ruled that the First Amendment's freedom of association prohibits states from interfering with public sector employees' right to join and form unions (*Atkins v. City of Charlotte*, 1969; *Keyeshian v. Board of Regents*, 1967; *Letter Carriers v. Blount*, 1969; *McLaughlin v. Tilendis* (1968).

These decisions invalidated the sovereignty doctrine, contributing to the growth of unions.

The Supreme Court held in *Smith v. Arkansas State Highway Employees, Local 1315* (1979), however, that nothing in the Constitution requires public employers to either recognize or collectively bargain with public employee unions. Employees can form and join unions without the benefit of protective legislation, but public employers are not compelled to recognize or bargain with unions (Dilts, 1993, p. 308). Public employers are required to bargain only under laws that mandate bargaining. The duty to bargain can be imposed only by statute.

Collective bargaining does occur, however, in states that do not provide statutory protection and procedures. For example, in Arizona, local governments have passed protective ordinances to permit de facto bargaining. Indiana permits de facto bargaining, and in Louisiana and West Virginia state courts have in effect permitted collective bargaining in limited applications (Dilts, Boyda, & Scherr, 1993, p. 260).

Limitations of civil service. With the growth of government, public agencies became larger, more impersonal, and more dominated by civil service regulations and boards. This depersonalization of public service helped to isolate and alienate individual employees. Employees looked to unions for support. Civil service and/or merit systems were no longer perceived to be neutral advocates for employees. In many cases, merit systems were viewed as alternative forms of favoritism, reifying employers subjective biases.

The need to reconcile collective bargaining and the merit system has been recognized by public sector unions. Jerry Wurf, former president of AFSCME saw both the merit system and collective bargaining as legitimate in government labor-management relations. AFSCME's International Constitution lists among the union's central objectives "to promote civil service legislation and career service in government" (Wurf, 1974). In fact, the early years of AFSCME's history were part of the movement to reform government and advocate for the enactment of civil service laws. Merit systems existed in only eleven states. Civil service was viewed as a means to end political kickbacks and protect members who might be fired because of political behavior.

Today, it is common to find both unions and civil service systems in public organizations. As noted earlier, however, many statutes have management rights clauses that limit the scope of mandatory topics of bargaining. Some statutes state that when in conflict, civil service regulations take precedence over contract terms.

While union membership rates in the private sector have continued to fall during the 1980s and 1990s, the Bureau of Labor Statistics reports an increase in public sector membership rates for the first time in fourteen years (Bureau of National Affairs, 1994b). Despite the stability of union membership in the 1980s, there was an erosion in the organizational, economic, and political influence of public unions (Klingner, 1993). To regain their influence, the unions have refocused their energies on issues of the new and diverse workforce. The number of females and minority members in the public workforce has increased. Issues such as pay equity, comparable worth for equitable job classifications, health and safety protection, training and retraining, quality-of-work life, job enlargement, and broader job classifications have replaced the previous emphasis on wages, seniority, and work rules.

Nonprofit Sector Distinctions

Unions and nonprofit organizations are not typically linked together in most people's thoughts. That may be because many nonprofits are small and do not meet the NLRB's jurisdictional standards. Another reason may be because nonprofit agencies often respond to new societal needs and thus become desirable places to work even if salaries are lower and working conditions are less comfortable than in more established institutions. Initiatives such as rape crisis and domestic violence centers, agencies that provide support and respite services to parents of special needs children, hospices for the terminally ill, and homes for people with AIDS are some of the services provided by voluntary agencies. Other nonprofit organizations that often pay their employees lower salaries include cultural, social, and educational institutions, day care centers, social welfare agencies, and health care facilities.

The research on unionization and nonprofits tends to focus on social workers and health care professionals (Benton, 1993; Hush, 1969; Sherer, 1994; Tambor, 1973). The dismantling of human service programs under President Reagan in the 1980s resulted in less job security and a decline in real wages (Tambor, 1988a). During this time there were also changes in working conditions. There has been increasing pressure toward greater productivity, and a decreasing influence in policymaking that has led to declines in professional autonomy. For human service professionals, unionization has been viewed as a vehicle for defending professional autonomy and improving working conditions. Unions have sought to expand the scope of bargaining to include such issues as agency-level policymaking, agency missions, standards of service, concerns about job satisfaction, and professional judgment (Tambor, 1988a), as well as malpractice and professional liability insurance, legal representation of workers, sabbatical leaves, minimum required training, workload issues, advance training sessions, in-service training, conferences, degree programs, licensing examination assistance, and remuneration for enhanced education (Tambor, 1988a).

Human service workers are not the only employees of the nonprofit sector who have joined unions. The International Brotherhood of the Teamsters represents 106 nonprofit bargaining units, with approximately 10,269 members, including hospitals, nursing homes, and health care facilities, as well as Masonic homes, retirement communities, Goodwill Industries, and the Association for Advancement of the Blind and Retarded. Bargaining-unit employees run the gamut from social workers, teachers, secretaries, housekeepers, nurses, dieticians, cooking staff, dishwashers, groundskeepers, maintenance activity aids, stock clerks, paramedics, emergency medical technicians, X-ray technicians, accountants, receptionists, cashiers, mechanics, painters, electricians, youth care workers, vehicle drivers, and dispatchers. The Communications Workers of America also represents a large number of workers employed by such nonprofit agencies as museums, housing authorities, social service and health care agencies, libraries, and foundation organizations. The AFSCME represents more than sixty thousand nonprofit agency employees who work in the areas of health, social, community, and educational services.

An AFSCME publication that promotes unionization addresses the similarities between public and private nonprofit employees: both look for recognition, for dignity and respect, and for decent wages and improved benefits. Private nonprofit employees work in highly stressful occupations, yet they receive salaries that may not be commensurate with the responsibilities and complexities of their jobs. Employees of nonprofits share many of the same desires as their public sector counterparts: for better pay and benefits, contract language protection, career mobility, and safer work environments (AFSCME, 1988, p. 1). Yet the vast majority of these workers have no union representation. AFSCME has taken the position that to win better working conditions and benefits, nonprofits need the clout of union representation.

Hush (1969) and Tambor (1973) observed that the unionization of nonprofits challenges the traditions that voluntary agencies have defined for themselves: altruistic roles and the denial of self-interest as wage earners. The impact of a union contract operating as the authority in place of the board of directors, personnel committee, or administrative staff members seems to contradict the values of openness, dignity, and communication often associated with nonprofits. For the boards and administrators of volunteer agencies, union interest among staff represents a threat to existing relationships. Nevertheless, more and more nonprofit employees are seeking union support. Nonprofit administrators, boards of directors, and personnel committee members must work with their staff to develop progressive and relevant human resources management policies.

Summary

Public sector and nonprofit unions have adapted strategies to meet the challenges of the future. Union contracts with federal, state, and local agencies recognize that new issues have emerged and that labor-management understanding and cooperation are important. The report of the National Performance Review (1993) recommended that a joint labor-management National Partnership Council be created to work on emerging issues. Following that recommendation for cooperation and collaboration, Executive Order 12871 established Labor-Management Partnership Councils to involve employees and union representatives as full partners with management representatives. In an attempt to minimize the adversarial relationship that often mars collective bargaining, Executive Order 12871 also provided for the systematic training of appropriate employees in alternative dispute resolution techniques and interest-based bargaining approaches.

Across the states and cities, cooperation between unions and management had already begun (Armshaw, Carnevale, & Waltuck, 1993; Hayes & Kearney, 1994; Hodes, 1991; Walters, 1994a). In response to the attention focused on reinventing government, privatization, and well-publicized battles in which mayors of large unionized cities such as Philadelphia, Indianapolis, and New York pounded the unions for their high wages and generous benefits, labor leaders have modified their traditional combative posture and have become more creative in shaping new initiatives (Walters, 1994a).

Acknowledging that the public's perceptions have changed and that a new collective bargaining environment exists, Steve Fantauzzo, executive director of AFSCME Council 62 in Indianapolis, stated the following: "But for many of us in the public sector, there is the realization that government—whether it's a state or city or school district—can and needs to be made more efficient. So the question is: Are you going to be part of the process and try to protect the interests of your members in that process? Or are you going to stand outside and let others shape the change?" (Walters, 1994a).

The scope of bargaining has also been expanded to include new employee benefits, including the introduction of labor-management committees, the provision of mental health and substance-abuse benefits, child-care benefits, employee individual development plans, incentive awards, counseling for tests, alternative work schedules, safety precautions such as guidelines covering the use of video display terminals, and tax-sheltered annuities.

For public and nonprofit organizations that are not yet unionized, it is important to have a progressive human resources management system in place that respects employees. Examinations, performance appraisals, promotions, and merit pay systems must be administered in an equitable and consistent manner. Jobs must be enriched to eliminate tasks that are routine and boring, and career enrichment opportunities must be provided. Employees must feel that their jobs are important and that they are contributing to the mission of the agency. Whether or not workers join unions depends on their perceptions of the work environment and on their desire to participate in or influence employment conditions. Organizations that provide employees with the opportunity to participate in the decision-making process are less likely to be the targets of unionization.

Part Three

Human Resources Management Challenges in Public and Nonprofit Organizations

This book concludes with three chapters that discuss some of the pending human resources management (HRM) challenges. Volunteers are used by public and nonprofit organizations to provide a range of services. Some volunteers serve as board members for nonprofit organizations or on local government commissions or boards. Other volunteers provide assistance where needed in cultural, social service, health care, and educational agencies. Still other volunteers are used to supplement paid staff in professional roles. Chapter Twelve discusses the importance of managing volunteers. In both public and nonprofit organizations, attention should be paid to the recruitment, selection, training, evaluation, and management of volunteers. While volunteers can be a tremendous asset to an agency, they also present challenges that need to be addressed through strategic human resources planning.

Part One of this book addressed many societal changes that have begun to impact public and nonprofit organizations. Contracting-out services, alternative dispute resolution, violence in the workplace, and the integration of computers into the workplace are the result of societywide economic, technological, legal, and cultural changes. Chapter Thirteen summarizes these topics that have resulted in new workplace structures and employee concerns, as well as how HRM practices have been affected.

Chapter Fourteen summarizes the main points addressed in the book and discusses how strategic human resources management (SHRM) can be used to help organizations cope with the challenges that lie ahead. Some of the challenges of SHRM include accommodating a more diverse workforce through family-friendly policies and recognizing the change in skill requirements. More and more public and nonprofit positions are professional in nature, requiring higher levels of education.

Organizations are being evaluated on the new performance standards of efficiency, quality, variety, customization, convenience, and timeliness. These new performance standards require improved skills and competencies. To remain competitive, organizations will have to elevate training and career development programs to organizational priorities.

Chapter Twelve

Volunteers in the Public and Nonprofit Sectors

There is a tradition of volunteerism in this country that began with churches, synagogues, and other religiously affiliated organizations as well as local government councils. Today a wide range of nonprofit and public sector organizations provide a variety of volunteer opportunities ranging from serving as board members of nonprofit organizations to serving on local government boards and commissions. Parents volunteer as coaches of nonprofit- and municipality-sponsored sports and recreation activities, and volunteers providing myriad services can be found in public and nonprofit cultural, educational, social service, and health care agencies. Volunteers are used to assist employees in meeting their agency's mission, and thus become an important part of strategic human resources management and planning. Following are some examples of how public and nonprofit agencies utilize volunteers; the last two examples illustrate how for-profit companies promote volunteerism.

- In the city of Virginia Beach, Virginia, volunteers serve as judicial information clerks in the circuit court, nutritionists in the health department, probation aides with the juvenile court, and family counselors at a child service center, in addition to other roles (Lane, 1995).
- The Kansas City Alzheimer's Association needs additional Helpline volunteers to provide families with information and support.
- In the City of Fairfield, Ohio, volunteers provide support to victims and witnesses of crime. Assigned through the courts,

volunteers keep people informed about upcoming court dates and about what to expect during court proceedings (Lane, 1995).

• Volunteers are needed for the Court Appointed Special Advocates program to speak up for children who have been determined by the family court to be abused, neglected, or abandoned.

• More than seventy thousand people from all walks of life volunteer their time and talents to the national parks. They serve in positions ranging from interpretive ranger to maintenance worker and are involve in community-based friends-of-the-park support groups (National Park Foundation, 1995).

• The Pillsbury Company promotes volunteerism as a way for employees to gain skills while giving to the community. To encourage volunteer efforts, the company allows workers release time from their jobs to participate in community projects (Bureau of National Affairs, 1994b).

• Electronic Data Systems Corporation organizes volunteer days to strengthen employees' commitment to volunteering and to contribute to the communities in which the company operates. Employees participate in community involvement projects (Bureau of National Affairs, 1994b).

When one thinks of volunteers and civic participation, nonprofit agencies typically come to mind, but as some of these examples illustrate, the public sector has also come to rely on volunteers for an assortment of purposes and in a variety of environments.

While the use of volunteers in the public sector has grown, volunteer use has become even more pervasive in the nonprofit sector. Hodgkinson, Weitzman, Toppe, and Noga (1992) report that in 1989 46.5 percent of the civilian noninstitutional population in the United States volunteered in nonreligious voluntary agencies, compared to 33.6 percent who volunteered in public sector agencies. Van Til (1988) notes the increasing professionalism of volunteer administration. Organizations such as the National Volunteers Center, the National Information Center on Volunteerism, the National Center for Voluntary Action, the Association of Volunteer Bureaus, the United Way's Voluntary Action Center, and the Minnesota Office on Volunteer Services provide books, pamphlets, training materials, and videos targeting the recruitment and management of volunteers. These agencies also provide training related to the recruitment and use of volunteers. The Association for Volunteer Administration even has a certification program for managers of volunteers.

In both public and nonprofit agencies, attention should be paid to the recruitment, selection, training, evaluation, and management of volunteers. While volunteers can be a tremendous asset to any organization, they also present new human resources management challenges. Administrative responsibilities are increased as agencies must keep records and extend their liability insurance and worker's compensation policies to volunteers. Managing volunteer programs requires the development of personnel policies and procedures to assist with the integration of volunteers into the everyday operations of the agency. Paid staff, unions, and board members need to support the use of volunteers; oversight needs to be provided so that volunteers are properly utilized; and strategies need to be developed to motivate and retain volunteers. This chapter addresses these issues. At the end of the chapter, special attention is given to volunteers who serve on governing boards.

Use of Volunteers

As dollars have become tighter, public and nonprofit agencies have come to rely on use of volunteers as a way to deliver services. Agencies are establishing programs to eliminate voids in service or to allow expansion of programs without a significant increase in costs (Brudney, 1990, 1993; Chase, 1992; Duncombe, 1985, 1986; Farr, 1983; Gerber, 1992; Lane, 1995).

Volunteers are an attractive resource for agencies because they cost little, they can give detailed attention to people for whom paid employees do not always have the time, they often provide specialized skills, they provide an expansion of staff in emergencies and peak load periods, they enable agencies to expand levels of service despite budgetary limitations, and they are good for public relations. Local governments use volunteers to serve on task forces; to oversee recreation programs; to staff libraries; as advocates for community causes; and as firefighters, police auxiliary officers, senior citizens center assistants, park maintenance workers, file clerks and office workers, hospital and nursing home attendants, teaching assistants in schools and correctional facilities, activity assistants for the developmentally and physically disabled, and museum guides. Volunteers have also begun to participate in community programs such as public safety, services for the homeless, AIDS prevention, and programs addressing the health and well-being of children (Lane, 1995). Peter Lane, a research associate with the Volunteerism Project of the National Association of Counties, believes that "beyond the millions of dollars of donated services, volunteer programs also deliver an unexpected fringe benefit: a more involved and informed citizenry. Rather than throwing up their hands in disgust at government, citizens are rolling up their sleeves and pitching in" (Lane, 1995, p. 12).

While the use of volunteers is promising, agencies must also be aware that there are costs associated with volunteer programs. Ellis (1995a, p. 3) notes that "because volunteers are agents of the organizations, their work poses potential risk management questions and insurance needs. Anyone acting on behalf of an organization can put others at risk or can be at risk. Volunteers are not inherently more or less likely to have accidents or make mistakes. However, the board should make sure that the organization has taken all the necessary steps to protect the client, the volunteer and the paid staff." This means that volunteers need to be screened for possessing the appropriate qualifications, and they need to be trained. For example, volunteers who would not be hired as police officers because of antisocial or aberrant personalities should not be selected as police auxiliary volunteers. Individuals who exhibit short tempers or low frustration levels should not work with children, senior citizens, or the disabled in capacities that require patience or in situations that, despite planning, often become unstructured. To minimize the frequency and severity of mistakes, volunteers need to receive general training concerning the agency's mission, policies, and regulations, as well as training that is tailored to the specialized tasks or responsibilities they will perform.

Agencies must anticipate the reactions to paid staff and unions if they plan to use volunteers as replacements for paid employees. For example, protests from unions have influenced the Voluntary Action Center in Lansing, Michigan, not to refer volunteers to state agencies where they would replace laid-off staff members. And in Chicago, corporate volunteers are used as troubleshooters for specific projects with a beginning, middle, and end, not as substitutes for paid employees (Chase, 1992). Other agencies have successfully integrated volunteers to work alongside paid staff to investigate complaints of discrimination, write case dispositions, interview witnesses, and act as testers. For example, because of its extensive workload, the Massachusetts Commission Against Discrimination uses volunteers to perform the same tasks as salaried employees. Volunteers are used to locate landlords who discriminate against prospective apartment renters with Section 8 subsidized housing certificates. John Ahearn, who supervises volunteers and paid staff, says that the employees see the volunteers as partners. "The people who work here are devoted to civil rights. They are sophisticated enough to realize that 3,000 people are going to come in here anyway. It's whether they're going to wait one year or 10 years" (Chase, 1992, p. 24–25). The Complaint Handling Unit of the Maryland Attorney General's Division of Consumer Protection is staffed by fifty to seventy-five volunteers who are supervised by paid employees. The volunteers are primarily retired senior citizens who work ten hours a week and commit to the job for six months (Chase, 1992).

If volunteer programs are going to be effective, agencies must work with employees to establish the parameters of volunteer programs. The volunteers with the Massachusetts Commission Against Discrimination were helpful in reducing the workload of the paid staff, but in other situations, such as in Michigan, where layoffs had occurred, volunteers being used to replace paid staff were resented. In most instances, volunteers are used to enhance the effectiveness of paid staff, not to eliminate paid positions or to compensate for deliberately understaffed programs. According to Brudney (1993, p. 130), "The literature leaves no question, however, that volunteer scholars and managers endorse labor's stance that the substitution of nonpaid workers for paid is unethical. No evidence exists that volunteers feel any differently. Hence, if agency administration intend to use volunteers to reallocate funds away from designated positions, they can anticipate resistance from not only employees but also from volunteers."

Attracting Volunteers

The demand for volunteers is rising. Duncombe (1985, 1986) found that in cities with a population of 4,500 or more the problem cited most frequently—more than volunteer supervision, liability coverage, support for managers, and volunteer absenteeism—was "getting enough people to volunteer." A 1994 survey conducted by the Gallup Organization for the INDEPENDENT SECTOR found a decrease in the number of adults over seventeen who volunteered. The survey of 1,509 people revealed a reduction in volunteering from 54 percent in 1989 to 48 percent in 1994 ("Americans Give, Volunteer Less," 1994). Brudney (1993) found that there has been an increase in competition among agencies, both public and nonprofit, for volunteer talent. This increased competition means that agencies have to work harder to attract volunteers.

Volunteer Motivation

Why do individuals volunteer? When surveyed, volunteers expressed a variety of reasons. It appears that both intrinsic and extrinsic rewards motivate volunteers. *Intrinsic rewards* are such things as satisfaction, a sense of accomplishment, and being challenged, which result from the work itself. *Extrinsic rewards* are benefits granted to the volunteers by the organization.

For example, many individuals use volunteering as a means for career exploration and development, such as individuals volunteering at a community nonprofit for developmentally disabled adults, who can thus experience what it is like to work with that population. By volunteering as a reserve police officer, individuals can receive enough exposure to determine whether law enforcement is a correct career choice for them. Some people volunteer to develop skills that might enhance their paid positions. For example, volunteering to make presentations in front of large groups, write grants, or prepare budgets develops essential skills needed by employers.

Some people volunteer because it provides them with the opportunity to meet new and different people. Some volunteer as a way to contribute or give back to the community in which they live. Some professionals, such as nurses and social workers, who are raising small children keep active professionally through volunteer work. Others volunteer as a way to interact with community leaders, or because they value the goals of the agency. Still others volunteer because they are concerned about people, or because they desire personal growth or external recognition (Cnaan & Goldberg-Glen, 1991; Dailey, 1986; Fisher & Cole, 1993; Pearce, 1993).

There is no one reason that individuals volunteer. What motivates one volunteer may not motivate others. Therefore the volunteer experience should attempt to provide both intrinsic and extrinsic rewards, by promoting satisfying and interesting opportunities and some form of external recognition.

Recruitment

The components of recruitment for paid staff discussed in Chapter Six also apply to the recruitment of volunteers, along with some additional issues that need to be addressed. Volunteers are individuals who donate their time, efforts, and experience to an organization without receiving money or in-kind payment (Brudney, 1990). Consequently, there is a lot of competition among public and nonprofit agencies for these quality people.

Unlike paid staff, who typically initiate the employment process themselves, volunteers need to be actively recruited. Communication is the key to finding volunteers. People need to know that the agency is looking for and receptive to volunteers. Word-of-mouth referrals from other volunteers or paid staff, newspaper articles and advertisements, radio and television spots, presentations before community or professional groups, and tapping the relatives and friends of clients have proven to be successful methods for recruiting volunteers. Ellis (1995b) explores the possibilities of using the Internet to recruit volunteers. Individuals with special skills or mutual interests could be targeted. Ellis provides an example of a youth center recruiting a volunteer to run its after-school book club by posting a notice on a computer bulletin board used to discuss book reviews.

The Prerecruitment Process

Before recruitment begins, it is important to identify what type of volunteer is needed and the specific skills that are required. Some agencies might need volunteers to perform clerical or reception-ist duties, which require generic skills, while other agencies may need volunteers capable of coaching an athletic team or writing grant proposals, which require specific skills. Some agencies may need a combination of specialized volunteers and volunteers who can be trained to provide support services to paid staff. Still others can be expected to want volunteers who are qualified to serve by specific education and/or experience, such as city planning com-missions that want to use volunteers to develop and administer zon-ing laws. Some agencies need volunteers for a finite amount of time to focus on one project or program, while other agencies need volunteer support on a continuing basis, such as for a G.E.D. or tutoring program.

During the prerecruitment process it is also important to note whether certain days of the week or set hours are required or whether volunteers may select the days and hours that are most convenient for them. This is important because more women are entering the paid labor force, leaving fewer volunteers available to work traditional daytime hours. Individuals who work full-time jobs may be reluctant to volunteer on an on-going basis. Agencies may need to identify and/or develop projects that do not require long-term commitments. Albuquerque, New Mexico, for example, held a "Paint the Town Day" on which more than five thousand residents volunteered to paint over graffiti that had defaced build-ings. City Hall coordinated the effort, which included local media assisting with publicity, and local businesses and the Air Force base providing materials and volunteers ("Mayors Share Programs That Work," 1995). If one-day programs are not possible, agencies should try to create positions in which the volunteer does not have to be in the office for long periods or can work independently at home (Mergenbagen, 1991). For programs that require consis-tent hours and long-term commitments, agencies may target retired citizens or students, who are likely to be more flexible than working adults.

The agency must be able to communicate what a volunteer position requires, both verbally and with written job descriptions. Each volunteer position should have a description that outlines the job's duties and responsibilities as well as the knowledge, skills, abil-ities, and other characteristics (KSAOCs) required to perform it.

For example, a volunteer bus or van driver might need a chauffeur's license or be required to take a driving test. Work hours should also be included in the description. Prospective volunteers need to be told whether the working hours for a position are flexible or will require a commitment to meet a specific number of hours per week or specific days. In this way they can understand what is expected of them (Alexander, 1991; Anderson & Baroody, 1992).

Volunteers should be asked to complete applications to identify their interests, special skills, and preferred working days and hours. This information enables the organization to match the interest and skills of the volunteers with the positions available in the agency. For example, someone who volunteers for social interaction would be unhappy working in isolation. Exhibit 12.1 presents the application form used by a local government and the accompanying descriptions for volunteer citizen boards and commissions. Notice the variety of skills that the different boards and commissions are seeking. Included are the term lengths and how often meetings are held.

The key to motivating and retaining volunteers is finding the best employee-position match. Research by Dailey (1986) found that job satisfaction plays a critical role in understanding the commitment to volunteer. Because volunteers often fill their higher-order needs through their volunteer activities, it is necessary to design volunteer tasks so that volunteers are enriched. Dailey found that work autonomy, job involvement, and feedback from the work itself were strong predictors of organizational commitment.

An organization wanting to make itself more attractive to potential volunteers might consider reimbursing clients for out-of-pocket expenses such as meals and transportation, providing flexibility in scheduling volunteer hours, increasing position responsibilities, and working with private sector agencies that encourage employee volunteerism. To be competitive in attracting volunteers, agencies must be creative (Brudney, 1990; Mergenbagen, 1991; Watts & Edwards, 1983).

Managing Volunteers

Within organizations that use volunteers, there are two or even three hierarchies: volunteers, paid staff, and professionals (Anderson &

Exhibit 12.1. Information Sheet on Prospective Appointee for Citizen Board or Commission.

1. Name in full_____
   (State whether Mr., Mrs., Miss, or Ms.)

2. Address _____
   (Number)   (Street)   (Ward)

3. Phone_____(Home); _____(Business)

4. Occupation _____ How long?_____

5. Business address_____
   (Number)   (Street)   (City)

6. How many years have you lived in this city?_____

7. Are you a registered voter in this city? ___(Yes) ___(No)

8. Have you ever served on a city board or commission? If so, state name of board or commission _____ (Years)____

9. Comment on your professional background, specialties, training, or abilities.

10. List civic, social, and professional organizations to which you belong.

11. Are you interested in appointment to any particular board or commission?

(Signature)_____

(Date)_____

Please return to: City Clerk

Exhibit 12.1. Information Sheet on Prospective Appointee for Citizen Board or Commission, *continued.*

Descriptions of Volunteer Boards and Commissions

Park Commission

The Park Commission is an advisory body whose duties are to survey and plan for an adequate system of parks and recreational facilities, to approve Park Department rules and regulations, and to advise and investigate problems in administration of the parks. There are nine members on the commission, all of whom must be residents for two years prior to appointment. The Park Commission meets at 7:30 P.M. on the fourth Tuesday of the month (except in December). The term of office is three years.

Board of Appeals

The Board of Appeals (Board of Building Code Appeals) has jurisdiction to hear and decide appeals when it is alleged that there is error in any order, requirement, or decision made by the building commissioner. The board has five citizen members and meets on call. At least three of the members must have ten years of experience as a licensed architect, builder, superintendent of building construction, or licensed professional engineer with structural, civil, or architectural engineering experience. The term of office is five years.

City Plan Commission

The City Plan Commission is responsible for preparing and submitting to the council a master plan for the physical development of the city, and for recommending changes to the plan in the city's interest. The commission also acts as the zoning commission and recommends such changes or amendments as may seem desirable. The commission has seven members, who must have lived in the city for at least two years and be qualified by knowledge and experience to act on questions pertaining to the development of the city and the administration of the zoning laws. The term of office is three years. Ex-officio, nonvoting members include a member of the city council, the city manager, the director of planning, and the zoning administrator. The commission meets on the fourth Wednesday of the month at 7:30 P.M.

Civil Service Board

The Civil Service Board advises the council and director of personnel on problems concerning personnel administration, hears appeals for disciplinary action, makes investigations that it considers necessary into the administration of personnel in the municipal service, and approves civil services rules. The board consists of five members, who must have resided in the city for at least two years prior to their appointment. The term of office is three years. Members of political party committees are not eligible to serve. The board meets quarterly, with additional meetings called by the chair, if necessary.

Baroody, 1992; Fisher & Cole, 1993; Selby, 1978). Volunteers must understand their roles relative to the paid and professional staff. Farr (1983, p. 18) states that "there are two aspects of the staffing issue—who will oversee and coordinate the volunteer effort and how other staff will be involved in working with volunteers." The effectiveness of volunteers will depend on how they are integrated into the organization.

Fisher and Cole (1993) recommend that volunteer programs and positions be developed that directly relate to the organization's mission, and that the organization's mission should reflect a commitment to volunteers. They provide the following example of a program mission statement (p. 28):

The agency's volunteer program promotes quality involvement in the delivery of agency services to families based on the following beliefs:

1. Volunteers bring unique contributions to the delivery of services to families; areas such as prevention, education, and support are best served by their involvement.
2. Volunteers allow the agency to expand its resources and reach more families than it could with paid staff alone.
3. Volunteers bring a useful community perspective to program planning, implementation, and evaluation.
4. Volunteers are strong representatives of the agency throughout the community.

Employee relationships with volunteers are critical. Often there is tension between employees and volunteers. To eliminate this tension, the plans for volunteer staffing should be developed in two distinct phases. First, the organization should examine the tasks that might best be performed by volunteer staff in light of the organization's mission, structure, and personnel policies. Secondly, specific volunteer positions and position guides need to be developed. This step should involve the participation of board members, union leaders, paid staff, direct service volunteers, and clients. It serves to encourage broad support for the volunteer program, as well as to make sure that the creation of volunteer jobs balances the needs of clients, paid staff, and volunteers (Fisher & Cole, 1993, pp. 27, 30–31).

Questions to be considered in the development of volunteer positions and position guides include the following (Fisher & Cole, 1993, pp. 30–31):

What are the characteristics, strengths and needs of the target population?

What qualifications will volunteers need in order to serve this population effectively through the program?

What are the preferences of the target population regarding service delivery by paid staff or volunteers?

How do the possible volunteer positions relate to the overall mission of the agency?

Ellis (1995a) recommends that boards should play key roles in supporting volunteer programs. She suggests that they should expect reports on volunteer involvement, that they should schedule time to discuss volunteers, that board members should refer volunteer candidates to the agency and carry recruitment materials with them to distribute, and that they should take part in volunteer recognition events. Ellis also advises agencies to remember that board members themselves are volunteers despite their legal and fiduciary responsibilities, and attempts should be made to occasionally link board members and direct-service volunteers.

As important as it is for board members to understand the benefits of volunteers, it is more important for paid staff to support volunteer programs. Employees must not feel that volunteers are clients who need attention. Volunteers and staff must be trained to work with each other. Volunteers need to know their scope of authority and when to retreat from interfering with the employees and/or clients.

Organizations that have volunteer programs must also decide whether they need to add a position such as a volunteer coordinator to administer the volunteer program or whether existing employees can assume the responsibilities. According to September McAdoo (former director of development for Places for People in St. Louis, Missouri), the latter is the biggest mistake an organization can make. According to Farr (1983, p. 18) major program management responsibilities include the following:

Obtaining and maintaining support for the volunteer program

Developing, monitoring, and evaluating the volunteer program budget

Keeping key officials informed about the scope of volunteer services

Establishing and monitoring program goals

Assigning volunteer responsibilities and monitoring results

Recommending policy changes or action steps to top management to maintain, improve, or expand the volunteer effort

A variety of administrative tasks need to be taken care of as well. Someone needs to recruit volunteers, provide training and orientation, keep records of their attendance and any expenses for which they might need to be reimbursed, secure liability insurance for volunteers or verify their coverage, work with departments to establish the need for volunteers and develop job descriptions, work with agency supervisors to integrate volunteers into their departments or programs, decide how incentives and rewards will be used to motivate volunteers, and keep volunteers informed about issues that will affect them (Farr, 1983; Fisher & Cole, 1993). Pearce (1993) notes that organizations have less control over the time of volunteers than of employees; thus there needs to be a large pool of volunteers to accommodate different preferences, talents, and time constraints (Montjoy & Brudney, 1991). For these reasons, more and more organizations that rely on volunteer assistance for executing their missions are hiring volunteer coordinators to assume the management and administrative responsibilities.

Orientation and Training

Volunteers should be oriented to the agency's mission, history, accomplishments, fiscal goals, and strategic plan (Alexander, 1991), as well as to what the agency expects from them. It has been suggested that an agency's mission statement should be translated into operational objectives, making it easy for volunteers to see how their contributions reinforce the mission (Muson, 1989). Understanding what the agency is about should increase commitment to its programs.

Volunteers need to be trained. Often employees expect volunteers to be clairvoyant and to know what to do, how to do it, or what the standard operating procedures are. This is a mistake; volunteers do not necessarily have the same expertise or experience that employees have. On-the-job training time should be devoted to providing instructions, answering questions, and allowing the volunteer to witness and absorb how the agency operates. This experience will reduce their insecurity about performing new tasks. Volunteers working for social service or public organizations may need to receive training in appropriate laws or policies, such as client confidentiality; in what to do in case of an emergency; or in how to handle citizens' questions or complaints.

Alexander (1991) found that the organizations with the most formalized training and orientation programs had the least turnover. These programs not only teach volunteers necessary skills; they also serve to clarify expectations and to integrate volunteers socially into the organization. Orientation and training programs also reinforce agency expectations.

Volunteer Recognition

Volunteers and the paid staff who supervise them should be recognized for their efforts. Recognition impresses upon volunteers and staff that their contributions are appreciated by the organization. Research by Cnaan and Goldberg-Glen (1991) indicates that volunteers not only give to the organization, but they also get back some type of reward or satisfaction from volunteering. As discussed earlier, some of these rewards and satisfactions are intrinsic—that is, they are an inherent part of doing the job—such as the satisfaction of task accomplishment, self-development and learning opportunities, self-fulfillment, opportunities for social interaction, and the opportunity to help other people. Other rewards and satisfactions are extrinsic; they are external to the work. Extrinsic rewards are reinforcers that are controlled by the agency—tokens of recognition that compliment volunteers for jobs performed well, including letters of appreciation, awards, and pictures or articles about the volunteer published in the newspaper or agency newsletter. Praise from supervisors and the paid staff, the opportunity to train other volunteers, and expanding the volunteer's area of responsibility are other intangible rewards that agencies often bestow on volunteers. Because individuals volunteer for different reasons, organizations must be prepared to recognize volunteers in a variety of ways.

Evaluation

Performance evaluations inform volunteers about whether they are meeting the supervisor's and agency's expectations. The evaluation must be job related. Volunteers should be assessed on the tasks they perform and on their contributions to the agency. Supervisors and volunteers need to understand each other's expectations and to establish specific goals and objectives to use as evaluation standards. A schedule should be developed so that the performance evaluation takes place at regular intervals.

The primary purposes of evaluation should be to provide feedback and to develop volunteers. Sometimes, however, a volunteer does not meet the agency's expectations. Should this occur, McCurley (1993) recommends that the following steps be taken:

1. *Resupervise:* You may have volunteers who do not understand the policies of the organization, or they may be testing the rules to see what can be expected.
2. *Reassign:* Move volunteers to different positions. The volunteer coordinator may have misread the volunteer's skills, or the volunteer may not be getting along with paid staff or fellow volunteers.
3. *Retrain:* Send the volunteer back for a second training program. Some people take longer to learn new techniques. Do not let the new volunteer's lack of knowledge lead you to believe that he or she is not motivated.
4. *Revitalize:* Long-time volunteers may need a rest. They may not be aware that they are burned out.
5. *Refer:* Refer volunteers to other agencies that are more appropriate to their needs.
6. *Retire:* Allow long-time volunteers the dignity of resigning.

If these steps do not work, you will have to terminate the volunteer. It is important to have policies in place to insure consistent termination procedures. Supervisors should be trained in these steps and in the documentation that may be required before terminating a volunteer.

Governing Boards

Governing boards in the public and nonprofit sectors bear the ultimate accountability for organizational activity and accomplishment; they make policy and provide oversight (Carver, 1990). The duties and authority of public governing boards are regulated by ordinances or statutes, while nonprofit governing boards are regulated by the organization's bylaws. Public boards, whether they are elected or appointed, are typically more bound by legal requirements than are nonprofit boards. There are also a greater variety of statutes establishing and charging public governing boards (Carver, 1990, p. 215).

Public sector governing boards deal primarily with particular aspects of policymaking, such as planning, personnel or civil service, parks and recreation, zoning and building, and probation and corrections (Baker, 1994). What differentiates most public sector governing boards from those in the nonprofit sector is that they typically serve in only an advisory capacity; final approval or decisions are made by the legislative body (Baker, 1994). Governmental board members may be appointed by elected officials, or elected directly by citizens. The provisions that govern local government boards and commissions are typically found in the community's ordinances, or they are required by state statute. Members of both types of boards, however, play important policymaking roles and serve as volunteers.

In nonprofit organizations, directors or trustees typically develop policies relating to the organization's management. It is the responsibility of the directors to make sure that the public purpose of the nonprofit organization is carried out. Ingram (1988) identifies the basic responsibilities of nonprofit boards:

1. Determining the organization's mission and purposes and setting policies for its operation
2. Selecting the executive and evaluating executive performance
3. Ensuring effective organizational planning by engaging in long-range planning to establish its future course

4. Ensuring adequate resources by establishing fiscal policy and boundaries and seeing that resources are managed effectively
5. Determining and monitoring the organization's programs and services
6. Enhancing the organization's public image by promoting the work of the organization
7. Serving as a court of appeal for employees with grievances
8. Assessing its own performance in relation to its responsibilities

As the following excerpts from newspaper editorials indicate, the oversight responsibilities of nonprofit governing boards have come under closer scrutiny following the well-publicized controversies of prominent nonprofit organizations ("Sampling of Newspaper Editorials," 1995):

From *The New York Times:*
The Aramony scandal hurt local United Ways all over the country, although they had no hand in it. More important, it signaled the businessmen and women who sit on charity boards—Mr. Aramony's and others as well—they are guardians of the public's trust, and must not treat the responsibility casually. . . . The United Way of America may be clean these days, but only because of a crisis that could have been avoided if its trustees had not been so trusting.

From *The Washington Post:*
Charity depends on trust. The United Way, nationally and locally, is at work rebuilding trust. But it's hard work and apparently will take a long time. While the crimes are Mr. Aramony's—and those of the two subordinates, Stephen J. Paulachak and Thomas J. Merlo, who were convicted with him—much blame also rests with the board of directors that was responsible for United Way of America in the years these offenses took place. The whole case is a terrible warning to charitable boards to resist the temptation to turn meetings into pleasant social events only briefly interrupted by a cursory glance at a sheet of figures.

From *The Chronicle of Philanthropy:*
The collapse of a double-your-money fundraising scheme may have seriously damaged the credibility of many American charities. The Foundation for New Era Philanthropy had promised that anonymous philanthropists would match money put up by charities and

donors. But New Era filed for bankruptcy last month and faces lawsuits by federal and state regulators and at least one charity. The immediate losers are the roughly 300 charities and donors with millions of dollars on account with New Era. The group owes about $200 million but has only $30 million, according to the U.S. Bankruptcy Court.

The effects could be much wider. A *Chronicle of Philanthropy* survey has found that the New Era scandal damaged donor confidence in fundraisers and charities. In the survey, 95 percent of wealthy donors from across the country said that they would now be more skeptical of claims made by fundraisers and nonprofit executives ("A Debacle for Charities' Credibility," 1995, p. 1).

Houle (1989, p. 6) defines a governing board as "an organized group of people with the collective authority to control and foster an institution that is usually administered by a qualified executive and staff." Board members are volunteers, and like most volunteers, they join boards for a variety of reasons. Research on the motivations of citizens serving on public sector boards indicates that they expect to receive certain benefits, and there are a number of selective incentives. Baker (1994), citing Clark and Wilson (1961) and Widmer (1985), identifies five types of incentives: material, solidary, purposive, developmental, and service. *Material incentives* are tangible rewards such as the opportunity to advance politically or the opportunity to make professional contacts. *Solidary incentives* are intangible rewards such as socializing, a sense of group membership, status, and sense of involvement. *Purposive incentives* are also intangible and relate to the satisfaction or gratification of working toward the stated goals of the organization. *Developmental incentives* are intangible rewards such as the ability to assume civic responsibility or to use acquired knowledge; they are geared to improving or using one's capabilities. Finally, *service incentives* include fulfilling or reducing a sense of civic responsibility; they are focused on relieving or fulfilling one's sense of obligation. Different board members, like other volunteers, are motivated by different incentives. Personal enrichment, substantive interest, social and business contacts, and feelings of accomplishment are just some of the reasons why individuals become board members.

But what should an organization look for in board members?

Characteristics identified by O'Connell (1988) and Houle (1989) include distributions in age, sex, location of residence, representatives of the constituency being served by the organization, political contacts, clientele, expertise, and training in the following areas: personnel, finance, law, fundraising, and public relations. Each board member should have KSAOCs that enhance the policymaking and oversight responsibilities of the board as a whole.

To select new board members, the existing board or nominating committee should identify the characteristics needed in new board members. The KSAOCs should relate to the organization's mission and objectives. To determine what KSAOCs are needed, the incumbent board members should be evaluated (Houle, 1989; Joyaux, 1991). Exhibit 12.2 presents a grid that identifies the match among the relevant criteria and the incumbent board members. Notice that space is permitted to add prospective board members to the grid.

The grid identifies five criteria for determining the composition of the board:

1. There should be a greater spread in the ages of the members of the board.
2. The board should be representative of the whole urban community.
3. The board should be evenly divided between men and women.
4. Major ethnic groups should be represented in roughly the same proportion as is found in the population served.
5. Board members should have expertise or substantive knowledge about the programs provided by the agency, or skills in personnel, finance, public relations, law, and building maintenance and acquisition.

This particular board has fifteen members serving three-year terms. Look at the members with expiring terms and determine which characteristics are needed to balance out the board member grid.

After reviewing the KSAOCs needed by new board members, the names of possible new members should be identified. These names might be retrieved from a list of people previously considered as board members; professional people whose names are

Exhibit 12.2. Grid for Matching Present and Potential Board Members.

Criteria	Present Board Members										Potential Board Members				
	A	B	C	D	E	F	G	H	I	J	V	W	X	Y	Z
Age															
Under 35	X	X					X								
From 35 to 50					X										
From 51 to 65															
Over 65		X		X		X		X	X	X					
Gender															
Women	X	X		X		X		X	X						
Men			X				X			X					
Residence															
Central city	X		X		X	X		X		X					
North side		X	X					X							
West side									X						
South side															
Suburbs				X			X								
Background															
Black	X														
White		X	X	X		X		X	X						
Hispanic					X					X					
Asian															
Responsibilities															
Program		X	X	X		X	X	X							
Personnel	X		X						X	X					
Finance	X									X					
Public relations		X				X	X	X	X	X					
Legal								X		X					
Building					X										

Source: Houle, 1989, p. 40. Used by permission.

given to the agency by a board bank sponsored by the United Way or Junior League; other volunteers; or individuals providing professional services to the agency. People associated with the agency, such as clients, employees, or present board members, often recommend prospective board members.

Nonprofits need to be vigilant about recruiting board members committed to serving the organization's best interests. For example, for many years before John Ott became the executive director of the Atlanta Historical Society, the board functioned more as a social group than a policymaking body. Since Ott became executive director, the board's focus has changed. One board member stated, "Now it's much more serious. We discuss puzzlements and long-range planning" (Knauft, Berger, & Gray, 1991, p. 10).

Agencies need to seek members who have special skills they can bring to the board. For example, Seattle Emergency Housing made a point of recruiting a former budget analyst at the United Way to review its financial statements, as well as a city employee with expertise and knowledge about public funding (Knauft, Berger, & Gray, 1991). Bylaws or statutes usually specify the procedures that should be followed to formally nominate candidates, as well as the selection procedures. Refer to the relevant policies and procedures for your organization.

After new board members have been selected, they should be provided with an orientation outlining their responsibilities as board members. They should also be informed about the organization's mission, objectives, and administrative/management structures. Morrison (1994, p. 43) recommends that the following information be provided to board members:

Constitution and bylaws

Organization's mission or purpose statement

Organization's goals and current plans, strategic and long-range

Annual report

Budget and financial report

Program description/goals and objectives

Organization chart (staff names and numbers)

Committees—their goals and plans, such as fundraising expectations and commitments, and public relations strategies

Personnel policies and expectations

List of board members with names, addresses, and phone numbers

Meeting information and attendance/time requirements

Minutes from meetings for previous fiscal year

Any appropriate procedures governing conduct of meetings

Any evaluations conducted during the previous year

Training and orientation are important for all board members regardless of their professional expertise and experience. Bowen (1994) acknowledges that when people from the for-profit sector join a nonprofit board they often lack an appropriate frame of reference as to the nature of the missions served by nonprofits. Bowen cites the following example: "A business man on the board of directors for a church kept pushing for 'double-digit' growth no matter what the implications were for the church's capacity to fulfill its mission" (p. 41). Herzlinger (1994) notes that board members may be perplexed about their appropriate roles. Because some board members are intimidated about the talent and professional expertise of the organization's employees, they abandon their oversight role. "How can I tell a symphony orchestra how to play Beethoven? How can I tell a doctor how to operate?" (p. 53). Other board members become overly involved in the organization's work. They feel free to give unsolicited and unwanted counsel on orchestra programs, museum exhibitions, educational curricula, or social service intervention strategies. Still other board members pour themselves into fundraising, while others use their appointment for status seeking and social climbing. According to Herzlinger, the role of a board's director is to ensure that the organization's mission is appropriate to its charitable orientation, and that it accomplishes its mission efficiently.

Board members must be prepared to assume responsibility for guiding the agency. Bowen (1994) notes that often hard-nosed businesspeople become permissive when serving on a board of directors. He provides an example of the board at a private school with severe financial difficulties that approved a request for new equipment the school could not afford because the board could not say no to such dedicated teachers (p. 39). In another case, a board of directors felt guilty about the low salary given to the director of a small arts organization, so it granted her permission to take the summer off (p. 39).

Board members, like other volunteers, should be evaluated on their performance and the contributions they make to the agency. Board members who miss meetings, or who are unprepared when they do attend should be held accountable. The fiduciary and oversight responsibilities of governing boards necessitate that members be individuals who are committed to the agency for the length of their terms. Organizations cannot afford to retain board members who dismiss their responsibilities.

(Further in-depth knowledge of governing boards is also provided by Carver, 1990, and Houle, 1989, and by publications from the National Volunteer Center.)

Summary

Volunteers have become an integral part of public and nonprofit organizations. Despite the belief of some that volunteers take paid positions away from employees, volunteers typically perform tasks that otherwise would not get done or would have to be handled by already overextended employees.

The guidance and support provided to volunteers and incumbent staff are essential to the successful integration of volunteers into the agency, to their performance, and to the achievement of agency goals. To minimize any conflicts, staff-development programs should be provided that communicate the differences in authority and responsibilities between paid staff and volunteers.

Agencies should develop volunteer recruitment strategies to reach individuals whose interests and skills are likely to match the needs of the organization. To facilitate good staffing decisions, key staff should be involved in the development of job descriptions for the volunteers they will supervise or work beside. Volunteers should receive training on how to perform their tasks and on the performance standards of the agency.

Agencies alone should not benefit from the use of volunteers. The volunteer experience should provide individuals with opportunities for personal and professional growth.

Chapter Thirteen

Emerging Issues

Part One of this book addressed many of the changes that are impacting public and nonprofit sector workplaces. Public and non-profit administrators must contend with new workplace structures and employee concerns brought on by a variety of economic, technological, legal, and cultural changes. Privatization or contracting-out services, violence in the workplace, alternative dispute resolution, the expansion of computer technology in the workplace, and technological advances that are changing the administration of human resources responsibilities are a few examples of the issues that need to be addressed by management, if they have not already been addressed.

Consider the following examples:

- In 1992, the Massachusetts Highway Department (MassHighway) privatized 1,450 miles of highway in Essex County along the state's north shore for a one-year trial period. A study by the John F. Kennedy School of Government at Harvard University found that the quality of maintenance was improved and the contractor was more cost-effective (Kostro, 1994).
- In Alton, Illinois, a client of a community mental health center that housed a methadone treatment clinic shot and killed the director of the treatment program while another client was in the director's office. The client with the gun ran through the hallway and threatened to kill his counselor before exiting the building and shooting himself in the parking lot.
- The Texas Commission on Human Rights implemented a pilot alternative dispute resolution program to process employment discrimination complaints. During the pilot program, 30 percent

of the cases that were referred to mediation were resolved within thirty days ("New Processes May Speed," 1995).

• In Escondido, California, public library patrons check out books on their own. A color monitor guides customers through each step of the transaction with graphics and on-screen prompts. A library card is placed inside the unit, which accesses a personal account. A scanner reads the book's bar code, records the transaction, electronically deprograms the book so it will pass through security, and prints a due-date slip to complete the transaction. This technology has freed up staff to serve customers and perform other functions ("Public Library Patrons," 1995).

• The federal government has established a satellite work station located seventy-five miles outside of Washington, D.C. The work station is equipped with telephones, computers, and fax machines that allow employees who live in the area to telecommute to their jobs in Washington for part of the work week (U.S. Office of Personnel Management, 1994).

This chapter provides a cursory overview of privatization or contracting-out services, violence in the workplace, alternative dispute resolution, and changes in information and computer technology.

Privatization or Contracting-Out Services

Privatization or contracting-out occurs when public sector agencies contract with nonprofit, private, or other public agencies to provide specific services. A typical privatization agreement specifies that a private or nonprofit entity is responsible for producing particular services. The public employer chooses the service level and pays the amount specified in the contract, but leaves decisions about production methods to the contracted firm. From an administrative perspective, privatization is often viewed as a way to save tax dollars, reduce the public payrolls, minimize government spending, and boost productivity. Supporters claim that contracting-out government programs will lead to greater efficiency and more effective operations. They maintain that competition and fewer restrictions allow the contractors to be more cost-efficient and responsive, and that cost savings can be achieved through the economies of scale used by one vendor to provide services to many communities and organizations. It is believed that nonprofit and private firms, not hampered by bureaucratic rules and regulations, can be more innovative than public sector ones. When Hinesville, Georgia, for example, contracted out its entire public works department, it found that computerization introduced by the company made city functions more efficient (Ward, 1993, p. 48). Other services that have been contracted out are refuse collection, street cleaning, ground maintenance, and the management of sports and leisure facilities. Mayor Daley of Chicago has privatized janitorial services, parking garages, tire collection, abandoned car removal, golf course management, window washing, equipment and fleet maintenance, and drug addiction treatment (Mahtesian, 1994, p. 26).

Privatization is controversial. It often results in job loss, invokes the ire of public unions, in some cases has led to poorer service, and establishes the need for oversight responsibilities and monitoring of the contractee's performance. Monitoring is designed to uncover discrepancies between the contract provision and the contract itself (Prager, 1994). In the public sector, elected officials are still responsible to the citizens for the provision of efficient and quality services. After a snowstorm, for instance, snow needs to be removed in a timely fashion, whether it be by public employees or a contracted firm.

When public services are contracted-out, the employees who used to provide them may be adversely affected. They must be transferred to different departments or hired by the contractor at lower salaries and with fewer benefits. Needless to say, contracting-out is typically opposed by public sector unions. The job security of union members is put at risk, as well as the union's survival. Public services not represented by a union are more likely to be contracted-out (Chandler & Feuille, 1994).

If agencies decide to privatize, they should attempt to make the transition fair to employees. If the contractee will not hire incumbent employees, then the incumbents should be provided with severance packages or retraining. An adversarial shift to privatization will spill over to other areas of governance. Other employees will view the administration with suspicion and feel insecure about their positions.

When one thinks of privatization or of contracting-out services, typically whole departments are envisioned. But another option for employers is to contract-out for specific skills when they are needed. According to Durning (1995), contracting-out provides options for employers when hiring permanent staff is not feasible. Individuals with specialized technical skills such as accounting, architecture, building and safety, finance, purchasing, and telecommunications can be hired on an as-needed basis for a fixed amount of time. This allows organizations to be more flexible and to provide greater control over labor costs. In these cases, a nonprofit or private company refers to the employer one or more candidates to do the desired work. The employer or department head assumes day-to-day supervisory responsibility while the contracting company is responsible for payroll preparation, distribution and tax deposits, workers compensation, fringe benefits, and federal and state governmental reporting requirements.

A variety of services are contracted-out by public employers. Tarpon Springs, Florida, contracts-out day care services; Palmetto, Florida, contracts-out its wastewater treatment plant; Richmond Heights, Missouri, contracts-out animal control; Farmers Branch, Texas, contracts with private tax attorneys for delinquent tax collection services; Florence, Kentucky, contracts-out payroll services; Warren, New Jersey, contracts-out public health services for the operation of its Tuberculosis Lab and Sexually Transmitted Disease Clinic; West Hollywood, California, contracts-out its parking meter maintenance and parking enforcement services; and Cadillac, Michigan, contracts-out its fall leaf collection services ("Tap into 3,000 City Programs," 1995).

As with most decisions, there are pluses and minuses to privatization. For privatization to be effective, certain conditions must be present. There needs to be competition, because without competition there is little reason to be efficient. Monitoring is critical; government must provide oversight and hold the contractee accountable for poor service. And finally, the public's interest should be a priority (Hass, 1993). Some services are best left in-house. Prager (1994) uses as an example the services provided by an emergency hospital. It may be cost-efficient to contract-out emergency services, but what if the contractee left the community or was forced to close its doors due to fiscal hardships? The community would be left without a care provider. The decision to privatize should not be capricious; instead, it should be the result of a thoughtful and comprehensive decision-making process. The reactions of employees, clients, and citizens as well as the fiscal implications and quality of services must all be considered.

Violence in the Workplace

More than one year after being fired and vowing revenge, on February 9, 1996, Clifton McCree returned to his former place of employment and killed five former coworkers and himself. Fourteen months earlier, McCree had been fired for flunking a drug test, harassing and threatening coworkers, and being rude to the public. The gunman accused his ex-bosses of racism and economic lynching. He claimed he could no longer support his family and wanted to punish coworkers who had contributed to the loss of his job. McCree had worked for the City of Fort Lauderdale as a park department beach cleaner for eighteen years. According to the city manager, counseling was offered to McCree, who refused it, because "he felt as though nothing was wrong with him" ("Man Takes Revenge," 1996).

On July 9, 1995, postal supervisor James Whopper III was shot to death by postal employee Bruce Clark. Both employees had blemish-free personnel files, and witnesses said that Clark and Whopper did not appear to be arguing when Clark shot Whopper twice during their Sunday morning graveyard shift. A postal union official said that Whopper was known as a strict disciplinarian, and a friend of Clark's said that Clark had complained that he was being singled out for discipline (Johnson & Glionna, 1995).

Nearly one million individuals per year become victims of violent crime while working or on duty. The National Crime Victimization Survey reports that "crime victimization occurring in the workplace costs about half a million employees 1,751,000 days of work each year, an average of 3.5 days per crime" (Bachman, 1994, p. 1). Federal, state, or local government employees are the most likely victims of workplace violence. Thirty-eight U.S. Postal Service (USPS) employees have been killed since 1986 (Duncan, 1995). The death of James Whopper in the summer of 1995 brings the total to thirty-nine.

In an attempt to eliminate the violence in its work sites, the USPS has established six strategies designed to defuse hostile situations. The areas to which these strategies pertain are the selection of job candidates, the physical security of the work environment, the establishment of an overall policy on violence, improvement of the workplace climate, the provision of support systems for employees, and the development of new separation procedures. Local USPS managers, supervisors, and union officials are also being required to attend an eight-hour training program that includes a videotape depicting three scenarios of workplace problems and presents information on conflict resolution, crisis management, and identifying management tools that can be used to avert violence (Winsten, 1995).

Other vulnerable employers are health care facilities. The violence they face, however, is usually not from employees but from outsiders, usually family members. To protect its approximately one thousand employees from outside threats, the National Rehabilitation Hospital in Washington, D.C., has established a security program that includes careful sign-in procedures and cameras that monitor secluded areas. Employees are advised to avoid isolated areas like stairwells. An escort program is utilized to protect employees as they travel to and from their jobs, and self-defense programs are provided. The Mount Sinai Medical Center in New York City trains its approximately fourteen thousand employees in how to handle problem patients. Employees providing direct services receive special instruction on how to recognize and handle potentially dangerous or abusive patients (Overman, 1995).

Because violence in the workplace has become so pervasive, the North Carolina State Government has formed the Task Force on Violence in the Workplace, with the following mission: "To develop policy, procedures, strategies, and training for the prevention and management of violence in the workplace for North Carolina State Government" ("Stop the Violence," 1995). The task force developed a survey to study the existing climate, attitudes, and needs of the workforce. The survey was administered to more than one thousand state employees. Twenty-four percent of the respondents felt that harassment, threats, physical attacks, or intentional property damage was a problem; 36 percent were aware of some forms of violence. Name calling and the use of obscenities in the workplace were the most common abuses at 83 percent, followed by physical violence at 63 percent, pushing at 33 percent, and hitting with hands at 29 percent. Sixty percent of the respondents said that customers or clients were the most frequent offenders, that other employees contributed to 30 percent of the incidents, and that supervisors contributed to 23 percent of the violent acts. The predominant causes for the violence were conflicts with colleagues, autocratic supervisors, and racial tension.

The increase in the number of violent workplace incidents over the last decade has focused attention on its causes as well as on the employer's responsibilities (Elliott & Jarrett, 1994; Johnson & Indvik, 1994; Travnick, 1994). Some of the reasons suggested for the increase include

Organizational downsizing and layoffs, leading to concerns about economic security

Autocratic work environments, leading to feelings of powerlessness and frustration

Domestic violence spilling into the workplace

Lack of recourse for employees who have been fired or who feel they have been mistreated

Demands for increased productivity with no increases in pay

Drug and substance abuse in the workplace, leading to decreased inhibitions against violence

Organizations that fail to take any precautions against potentially violent situations may find themselves facing a lawsuit over negligent security. Specific danger areas are negligent hiring, negligent supervision, and negligent retention (Johnson & Indvik, 1994).

Because violence is in part an uncontrolled expression of built-up stress, it has been suggested that organizations should review which elements of their human resources management (HRM) system can be used to defuse stress (Elliott & Jarrett, 1994). Ten elements that merit review are discussed in the following paragraphs.

Job analysis. A systematic job analysis should identify the prerequisite KSAOCs required for a job. The job analysis should help agencies recruit individuals who possess those characteristics and who are able to perform or learn the tasks, which should minimize frustrated employees. Jobs with a high risk of violence should be identified, and precautions to minimize risk should be emphasized.

Selection process. The use of particular selection instruments should be validated. They should screen out candidates who are unable to adequately perform the required job duties. Tests, applications, interviews, and reference checks can be used to discover nonapparent personality or work-related attitudes. When feasible, thorough background checks should be conducted.

Performance evaluation processes. Supervisors need to be trained in providing timely, constructive feedback to their staff. The feedback should be provided in a helpful and nonconfrontational manner. Any verbal or physical threats should be documented and reported to management.

Training and development. Organizations need to provide training and development opportunities so that employees can upgrade their skills as the demands of their jobs change. All employees should receive training on how to recognize the signs of a potentially violent person. Warning signs of possible violent acts are being argumentative, not cooperating well with others, having problems with authority figures, frequently blaming others for one's problems, and being involved with alcohol or drugs (DeJong, 1994).

Probationary period. The probationary period should be used to closely monitor an employees' performance of job tasks and interactions with coworkers and management. Danger signals should not be ignored, and if warranted, the probationary period should be extended.

Grievance procedures. To resolve disputes in nonunionized environments, organizations should have a system to resolve employee grievances, thereby reducing employee feelings of powerlessness. The Labor-Management Relations Act, the Federal Labor Relations Authority, and the public employee relations acts require that a grievance procedure be included in every collective bargaining contract.

Employee assistance programs (EAPS). EAPs should be available to employees who need counseling and other types of assistance. Chronically poor work performance, conflicts with supervisors and other employees, unfounded grievances and complaints, and the abuse of sick leave are symptoms of stress. Providing stress management, employee wellness services, financial advice, and out-placement services may help to decrease incidents of workplace violence.

Disciplinary policies and procedures. Due process protections and progressive discipline policies should be in place. The objective of the disciplinary process should be to improve performance and not to punish or denigrate the employee.

Rewards and incentive systems. Organizations must ensure that superior performance is recognized and that employees with unacceptable performance are held accountable. Discrimination, partisan loyalty, and favoritism do not belong in organizations' recognition and reward systems.

Crisis management system. There should be a comprehensive plan to address violence in the workplace. Issues such as the physical arrangement of offices, the distribution of keys, and access of visitors to employees, files, and computers should be reviewed. Should a violent incident occur, a crisis management team should be available to direct employees and handle emergency procedures.

Alternative Dispute Resolution

Alternative dispute resolution (ADR) is the name given to a variety of techniques used by organizations to resolve workplace disputes. ADR has been credited for minimizing the expenses, time delays, and adversarial postures typically found in litigation. ADR techniques have been instituted as a means to preserve and improve workplace relationships, and to reduce lawsuits (Carver & Vondra, 1994; Fitzpatrick, 1994; Wilensky & Jones, 1994; Yarborough, 1994).

Forty-six states and approximately twelve hundred courts are utilizing ADR as a way to resolve workplace disputes (Dick, 1994). The use of ADR is supported by the courts as a way to reduce their backlog of cases. The National Center for State Courts indicates that the average civil case filed with state courts takes approximately fourteen months to be resolved, and in some locations, even longer. In Chicago, civil cases are backlogged up to eight years, and in New York some judges have as few as seventeen minutes to review a civil case (Ide, 1993). Employers and employees may have to wait for years before their cases reach the federal courts.

Employees, unions, and management all promote ADR as a way to resolve workplace disputes. ADR has been successful in settling grievances; it is considered to be more cost-effective than going to trial, and decisions are made in a shorter time frame. Better results are often achieved because employees and management participate in reaching the agreement together without much of the acrimony that permeates formal trials or hearings (Carnevale, 1993; McDermott, 1995).

The USPS developed an ADR program called Union Management Pairs (UMP). UMP are teams that comprise a National Association of Letter Carriers union representative and a management representative. The teams work with frontline supervisors and union stewards to settle any contract violations or misunderstandings when they first arise, before they escalate into major confrontations. UMP teams are called in after supervisors, union stewards, or, if necessary, upper-management cannot resolve a problem. A UMP team reviews the facts surrounding the case, analyzes the information collected by the steward and supervisor, and suggests nonbinding recommendations. If the parties are dissatisfied with the recommendation of the UMP team, they still are provided with the opportunity to file a formal grievance and proceed through the grievance procedure established in the collective bargaining contract. The intent of the UMP process is to resolve the dispute by the use of objective parties before a formal hearing becomes necessary (Anfuso, 1994; Hughes & Grote, 1993; Seeley, 1992; Wilensky & Jones, 1994).

Nonunionized employers also use a variety of ADR techniques. Some of these are described in the following paragraphs.

Settlement conference. Settlement conferences are meetings of the disputing parties designed to resolve the dispute early on. Usually each side is represented by an executive with decision-making authority who is not involved in the dispute.

Mediation. Mediation uses the services of a neutral third-party, who helps the parties reach a settlement. As in collective bargaining contract impasses, the mediator's involvement is not binding on the parties. The purpose of mediation is to get the parties to talk to one another and suggest possible solutions.

Summary jury trials. In a summary jury trial, a court will direct the parties to present arguments before a mock jury panel. Such trials are used to help the parties better understand how cases might be considered by a jury, and thus encourage settlements.

Arbitration. In arbitration the parties present the facts of their case to a neutral third party who renders a decision that is binding.

Minitrial. The procedures for minitrials vary. Typically, one high-level executive from each side (but one not involved in the case) and one neutral individual preside over a trial. The parties exchange documents and briefs, and they may engage in discovery motions and take witnesses' testimony. The case is presented before the panel, which settles the dispute.

Peer review boards. Peer review boards are panels composed of employees who have volunteered and received training to be peer review panelists. Employees who have a complaint that cannot be resolved by their supervisors have the opportunity to take their grievance or complaint to a panel composed of employees and some management representatives. While peer review boards differ across organizations, usually there is at least one member from management on the panel. The panel will hear the grievance and render a decision. Peer review boards may not determine policy; instead, they interpret how policies have been applied.

Employers should consider using ADR to resolve workplace disputes. ADR has been found to expedite workplace justice, minimize the costs typically associated with grievance arbitration or lawsuits, and establish a more supportive relationship between labor and management.

Computer Technology and HRM

Computers and information technology have been changing the way public and nonprofit organizations operate (Dawes, 1994; Halachmi, 1991). In the early days of computer use in organizations, they were used mostly for repetitive functions such as billing and processing taxes. Today computers are used to track child support payments, and some cities are using voice-automated systems that enable citizens to call local governments at any time to reserve public facilities or schedule a round of golf. In Louisiana, the state's Child Support Enforcement Division created an automated telephone system to provide public access to specific case information twenty-four hours a day, seven days a week. In Sacramento and San Diego counties, residents can use video kiosks placed in malls, supermarkets, and government offices to find out about job openings, to order copies of birth certificates, to check on beach conditions, and to learn how to apply for government services and benefits (Polilli, 1993).

In some instances, the use of computers has enabled organizations to grow without having to add more staff. The Texas Rehabilitation Commission converted paper files to a computer-assisted retrieval system. With the new system, one clerk was able to handle a job that previously required three clerks (Calbreath, 1986). In Dade County, Florida, the public can dial in by computer to get civil and criminal court information, property appraisal records, tax collection information, occupational licenses, and building and zoning information ("Broward Courts to Go Online," 1995).

The Connecticut State Police and the Hartford Police Department are two law enforcement agencies that have adopted "pen computing." Pen computing is a pen-based technology that operates as handwriting on a computer screen. The pen also acts as a mouse for choosing icons and enables the computer to decipher its user's handwriting. It is a battery-operated, lightweight, hand-held device. Police officers can fill out incident forms right on the screen. The pen eliminates the need for data processors to input the report. One pen-computing system also offers accident and crime scene diagrams. Officers can select roadway configurations and then drag icons across the screen or draw directly on it to depict accident scenes. Officers in Connecticut estimated that using the computer pen they saved approximately eight hours a week in the reporting process (Massino, 1995).

Nonprofits are also relying more on computers to disseminate and receive information. The Foundation Center uses the Internet to list Foundation Center libraries and to provide tips for seeking grants. It also has an electric version of the center's biweekly publication, *Philanthropy News Digest* ("Foundation Center Puts Information," 1995).

Two graduate students at the University of Michigan's School of Information and Library Studies compiled a listing called *Internet Resources for Non-Profit Public Service Organizations*. It provides information classified according to various causes, from youth to emergency services to substance abuse. Impact Online, located in

Palo Alto, California, is using the Internet to encourage residents to fight homelessness and other social problems. It includes statistics, essays, and pictures about homelessness in its offerings. It also directs users to charities that deal with specific social problems. For example, it provides information on a charity called Golden Gate Community, which claims to turn a $15 donation into ten meals and ten nights of shelter for a homeless person. Impact Online has also prepared a guide for charity officials on how computer technology can advance their causes, including examples of charities already using the Internet ("New Guide to Resources," 1995).

Computer technologies are beginning to influence the way organizations are structured and work teams are formed. Employees can communicate through e-mail, teleconferencing, and videoconferencing, enabling them to work at diverse geographic locations and even at home. The federal government has established the Federal Flexible Workplace Program, commonly referred to as flexiplace, for employees who do not have to be in their office and in person to perform their jobs. Employees may work from their homes or satellite work stations close to their homes. Employees can log into the office server and access their e-mail or connect to the Internet. Employee participants in the program report increased job satisfaction and reduced commuting time and transportation costs. Flexiplace is an attractive option that employers can use to recruit and retain employees. It can also reduce facility costs by enabling coworkers with complementary telecommuting schedules to share the same work space. Research on the federal pilot programs found that flexiplace programs have positive impacts on job performance, quality-of-work issues, and operational costs, and bring about reductions in vehicle and sick leave usage and improvements in employee health and stress (Joice, 1993).

For flexiplace programs to be successful, certain operational guidelines should be established. For example, employers should consult with unions, if applicable, to make sure that the terms of collective bargaining agreements are not being violated; that only employees with experience in their jobs and who perform at satisfactory or higher levels are selected for participation; that supervisors and employees attend training and orientation sessions; that a work agreement or contract between employees and management is established so that in case the project fails to meet organizational needs it will be discontinued, or that employees may choose to discontinue participation if the program does not meet their needs; and that employees and supervisors schedule time to meet with one another. Comprehensive planning should take place before flexiplace programs are implemented.

Changes in organizational design and structure have resulted from flexiplace arrangements and from increased reliance on computers and other technology. One caveat to the increasing use of technology is the elimination of face-to-face personal interactions. Halachmi (1991) cautions that "as hardware and software become the gatekeepers that lower or deny access to group resources, the natural boundaries of the group are diffused. Intimacy, belonging, and the feeling of control over criteria for membership in the group are missing when a workgroup is formed only by the sharing of information" (p. 329). Interpersonal relationships that may be necessary for program or agency success may suffer. Organizations will have to work to integrate the concepts of total quality management, participative decision making, and work teams into long-distance employee relationships.

Computer technology is being used to monitor employee performance and productivity. Concerns have been raised in regard to invasions of work privacy through electronic monitoring and home inspections. Computers can be programmed to count the number of keystrokes per minute input by clerical employees.

The impacts of technology on the job security of employees is a matter of concern for public unions. Promotional material developed by the American Federation of State, County, and Municipal Employees (AFSCME) in 1985 stated the following: "AFSCME wants technology applied in ways which will benefit the people we represent, as well as the public we serve. Technology must be used to expand skills and responsibilities, not narrow them; and to affirm the worker's role in providing public services, not eliminate it (Klay, 1988, p. 59).

Another concern about the expansion of technology in the workplace is the affect it will have on employees' skills. Will a technology advance the skills of incumbent employees or replace them? Klay (1988, p. 60) offers this example: "The need for welfare intake counselors to spend many months mastering the intricacies of eligibility rules is giving way to computer programs that automatically determine eligibility. The position of intake counselor is deskilled if counselors become hardly more than reception clerks who only ask prescribed questions and enter responses into the computer, but the position is enskilled if counselors receive training in social work and can deal with a broader range of clients' problems." Organizations introducing new technology must be prepared to bear the expense and training time needed to develop new skills in their employees and involve unions in the planning process so that technology is not resisted.

Technological Changes in HRM Administration

Technological advances have not only changed how organizations are structured and work is performed, but they have begun to change the tasks of HRM specialists. Computers are being used to perform many of the functions for which employees were once responsible.

Computers are used to advertise job vacancies in public places and on computer bulletin boards. Citizens can dial in or push appropriate buttons to see what agencies are recruiting and for what types of positions. Computers have also been used to replace interpersonal screening and interviewing. Computer-assisted screening exists by which applicants are screened over the telephone. A digitized voice asks applicants to respond to a variety of job-related questions, inquiring about work experience, attitudes, interests, and skills.

Many civil service systems have adopted computerized testing. Applicants read questions off of a computer screen and use the computer to select the correct answer. Tests that require the ability to read, write, and follow oral and visual instructions have been developed that utilize interactive video and multimedia. The computer will score exams as soon as the candidates complete them, immediately notifying the candidates of the results.

Tasks that used to require many human hours of retrieving data from archival files can now easily be performed by computers. Administrative responsibilities such as tracking applicants and employees for equal opportunity and affirmative action goals and timetables is being done by computers. Computer programs are also being used for salary administration and performance evaluations. Benefits administration is increasingly being done through computer technology. Interactive voice response systems are providing twenty-four-hour access to retirement plan enrollment, savings plan inquiries and enrollment, and medical plan inquiries. With more and more information being compiled into agency databases it is imperative that security measures be developed that protect sensitive or confidential information such as medical records and employee personnel files.

Increases in the uses of information technology require different combinations of skills and other resources. As public and nonprofit organizations confront these challenges, strategic human resources management will become even more important. Innovative human resources strategies will be imperative and necessary to assist organizations to prepare for changing missions, priorities, and programs.

Summary

This chapter has addressed five workplace issues presently affecting public and nonprofit HRM: privatization or contracting-out services, violence in the workplace, alternative dispute resolution, the expansion of computer technology in the workplace, and technological advances that are changing the administration of human resources responsibilities. These issues are only the tip of the iceberg; administrators can anticipate even more changes as economic, technological, legal, and cultural changes result in additional downsizing, deregulation, and devolution.

Strategic human resources management requires that organizations continually analyze their external and internal environments and adopt strategies necessary to cope with the changes and remain viable. This means that administrators must take a proactive stance in developing innovative HRM practices.

Challenges for Public and Nonprofit Organizations

The chapters in Part One of this book addressed how society and workplaces have changed, and what the human resources management (HRM) implications of those changes are for public and nonprofit organizations. The chapters in Part Two explained seven HRM techniques and practices: job analysis, recruitment and selection, performance evaluation, compensation, benefits, training and development, and collective bargaining. The chapters in Part Three discussed some of the pending HRM challenges that will confront, if they have not already confronted, the HRM practices used in public and nonprofit organizations. This chapter will summarize the main points addressed in earlier chapters and discuss how strategic human resources management (SHRM) can be used to help organizations cope with the challenges that lie ahead.

What to Expect

As noted earlier in the book, public and nonprofit organizations are facing and will continue to be confronted with reduced budgets. Gridlock caused by different funding priorities characterized the 1995–1996 federal budget proposals, and similar scenarios were played out across most of the states. Reduced funding for civic and social service programs, health care, education, legal services, and arts and culture programs were part of the national debate. Cuts in those programs will have a dramatic impact on many public agencies at the federal, state, and local levels, as well as on most nonprofit organizations that provide many of these services and that are dependent on government support for a significant amount of their funding. Resources will continue to be tight, and wages and benefit increases are not likely to be forthcoming. Organizations are going to be less inclined to expand programs or to hire new employees. Instead, they must be prepared to invest time and money in training their present staff. For many agencies there is likely to be an increase in the use of contingency workers, of workers employed on a temporary or part-time basis, and of specific services contracted-out to independent contractors.

New cultural and social changes are affecting the workplace. There have been substantial increases in the number of female, minority, disabled, and older workers. Not only have the public and nonprofit workforces become more demographically diverse but the values of employees have also changed. They want challenging jobs, and they want to exercise discretion in those jobs. New organizational structures such as cross-functional and self-managing teams have emerged as alternatives to traditional bureaucratic structures.

Jobs are changing, and with those changes arise quality-of-life and quality-of-work issues. Employees want to satisfy their important personal needs by working in the organization. In addition to the desire for more autonomy, employees are also looking for a better fit between work and family responsibilities. They are seeking alternative work schedules such as flextime, compressed schedules, and part-time employment opportunities so they can spend more time with their families.

The legal environment has also changed. Public and nonprofit agencies must comply with federal, state, and local laws; with executive orders; with the rules and regulations promulgated by administrative agencies such as the Equal Employment Opportunity Commission; and with federal and state court decisions. Equal employment opportunity, compensation, labor relations, and employer contributions to benefits such as retirement plans and pensions, workman's compensation, and unemployment insurance are regulated by law. The legal environment must be monitored because it is always changing. By the time this book is published, some of the legislation discussed in earlier chapters that is pending before Congress may become law, once again changing the legal environment.

Technology has changed many jobs and has led to new skill requirements and organizational structures. The increased use of computers and telecommunication devices are changing the way organizations are structured and the way work is organized and managed.

All of these forces have implications for managing public and nonprofit organizations. Many jobs have been changed or eliminated, and employees must constantly upgrade their knowledge, skills, abilities, and other characteristics (KSAOCs). In some instances, upgrading incumbent employees' KSAOCs is not enough; organizations must recruit and hire people with advanced skills. For public and nonprofit organizations to survive, they need employees who can help them provide high-quality mission-related services. To be assured of this, organizations must link their HRM functions to the short- and long-term priorities of the organization.

Public and nonprofit organizations are subject to the capriciousness of funding, financial support, and market positions, in addition to public and political support that is often fickle. The demands placed on public and nonprofit organizations keep changing. Numerous reports suggest that government and nonprofit organizations need to be reinvented and reengineered if they are to fulfill their missions (National Performance Review, 1993; *Hard Truths/Tough Choices*, 1993; Governor's Human Resources Advisory Council, 1993; National Commission on the Public Service, 1989). Across both sectors there is the recognition that organizations need to restructure their HRM systems because they are often unable to attract and retain energetic and competent personnel. They need to reengineer management systems to best utilize their workforces to facilitate improvements in the quality of their services and in the productivity of their workforce.

Today, the expectation is that organizations will provide services characterized by timeliness, variety, customization, and convenience (Carnevale, 1991). Linden (1994) uses the term "seamless" to describe organizations that are not overbureaucratized and fragmented. Instead, seamless organizations provide a smooth, transparent, almost effortless experience for their customers. Staff in seamless organizations perform the full job, in direct contact with their end users (p. xii). Services are delivered in a holistic rather than a fragmented manner.

Lakeland Regional Medical Center in Florida is provided by Linden (1994) as an example of an organization headed in the "seamless" direction. Lakeland is an 897-bed hospital that provides a full range of health care services. An analysis in 1989 revealed that only 16 percent of the staff's time was spent delivering medical, technical, and clinical care. To increase the amount of time spent with patients, four hospital units developed teams of registered nurses and technicians to provide most services to the patient. They go through an intensive six-week training program in which they learn procedures previously performed by specialized departments, such as respiratory and physical therapy, laboratory testing, and diagnostic radiology. Once they pass a rigorous test in each area, they begin working as a team. Computer terminals are positioned in the patients' rooms that are linked to the hospital's mainframe computer and that can oversee admissions, discharges, and bed control. As a result, information and control rests with the teams of nurses and technicians. The service providers care for the whole patient, services are available at anytime, there are no sharp divisions among staff, the teams produce the whole job, and they are in direct contact with the end users (Linden, 1994, pp. 47–49).

Alternative service delivery programs require new skills. Employees and organizations can no longer possess tunnel vision or be overspecialized. To be effective requires a breadth of knowledge, an interest in learning, and a willingness to tap the knowledge of others (Bozeman & Straussman, 1990, p. 206). The immediate SHRM implication is that agencies must identify the KSAOCs needed both now and in the future, and they must audit their organizations to determine whether those KSAOCs are possessed by incumbent employees or can be obtained through training and development activities. If neither of these is the case, then HRM departments must work with department managers and line personnel to develop recruitment and selection strategies. Managers and employees need to think about the future and prepare for impending changes.

The requirement for flexibility and speed of response to market changes is likely to continue. This has implications for the practice of SHRM. Agencies need to invest in their workforces and to ensure that their members have sufficient security. Employees who fear losing their jobs will resist new innovations. Instead, agencies should provide learning environments, invest in development opportunities, and train and retrain their employees when dictated by changes in technology or demands for service.

Challenges of Strategic Human Resources Management

The demographic characteristics of the labor force have changed. As noted in earlier chapters, there have been increases in the number of women, racial and ethnic minorities, older employees, disabled, and homosexuals. Organizations must recognize underlying attributes, or nonobservable characteristics, such as different learning styles, different working styles and values, and different types of personalities, as well as differences in culture, socioeconomic background, educational background, occupational background, and professional orientation.

To accommodate the changing workforce and to minimize conflict, organizations should promote a greater awareness of diversity issues and cultural differences. It is also important that they audit their human resources functions to ensure that they are free from bias. Recruitment, selection, training and development, performance evaluation, and compensation and benefits should be administered in an equitable fashion. To avoid discriminating against the disabled, the essential functions of positions and the KSAOCs necessary for successful performance must be identified.

Under the Age Discrimination in Employment Act, employers can no longer force employees to retire when they reach a certain age, as long as they are still capable of performing their jobs. In fact, the U.S. Congress is encouraging individuals to work longer and delay retirement (thereby delaying when they will receive social security benefits). Fewer employees retiring at early ages combined with flatter organizational structures results in fewer promotional opportunities and career plateauing. To retain a motivated and energetic workforce, new types of career enhancement opportunities need to be developed to challenge incumbent employees. To older employees who are reluctant to retire, organizations may want to offer part-time work, phased retirements, or early retirement buyouts.

Families are another characteristic that differentiate workers. Many employees in the public and nonprofit sector are parents who need greater flexibility in work schedules and work patterns to accommodate family responsibilities. Flexible work arrangements are needed for parents to care for young children or in some cases for employees to care for their parents. More opportunities should be available for part-time work, and there should be greater variety in benefits programs, such as child care and elder care. Benefits packages should recognize alternative families and different priorities.

Alternative scheduling now being used in many public and nonprofit organizations includes job sharing, flextime, and compressed work weeks, in which a full week's work is compressed into fewer than five days. Working at home or telecommuting to work are other options.

Change in Skill Requirements

Today, public and nonprofit sector jobs are increasingly more professional in nature, requiring higher levels of education, and there is a decrease in jobs requiring routine tasks. Technology has taken on much of the workplace's mentally and physically repetitive tasks. Jobs today require employees to possess greater skills as they assume more challenging responsibilities (Carnevale & Carnevale, 1993). Organizations need to acquire the skills necessary for coping with the challenges brought on by today's competitiveness. This competitiveness is based on the ability of institutions to deliver quality, variety, customization, convenience, and timeliness (Carnevale, 1991).

Accompanying the change in competitiveness are changes in the way organizations are judged. The new performance standards are *efficiency*, defined as the ability to produce higher volume with the same or fewer resources; *quality*, defined as matching products or services to a human need with a consistent conformance to standards; *variety,* defined as providing choices to suit diverse tastes and needs; *customization,* defined as tailoring goods and services to individual clientele; *convenience,* defined as developing user-friendly products and services and delivering them with high levels of customer satisfaction; and *timeliness,* defined as delivering innovations to customers, making continuous improvement, and developing new applications quickly (Carnevale & Carnevale, 1993, p. 4).

These new performance standards require improved skills and competencies for employees throughout the organization, regardless of position. Skills deemed to be necessary include *the academic basics,* for example, proficiency in reading, writing, and computation; *self-management skills,* such as self-esteem, motivation, goal-setting ability, and willingness to participate in career development activities; *social skills,* such as interpersonal, negotiation, and teamwork skills; *communication skills,* such as the ability to listen and communicate clearly; and *influencing skills,* or leadership abilities (Carnevale & Carnevale, 1993).

Today's jobs require a more educated workforce with advanced knowledge. Training needs to be continuous; alternative training methods such as interactive videos and individual training modules can be used. Employees need to be trained not just for their present positions but also for future jobs and KSAOCs. Training must be available for all employees regardless of their level in the organization.

As skill requirements increase, job tasks often become less specific (Carnevale & Carnevale, 1993). In such situations, job requirements become more flexible and overlapping, making the development of standardized examinations more difficult. Due to changes in the workplace and the rapid changes in technology that necessitate a high degree of change and evolution, it will become necessary to develop selection examinations that capture a variety of KSAOCs. More accurate selection techniques will need to be used, utilizing many of the advanced techniques identified in Chapter Six, such as assessment centers or other combinations of techniques, in order to evaluate not only technical skills but also interpersonal or leadership skills. Selection techniques will have to assess many of the skills associated with the use of self-managing teams, which plan, implement, and evaluate their own work.

Employees will need to possess initiative, judgment, decision-making skills, leadership abilities, interpersonal skills, and other competencies often neglected during the selection process.

Information technology is changing rapidly and will lead to modifications in job knowledge and responsibilities, resulting in changed organizational structures. Earlier chapters provided some examples of the uses of technology and how it has and will continue to affect the workplace. While the use of technology can be exciting, there are some caveats of which employers need to be aware. Wooldridge (1994), for example, notes that the increase in the use of technology often places women, African Americans, Hispanics, and older employees at a disadvantage because of differences in experiences using technology, cognitive styles, and unevenly distributed workplace literacy. Wooldridge recommends that to combat illiteracy employers must make significant investments in expanded, continuous educational and training programs for all of their employees. To eliminate the gaps in gender, race, or age, he recommends that employers require computer and technological training for all employees in appropriate job categories. The training programs should be monitored to ensure that all eligible employees participate. Training in computer skills is not enough, however; any stereotypes that suggest that women, persons of color, and older workers are incapable of learning new technology should be purged from the workplace.

Summary

The underlying belief of SHRM is the conviction that public and nonprofit employees are important assets to an organization and critical for the organization's success. Human resources representatives should be part of the strategic planning process, along with representatives from other departments. After strategies are formulated, human resources specialists, department directors, line managers, employees, and in unionized organizations, union representatives should collaborate with one another to develop programs, policies, job tasks, and responsibilities that are compatible with the organization's overall strategies.

References

Adarand Constructors v. Pena, 115 S. Ct. 2097, 132 L. Ed. 2d 158 (1995).

A debacle for charities' credibility. (1995, June 1). *The Chronicle of Philanthropy, 7,* 1, 24, 29.

Age Discrimination in Employment Act, 29 U.S.C., Sec. 621 et seq. (1967).

Aho, K. (1989). Achieving pay equity. *American City & County, 104,* 14–15.

Albert, S. (1993). *Hiring the chief executive: A practical guide to the search and selection process.* Washington, DC: National Center for Nonprofit Boards.

Alexander, G. D. (1991, February). Working with volunteers: No pain, no gain. *Fund Raising Management,* pp. 62–63.

American Federation of State, County, and Municipal Employees. (1988). *Nonprofit agency employees: Working for people, not for profit.* Washington, DC: American Federation of Labor–Congress of Industrial Organization.

American Federation of State, County, and Municipal Employees v. State of Washington, F.2d 770: 1401–1408 (1985).

American Psychological Association. (1991). *Questionnaires used in the prediction of trustworthiness in pre-employment selection decisions: An APA task force report.* Washington, DC: Author.

American Psychological Association, Division of Industrial and Organizational Psychology. (1987). *Principles for the validation and use of personnel selection procedures* (3rd ed.). Washington, DC: Author.

Americans give, volunteer less, for charities, says poll. (1994, October 20). *St. Louis Post-Dispatch,* p. 14A.

Americans with Disabilities Act, PL 101–336, 42 U.S.C., Sec. 12101–12117.

Ammons, D. N., & Glass, J. J. (1989). *Recruiting local government executives: Practical insights for hiring authorities and candidates.* San Francisco: Jossey-Bass.

Andersen, D. F., Belardo, S., & Dawes, S. S. (1994). Strategic information management: Conceptual frameworks for the public sector. *Public Productivity & Management Review, 17,* 335–353.

Anderson, L. M., & Baroody, N. B. (1992, August). Managing volunteers. *Fund Raising Management, 23,* 43–45.

Anfuso, D. (1994). Peer review wards off unions and lawsuits. *Personnel Journal, 49,* 47–58.

Arline v. School Board of Nassau County, 479 U.S. 927 (1987).

Armshaw, J., Carnevale, D., & Waltuck, B. (1993). Cooperating for quality: Union-management partnership in the U.S. Department of Labor. *Review of Public Personnel Administration, 13,* 94–107.

Arvey, R. D. (1986). Sex bias in job evaluation procedures. *Personnel Psychology, 39,* 315–335.

Arvey, R. D., & Faley, R. H. (1988). *Fairness in selecting employees* (2nd ed.). Reading, MA: Addison-Wesley.

Arvey, R. D., Nutting, S. M., & Landon, T. E. (1992). Validation strategies for physical ability testing in police and fire settings. *Public Personnel Management, 21,* 301–312.

A sampling of newspaper editorials on the Aramony case. (1995, April 20). *The Chronicle of Philanthropy, 7,* 34.

Ash, A. (1994). Participants' reactions to subordinate appraisal of managers: Results of a pilot. *Public Personnel Management, 23,* 237–256.

Atkins v. City of Charlotte, U.S. Dist. Ct. 296 F. Supp. (1969).

Bachman, R. (1994, July). Violence and theft in the workplace. *National Crime Victimization Survey* (NCJ-148199). Washington, DC: U.S. Department of Justice, Bureau of Justice Statistics.

Baker, J. R. (1994). Government in the twilight zone: Motivations of volunteers to small city boards and commissions. *State and Local Government Review, 26,* 119–128.

Ban, C., & Riccucci, N. (1993). Personnel systems and labor relations: Steps toward a quiet revitalization. In F. J. Thompson (Ed.), *Revitalizing state and local public service: Strengthening performance, accountability, and citizen confidence* (pp. 71–103). San Francisco: Jossey-Bass.

Barber, A. E., Dunham, R. B., & Formisano, R. A. (1992). The impact of flexible benefits on employee satisfaction: A field study. *Personnel Psychology, 45,* 55–74.

Barciela, S. (1995, September 18). Leaving can mean beginning. *The Miami Herald,* p. B13.

Barnes v. Breedon, U.S.D.C. sTexas, No. H-92–0898 (January 25, 1996).

Barnum, P. (1991). Misconceptions about the future U.S. workforce: Implications for strategic planning. *Human Resources Planning, 14,* 209–219.

Barrett, G., Phillips, J., & Alexander, R. (1981). Concurrent and predictive validity designs: A critical reanalysis. *Journal of Applied Psychology, 66,* 1–6.

Barrick, M. R., & Mount, M. K. (1991). The big five personality dimensions and job performance: A meta-analysis. *Personnel Psychology, 44,* 1–26.

Bartlett, D. K. III, & Lichtenstein, H. (1992). Retirement plans for not-for-profit groups. In J. S. Rosenbloom (Ed.), *The handbook of employee benefits* (Vol. 1, pp. 915–924). Homewood, IL: Business One Irwin.

Becker, F. W., Silverstein, G., & Chaykin, L. (1995). Public employee job security and benefits: A barrier to privatization of mental health services. *Public Productivity and Management Review, 19,* 25–33.

Bell, K. (1995, June 1). Veto will bring legislature back, Carnahan also Oks teacher pension bill. *St. Louis Post-Dispatch,* p. 2b.

Benton, T. (1993). Union negotiating. *Nursing Management, 23,* 70, 72.

Berman, E. (1994). Implementing TQM in state governments: A survey of recent progress. *State and Local Government Review, 26,* 46–53.

Bernardin, H. J. (1986). Subordinate appraisal: A valuable source of information about managers. *Human Resource Management, 25,* 421–439.

Bernardin, H. J., & Kane, J. S. (1993). *Performance appraisal: A contingency approach to system development and evaluation.* Belmont, CA: Wadsworth.

Bernardin, H. J., & Lee, B. A. (1993). Equal employment opportunity. In H. J. Bernardin and J. E. Russell (Eds.), *Human resource management: An experiential approach* (pp. 60–81). New York: McGraw-Hill.

Blumrosen, R. G. (1979). Wage discrimination, job segregation, and Title VII of the Civil Rights Act of 1964. *University of Michigan Law Review, 12,* 397–502.

Bowen, D. E., Ledford, G. E. Jr., & Nathan, B. R. (1991). Hiring for the organization, not the job. *Academy of Management Executive, 5,* 35–50.

Bowen, W. G. (1994). When a business leader joins a nonprofit board. *Harvard Business Review, 72,* 38–43.

Bowman, J. S. (1994). At last, an alternative to performance appraisal: Total quality management. *Public Administrative Review, 54,* 129–136.

Bozeman, B., & Straussman, J. D. (1990). *Public management strategies: Guidelines for managerial effectiveness.* San Francisco: Jossey-Bass.

Brotman, A. (1992). Privatization of mental health services: The Massachusetts experience. *Journal of Health Politics, Policy and Law, 17,* 541–551.

Broward courts to go online with legal data permanently. (1995, October 31). *The Miami Herald,* p. 2BR.

Brudney, J. L. (1990). The availability of volunteers: Implications for local governments. *Administration & Society, 21,* 413–424.

Brudney, J. L. (1993). *Fostering volunteer programs in the public sector.* San Francisco: Jossey-Bass.

Bryson, J. M. (1988). *Strategic planning for public and nonprofit organizations: A guide to strengthening and sustaining organizational achievement.* San Francisco: Jossey-Bass.

Bullard, A. M., & Wright, D. S. (1993). Circumventing the glass ceiling: Women executives in American state government. *Public Administration Review, 53,* 189–202.

Bureau of National Affairs. (1994a, December 15). Benefit expenses spiral higher. *Bulletin to Management, 45,* 400.

Bureau of National Affairs. (1994b, March 17). Volunteerism: An organizational booster. *Bulletin to Management, 45,* 88.

Bureau of National Affairs. (1995a, April 6). Reverse bias not widespread. *Fair Employment Practices, 31,* 37.

Bureau of National Affairs. (1995b, April 5). Employee benefit costs. *Bulletin to Management, 46,* 4.

Bureau of National Affairs. (1996a, March 21). Earnings of college graduates. *Bulletin to Management, 47,* 92.

Bureau of National Affairs. (1996b, September 19). Sexual orientation bias bill defeated. *Fair Employment Practices, 32,* 109.

Calbreath, L. (1986). Texas rehabilitation commission: High-quality service on a lean budget. *Journal of Information and Image Management, 19,* 12–16.

California Federal Savings & Loan Association v. Guerra, 42 FEP Cases 1073 (1987).

Campion, M. A., Pursell, E. D., & Brown, B. K. (1988). Structured interviewing: Raising the psychometric properties of the employment interview. *Personnel Psychology, 41,* 25–42.

Cardy, R. L., & Dobbins, G. H. (1992). Job analysis in a dynamic environment. *Academy of Management, Human Resources Division Newsletter, 16,* 4, 5–6.

Cardy, R. L., & Dobbins, G. H. (1994). *Performance appraisal: Alternative perspectives.* Cincinnati, OH: South-Western.

Carnevale, A. P. (1991). *America and the new economy: How competitive standards are radically changing American workplaces.* San Francisco: Jossey-Bass.

Carnevale, A. P., & Carnevale, D. G. (1993). Public administration and the evolving world of work. *Public Productivity and Management Review, 17,* 1–14.

Carnevale, D. G. (1993). Root dynamics of alternative dispute resolution: An illustrative case in the U.S. Postal Service. *Public Administrative Review, 53,* 455–461.

Carson, K. P., & Stewart, G. L. (1996). Job analysis and the sociotechnical approach to quality: A critical examination. *Journal of Quality Management, 1,* 49–65.

Carver, J. (1990). *Boards that make a difference: A new design for leadership in public and nonprofit organizations.* San Francisco: Jossey-Bass.

Carver, T. B., & Vondra, A. A. (1994). Alternative dispute resolution: Why it doesn't work and why it does. *Harvard Business Review, 72,* 120–124.

Cascio, W. F. (1991a). *Costing human resources: The financial impact of behavior in organizations* (3rd ed.). Boston: PWS-Kent.

Cascio, W. F. (1991b). *Applied psychology in personnel* (4th ed.). Englewood Cliffs, NJ: Prentice Hall.

CCH Business Law Editors. (1992). *Workers' Compensation Manual: For managers and supervisors.* Chicago: Commerce Clearing House.

Chandler, T., & Feuille, P. (1991). Municipal unions and privatization. *Public Administration Review, 51,* 15–20.

Chandler, T., & Feuille, P. (1994, Winter). Cities, unions, and the privatization of sanitation services. *Journal of Labor Research, 15,* 53–71.

Chase, A. (1992). Calling all points of light. *Governing, 5,* 24–25.

Chicago Tribune v. National Labor Relations Board, 974 F2d 933 (7th Cir. 1992).

Christensen v. State of Iowa, 563 F.2d 353 (8th Cir., 1977).

City of Richmond v. J. A. Croson Co., 488 U. S. 469 (1989).

Civil Rights Act, 42 U.S.C., Sec. 1981 (1866).

Civil Rights Act, 42 U.S.C., Sec. 2000 (1964).

Clark, P. B., & Wilson, J. Q. (1961). Incentive systems: A theory of organizations. *Administrative Science Quarterly, 6,* 129–166.

Cnaan, R. A., & Goldberg-Glen, R. S. (1991). Measuring motivation to volunteer in human services. *Journal of Applied Behavioral Science, 27,* 269–284.

Cohen, S. L. (1991).The challenge of training in the nineties. *Training and Development, 45,* 30–35.

Cohodas, M. J. (1996). Picture this. *Governing, 9,* 55–56.

Columbia University Graduate Program in Public Policy and Public Administration, School of International and Public Affairs. (1993, March). *New York City solutions II: Transforming the public personnel system.* New York: Columbia University.

Commerce Clearning House. (1989). Nonprofit organizations and "opting out." *Compensation,* p. 3250.

Commerce Clearing House. (1990). Jurisdiction of NLRB over nonprofits. *Employment Relations,* pp. 708–712, 736–739.

Conway v. Studeman, USDC EVa, No. 95–426-A (March 31, 1995).

Cook v. State of Rhode Island, Department of Mental Health, Retardation, and Hospitals, Docket Number 93–1093 (November 22, 1993).

Cornwell, C., & Kellough, J. E. (1994). Women and minorities in federal government agencies: Examining new evidence from panel data. *Public Administration Review, 54,* 265–270.

Cortina, J. M., Doherty, M. L., Schmitt, N., Kaufman, G., & Smith, R. G. (1992). The big five personality factors in the IPI and MMPI: Predictors of police performance. *Personnel Psychology, 45,* 119–140.

Cosier, R. A., & Dalton, D. R. (1993). Management training and development in a nonprofit organization. *Public Personnel Management, 22,* 37–42.

Cox, T. H., & Blake, S. (1991). Managing cultural diversity: Implications for organizational competitiveness. *Academy of Management Executive, 5,* 45–56.

Cranford, J. (1995). A guide to award-winning technology. *Governing, 8,* 61–70.

Crooker, K. J., & Grover, S. L. (1993, August). *The impact of family-responsive benefits on selected work attitudes.* Paper presented at the meeting of the Academy of Management, Atlanta, Georgia.

Dailey, R. C. (1986). Understanding organizational commitment for volunteers: Empirical and managerial implications. *Journal of Voluntary Action Research, 15,* 19–131.

Dawes, S. S. (1994). Human resource implications of information technology in state government. *Public Personnel Management, 23,* 31–46.

Day, D., & Silverman, S. (1989). Personality and job performance: Evidence of incremental validity. *Personnel Psychology, 42,* 25–26.

Deal, T., & Kennedy, A. (1982). *Corporate culture.* Reading, MA: Addison-Wesley.

DeJong, W. (1994, November). Preventing interpersonal violence among youth. *Violent Crime Control & Law Enforcement Act of 1994,* pp. 1–62.

Delaware Police Officers' and Firefighters' Employment Relations Act, 19 Del. C. Ch. 16 (1986).

Dellion, H., & Pearson, R. (1991, September 14). Edgar vetoes comparable worth. *Chicago Tribune,* North, Section 1, p. 13.

Dick, S. G. (1994). ADR at the crossroads. *Dispute Resolution Journal, 49,* 47–58.

DiLorezo, L. P., & Carroll, D. J. (1995). Screening applicants for a safer workplace. *HRMagazine, 40,* 55–58.

Dilts, D. A. (1993). Labor-management cooperation in the public sector. *Journal of Collective Negotiations in the Public Sector, 22,* 305–311.

Dilts, D. A., Boyda, S. W., & Scherr, M. A. (1993). Collective bargaining in the absence of protective legislation: The case of Louisiana. *Journal of Collective Negotiations in the Public Sector, 22,* 259–265.

Dobbins, G. H., Lin, T. R., & Farh, J. L. (1992). A field study of race and age similarity effects on interview ratings in conventional and situational interviews. *Journal of Applied Psychology, 77,* 363–371.

Doe v. City of Chicago, U.S.D.C. NIL, No. 94–4122 (February 14, 1995).

Drexel Homes, Inc., 182 N.L.R.B., No. 151 (1970).

Duncombe, S. (1985). Volunteers in city government: Advantages, disadvantages and uses. *National Civic Review, 74,* 356–364.

Duncombe, S. (1986). Volunteers in city government: Getting more than your money's worth. *National Civic Review, 74,* 291–301.

Duncan, T. S. (1995). Death in the office. *FBI Law Enforcement Bulletin, 64,* 20–25.

Durning, A. W. (1995, January 16). How public agencies can effectively use private services. *Nation's Cities Weekly, 18,* 6.

Edwards, H. T., Clark, R. T. Jr., & Craver, C. B. (Eds.). (1979). *Labor relations law in the public sector* (3rd ed.). Riverside, NJ: Bobbs-Merrill.

Elliott, R. H. (1985). *Public personnel administration: A values perspective.* Reston, VA: Reston.

Elliott, R. H., & Jarrett, D. T. (1994). Violence in the workplace: The role of human resource management. *Public Personnel Management, 23,* 287–299.

Ellis, S. J. (1995a). *The board's role in effective volunteer involvement.* Washington, DC: National Center for Nonprofit Boards.

Ellis, S. J. (1995b, March). Volunteers can be found in cyberspace. *The Nonprofit Times, 9,* 30, 32.

Ellison v. Brady, 924 F.2nd 872 (9th Cir. 1991).

Employee Polygraph Protection Act, U.S. Code, Title 29, Sections 2001–2009 (1988).

Employee Polygraph Protection Act, Pub. L., No. 100–347 (1988).

Equal Employee Opportunity Commission. (1989, July 1). Sexual Harassment, 29 C.F.R., Ch. XIV, Sec. 1604, 197–198.

Equal Employment Opportunity Commission v. Association of Community Organizations for Reform Now, USDC ELa, 93–0597 (March 8, 1995).

Erickson, P. R. (1990). Evaluating training results. *Training and Development Journal, 44,* 65–59.

Ewalt, P. L. (1991). Trends affecting recruitment and retention of social work staff in human services agencies. *Social Work, 36,* 214–217.

Executive Order No. 11246, C.R.F., Sec. 60.2.11 (1978).

Fair Labor Standards Act, Title 29, Part 541, C.F.R., Sec. 541.1, 541.2, 541.3.

Fair Labor Standards Act of 1985, Pub. L., 99–150.

Farr, C. A. (1983). *Volunteers: Managing volunteer personnel in local government.* Washington, DC: International City Managers Association.

Feldacker, B. (1990). *Labor guide to labor law* (3rd ed.). Englewood Cliffs, NJ: Prentice Hall.

Feuer, D. (1987). Paying for knowledge. *Training, 24,* 57–66.

Fine, M. G., Johnson, F. L., & Ryan, M. S. (1990). Cultural diversity in the workplace. *Public Personnel Management, 19,* 305–319.

Firefighters Local 93 v. City of Cleveland, 106 S. Ct. (1986).

Firefighters Local 1784 v. Stotts, 467 U.S. 561 (1984).

Fisher, J. C., & Cole, K. M. (1993). *Leadership and management of volunteer programs: A guide for volunteer administrators.* San Francisco: Jossey-Bass.

Fisher, M. J. (1990). Health benefits surging as strike issue. *National Underwriter, 94,* 7, 31.

Fitz-enz, J. (1990). Getting and keeping good employees. *Personnel, 67,* 25–28.

Fitz-enz, J. (1996). *How to measure human resources management* (2nd ed.). New York: McGraw-Hill.

Fitzgerald, W. (1992). Training versus development. *Training and Development Journal, 5,* 81–84.

Fitzpatrick, R. B. (1994). Let's end legal war in the workplace. *HRMagazine, 39,* 118, 120.

Frierson, J. G., & Jolly, J. P. (1988). Problems in employment application forms. *Employment Relations Today, 15,* 205–217.

Foundation center puts information on the Internet. (1995, February 9). *The Chronicle of Philanthropy, 8,* 33.

Gael, S. (1988). *The job analysis handbook for business, industry, and government* (Vols. 1 & 2). New York: Wiley.

Garcia v. San Antonio Metropolitan Transit Authority, 105 S.Ct. 1005 (1985).

Gaston, C. L. (1986). An idea whose time has not come: Comparable worth and the market salary problem. *Population Research and Policy Review, 5,* 15–29.

Gilmore, T. N. (1993). *Finding and retaining your next chief executive: Making the transition work.* Washington, DC: National Center for Nonprofit Boards.

Gordon, J. (1991). Measuring the "goodness" of training. *Training, 28,* 19–25.

Governor's Human Resources Advisory Council. (1993, September). *Final report: Recommendations for change in Illinois.* Springfield: Illinois Department of Central Management Services.

Graham, M. (1992). The drive for comparable worth: Has it sputtered out? *PA Times,* p. 8.

Greenberg, J. (1986). Determinants of perceived fairness of performance evaluations. *Journal of Applied Psychology, 71,* 340–342.

Greene, E. (1995, July 13). Non-profit groups show increased interest in bonuses for top-level executives. *The Chronicle of Philanthropy,* p. 39.

Gupta, N., Jenkins, G. D. Jr., & Curington, W. P. (1986). Paying for knowledge: Myths and realities. *National Productivity Review, 5,* 107–123.

Gurwitt, R. (1988). The computer revolution: Microchipping away at the limits of government. *Governing, 8,* 34–42.

Gutteridge, T. G., Leibowitz, Z. B., & Shore, J. E. (1993, November). When careers flower, organizations flourish. *Training and Development, 47,* 24–29.

Guy, M. E. (1993). Three steps forwards, two steps backward: The status of women's integration into public management. *Public Administration Review, 53,* 285–292.

Halachmi, A. (1991). Productivity and information technology: Emerging issues and considerations. *Public Productivity and Management Review, 14,* 327–350.

Halachmi, A. (1993). From performance appraisal to performance targeting. *Public Personnel Management, 22,* 323–344.

Hand, S., & Zawacki, R. A. (1994). Family friendly benefits: More than a frill. *HRMagazine 39,* 79–84.

Harkness, L., & Mulinski, P. (1988, July-August). Performance standards for social workers. *Social Work,* pp. 339–348.

Harris v. Forklift Systems, U.S. SupCt, 1993, 63 FEP cases 225 (1993).

Harris, C. (1995, January 23). Fewer and smaller cash awards expected. *Federal Times, 30,* 4.

Hass, N. (1993, August 3). Buy a bridge? *Financial World,* pp. 31–35.

Hays, S. W., & Kearney, R. C. (1992). State personnel directors and the dilemmas of workforce 2000. *Public Administration Review, 52,* 380–388.

Hays, S. W., & Kearney, R. C. (1994). Labor-management relations and participative decision making: Toward a new paradigm. *Public Administration Review, 54,* 44–51.

Healey v. Southwood Psychiatric Hospital, CA 3, 70 FEP Cases 439 (1996).

Healy, B., & Southard, G. D. (1994, April). *Pay for performance, Administrative policy manual, policy no. 30–19, City of Claremont.*

Heilman, M. E., Lucas, J. A., & Block, C. J. (1992). Presumed incompetent? Stigmatization and affirmative action efforts. *Journal of Applied Psychology, 77,* 536–544.

Henderson, R. (1988). Job evaluation, classification, and pay. In S. Gael (Ed.), *The job analysis handbook for business, industry, and government* (Vol. 1). (pp. 90–118). New York: Wiley.

Henderson, R. (1989). *Compensation management* (5th ed.). Englewood Cliffs, NJ: Prentice Hall.

Heneman, R. L. (1992). *Merit pay: Linking pay increases to performance ratings.* Reading, MA: Addison-Wesley.

Herman, R. D., & Heimovics, R. D. (1989). Critical events in the management of nonprofit organizations: Initial evidence. *Nonprofit and Voluntary Sector Quarterly, 18,* 119–132.

Herzlinger, R. E. (1994). Effective oversight: A guide for nonprofit directors. *Harvard Business Review, 72,* 52–60.

Hiring overhauled: Case examining replaces OPM's central registers. (1994, July). *Staffing Digest, 6,* 1–2.

Hodes, N. (1991). Achieving quality through labor-management participation in New York State. *Public Productivity and Management Review, 15,* 163–168.

Hodgkinson, V. A., & Weitzman, M. S. (1986). *Dimensions of the independent sector: A statistical profile* (2nd ed.). Washington, DC: INDEPENDENT SECTOR.

Hodgkinson, V. A., Weitzman, M. S., Toppe, C. M., & Noga, S. M. (1992). *Nonprofit almanac 1992–93: Dimensions of the independent sector.* San Francisco: Jossey-Bass.

Hogan, R. (1971). Personality characteristics of highly rated policemen. *Personnel Psychology, 24,* 679–686.

Hogan, R., & Kurtines, W. (1975). Personological correlates of police effectiveness. *Journal of Psychology, 91,* 289–295.

Hopwood, et al., v. State of Texas, et al. (5th Circuit Court of Appeals 1996). [On-line]. Available: http://www.law.utexas.edu/ 94–50569. html.

Horrigan, J., & Harriman, A. (1988). Comparable worth: Public sector unions and employers provide a model for implementing pay equity. *Labor Law Journal, 39,* 704–711.

Houle, C. O. (1989). *Governing boards: Their nature and nurture.* San Francisco: Jossey-Bass.

Hudson Institute. (1987). *Workforce 2000: Work and workers for the 21st century: Executive summary.* Indianapolis, IN: Author.

Hughes, M. A., Ratliff, R. A., Purswell, J. L., & Hadwiger, J. (1989). A content validation methodology for job-related physical performance tests. *Public Personnel Management, 18,* 487–504.

Hughes, P. A., & Grote, R. C. (1993). Peer review places trust with employees. *HRMagazine, 38,* 57–62.

Hunter, J. E. (1986). Cognitive ability, cognitive aptitude, job knowledge, and job performance. *Journal of Vocational Behavior, 29,* 340–362.

Hush, H. (1969). Collective bargaining in voluntary agencies. *Social Casework, 50,* 210–213.

Hyland, S. L. (1990, September). Helping employees with family care. *Monthly Labor Review,* pp. 22–26.

Ide, R. W. III (1993). ADR: A giant step toward the future. *Dispute Resolution Journal, 48,* 20–23.

Indiana United Way Cuts Staff. (1995, March). *The Nonprofit Times,* p. 4.

Ingraham, P. W., & Rosenbloom, D. H. (1990, June). *The state of merit in the federal government.* An occasional paper prepared for the National

Commission on the Public Service. Washington, DC: National Commission on the Public Service.

Ingram, R. T. (1988). *Ten basic responsibilities of nonprofit boards.* Washington, DC: National Center for Nonprofit Boards.

International City Managers Association. (1994). *Training courses catalogue.* Washington, DC: Author.

International Personnel Management Association. (1993). Award winning programs: Interviews with the winners. *Public Personnel Management, 22,* 1–5.

Jerrick, W., & Berger, K. A. (1994, February). How a homeless shelter cut employee turnover in half. *HR Focus, 71,* 17–18.

Joel, L. G. III. (1993). *Every employee's guide to the law.* New York: Pantheon Books.

Johnson, A. T., & O'Neill, N. (1989). Employee assistance programs and the troubled employee in the public sector workplace. *Review of Public Personnel Administration, 9,* 66–80.

Johnson, J. A., & Hogan, R. (1981). Vocational interests, personality, and effective police performance. *Personnel Psychology, 34,* 49–53.

Johnson, P. R., & Indvik, J. (1994). Workplace violence: An issue of the nineties. *Public Personnel Management, 23,* 515–523.

Johnson, R. E. (1988). Flexible benefit plans. In J. Matzer Jr. (Ed.), *Pay and benefits: New ideas for local government* (pp. 72–86). Washington, DC: International City Managers Association.

Johnson v. Santa Clara Transportation Agency, 107 S. Ct. 1442 (1987).

Johnson, T., & Glionna, J. M. (1995, July 11). Postal supervisor's shooting death baffles employees. *The Los Angeles Times,* pp. B1, B10.

Johnson, W. B. (1988). *Civil Service 2000.* U.S. Office of Personnel Management: The Hudson Institute.

Johnson-Bateman Co., 295 NLRB No. 26 (1989).

Joice, W. (1993). Flexiplace: Getting the job done at home. *The Public Manager, 22,* 22–24.

Joinson, C. (1995). Make your training stick. *HRMagazine, 40,* 55–60.

Karger, H. J. (1988). *Social workers and labor unions.* New York: Greenwood Press.

Kaye, B., & Leibowitz, Z. (1994). Career development: Don't let it fizzle. *HRMagazine, 39,* 78–83.

Kearney, R. C. (1992). *Labor relations in the public sector* (2nd ed., rev.). New York: Marcel Dekker.

Kellough, J. E., & Lu, H. (1993). The paradox of merit pay in the public sector. *Review of Public Personnel Administration, 13,* 45–64.

Kerr, J., & Slocum, J. W. (1987). Managing corporate culture through reward systems. *Academy of Management Executive, 1,* 99–108.

Keyeshian v. Board of Regents, 385 U.S. 589 (1967).

Kim, P. S. (1993). Racial integration in the American federal government: With special reference to Asian Americans. *Review of Public Personnel Administration, 13,* 52–66.

Kim, P. S., & Lewis, G. B. (1994). Asian Americans in the public service: Success, diversity, and discrimination. *Public Administration Review, 54,* 285–290.

Kirkpatrick, D. L. (1994). *Evaluating training programs.* San Francisco: Berrett-Koehler.

Klay, W. E. (1988). Microelectronics-based automation and the future of public labor relations. *Public Productivity Review, 4,* 57–68.

Klingner, D. E. (1993). Developing a strategic human resources management capability in public agencies. *Public Personnel Management, 22,* 565–578.

Knauft, E. B., Berger, R. A., & Gray, S. T. (1991). *Profiles of excellence: Achieving success in the nonprofit sector.* San Francisco: Jossey-Bass.

Kossek, E. E., DeMarr, B. J., Backman, K., & Kolar, M. (1993). Assessing employees' emerging elder care needs and reactions to dependent care benefits. *Public Personnel Management, 22,* 617–638.

Kostro, C. (1994). The road to cheaper services. *American City & County, 109,* 16.

Kovach, K. A., & Millspaugh, P. E. (1990). Comparable worth: Canada legislates pay equity. *Academy of Management Executive, 4,* 92–101.

Kramer, R. M., & Grossman, B. (1987). Contracting for social services: Process management and resource dependencies. *Social Service Review, 61,* 32–55.

Kraten, M. (1995, June). HR policies in the nonprofit arena. *The Nonprofit Times,* p. 29.

Kuhn, T. (1993, April 21). Fire department to come under city scrutiny: Board says give job back to paramedic. *Citizen Journal,* pp. 7A, 10A.

Laird, D. (1985). *Approaches to training and development* (2nd ed.). Reading, MA: Addison-Wesley.

Lane, P. (1995, March 13). Partners in public service. *Nation's Cities Weekly,* p. 12.

Lantigua, J. (1995, October 16). Fallout from O. J.: Chiefs say Fuhrman gives all officers a bad rap. *The Miami Herald,* pp. B1, B4.

Lauber, D. (1997). *Nonprofits and education job finder.* River Forest, IL: Planning/Communications.

Lauber, D. (1997). *Government job finder* (3rd ed.). River Forest, IL: Planning/Communications.

Lauber, D. (1997). *Professional's job finder.* River Forest, IL: Planning/Communications.

Lawler, E. (1989). *Pay for performance: A strategic analysis.* In L. R. Gomez-Mejia (Ed.), *Compensation and Benefits* (pp. 136–181). Washington, DC: Bureau of National Affairs.

Legal aid lawyers weren't striking against New York City. (1994, October 11). *The New York Times,* p. A14.

Lemons v. City and County of Denver, 620 F.2d 228 (10th Cir., 1980).

Leonard, B. (1995a). Creating opportunities to excel. *HRMagazine, 40,* 47–51.

Leonard, B. (1995b). Companies step forward with college savings plans. *HRMagazine, 40,* 49–50, 53.

Letter Carriers v. Blount, 305 F. Supp 546 (D.D.C., 1969).

Lewis, G. B. (1988). Progress toward racial and sexual equality in the federal civil service? *Public Administration Review, 48,* 389–397.

Lewis, G. B. (1994). Women, occupations, and federal agencies: Occupational mix and interagency differences in sexual inequality in federal white-collar employment. *Public Administration Review, 54,* 271–276.

Liebno v. Maryland State Police, USDC Md, No. JFM–92–740, (April 5, 1995).

Linden, R. M. (1994). *Seamless government: A practical guide to re-engineering in the public sector.* San Francisco: Jossey-Bass.

Lipsky, M., & Smith, S. R. (1989–1990). Nonprofit organizations, government, and the welfare state. *Political Science Quarterly, 104,* 625–648.

Loden, M., & Rosener, J. B. (1991). *Workforce America! Managing employee diversity as a vital resource.* Homewood, IL: Irwin.

Longenecker, C., & Ludwig, D. (1990). Ethical dilemmas in performance appraisal revisited. *Journal of Business Ethics, 9,* 961–969.

Mahtesian, C. (1994). Taking Chicago private. *Governing, 7,* 26–31.

Man takes revenge: kills self. (1996, February 10). *St. Louis Post-Dispatch,* p. 3A.

Martin, B., Harrison, P., & Ingram, E. (1991). Strategies for training new managers. *Personnel Journal, 70,* 114–117.

Martin v. Wilks, 109 S. Ct. 2189 (1989).

Massino, C. (1995). Pen computing: A "natural next step" for public safety field personnel. *Nation's Cities Weekly, 18,* 8.

Masterson, S. S., & Taylor, M. S. (1996). Total quality management and performance appraisal: An integrative perspective. *Journal of Quality Management, 1,* 67–89.

Mayors share programs that work. (1995, June 26). *Nation's Cities Weekly, 18,* 3.

McAdoo, S. (1992). *Impact of a public relations program on the development of a nonprofit mental health agency.* Unpublished master's thesis, Southern Illinois University, Edwardsville.

McAdoo, S., & Pynes, J. (1995). Reinventing mental health service delivery: One nonprofit's experience. *Public Administration Quarterly, 19,* 367–374.

McCurley, S. (1993). How to fire a volunteer and live to tell about it. *Grapevine,* pp. 8–11.

McDermott, K., & Gillerman, M. (1995, June 14). Retiring East St. Louis educators can cash in unused sick days repaid generously. *St. Louis Post-Dispatch,* pp. 1, 10.

McDonnel Douglas v. Green, 401 U.S. 424 (1973).

McEvoy, G. M. (1990). Public managers' reactions to appraisals by subordinates. *Public Personnel Management, 19,* 201–212.

McGill, D. M. (1992). Public employee pension plans, In J. S. Rosenbloom (Ed.), *The handbook of employee benefits* (Vol. 2, pp. 522–536). Homewood, IL: Business One Irwin.

McIntosh, S. S. (1990). Clerical jobs in transition. *Human Resources Magazine, 35,* 70–72.

McLaughlin v. Tilendis, 398 F. 2d 287 (1968).

Mergenbagen, P. (1991, June). A new breed of volunteer. *American Demographics, 13,* 54–55.

Meritor Savings Bank v. Vinson, 40 FEP Cases 1822 (1986).

Milliken, F. J., & Martins, L. L. (1996). Searching for common threads: Understanding the multiple effects of diversity in organizational change. *Academy of Management Review, 21,* 402–433.

Mohrman, A. M. Jr., Resnick-West, S. M., & Lawler, E. E. III. (1989). *Designing performance appraisal systems: Aligning appraisals and organizational realities.* San Francisco: Jossey-Bass.

Montjoy, R. S., & Brudney, J. L. (1991). Volunteers in the delivery of public services: Hidden costs . . . and benefits. *American Review of Public Administration, 21,* 327–344.

Moore, P. (1991). Comparison of state and local employee benefits and private employee benefits. *Public Personnel Management, 20,* 429–439.

Mormon Church v. Amos, 107 S. Ct. 2862 (1987).

Morrison, E. K. (1994). *Leadership skills: Developing volunteers for organizational success* (3rd ed.). Tucson, AZ: Fisher Books.

Murawski, J. (1995a, February 9). Cracks in non-profit nest eggs. *The Chronicle of Philanthropy, 7,* 27–29.

Murawski, J. (1995b, July 27). Audit questions spending by former NAACP chairman. *The Chronicle of Philanthropy, 7,* 36.

Murphy, K. R., & Cleveland, J. N. (1991). *Performance appraisal: An organizational perspective.* Needham Heights, MA: Allyn and Bacon.

Murphy, K. R., & Cleveland, J. N. (1995). *Understanding performance appraisal: Social, organizational, and goal-based perspectives.* Thousand Oaks, CA: Sage.

Muson, H. (1989, March). The nonprofit's prophet. *Across the Board, 26,* 24–38.

Naff, K. C. (1994). Through the glass ceiling: Prospects for the advancement of women in the federal civil service. *Public Administration Review, 54,* 507–514.

Nason, J. W. (1993). *Board assessment of the chief executive: A responsibility essential to good governance* (4th ed.). Washington, DC: National Center for Nonprofit Boards.

National Commission on the Public Service. (1989). *Leadership for America: Rebuilding the public service.* Washington, DC: Author.

National Commission on the State and Local Public Service. (1993). *Hard truths/tough choices: An agenda for state and local reform.* Albany, NY: The Nelson A. Rockefeller Institute of Government.

National Labor Relations Board. (1991). *A guide to basic law and procedures under the NLRA.* Washington, DC: U.S. Government Printing Office.

National Labor Relations Board v. Catholic Bishop of Chicago, 440 U.S. 490, 100 LRRM 2913 (1979).

National Park Foundation. (1995). Washington, DC: Author.

National Performance Review. (1993). *Creating a government that works better and costs less.* Washington, DC: Author.

National Treasury Employees Union v. Von Raab 109 S. Ct. 1384 (1989).

Nelson, W. R. (1982). Employment testing and the demise of the PACE examination. *Labor Law Journal, 35,* 729–750.

Nelson-Horchler, J. (1989). Elder care comes of age. *Industry Week, 238,* 54–56.

New guide to resources geared to nonprofit groups (1995, February 9). *The Chronicle of Philanthropy, 8,* 33.

New processes may speed EEOC dispute resolution. (1995, June 26). *Nation's Cities Weekly,* p. 6.

Newlin, J. G., & Meng, G. J. (1991). The public sector pays for performance. *Personnel Journal, 70,* 110–114.

O'Connell, B. (1988). *Finding, developing, and rewarding good board members.* Washington, DC: INDEPENDENT SECTOR.

O'Connor v. Consolidated Coin Caterers Corporation, No. 95–354, S. Ct. April 1, 1996. [On-line]. Available: ftp.cwru.edu/hermes/ascii/95–354.zo.fitt.

Odendahl, T., & O'Neill, M. (Eds.). (1994). *Women and power in the nonprofit sector.* San Francisco: Jossey-Bass.

Odendahl, T., & Youmans, S. (Eds.) (1994). Women on nonprofit boards. In T. Odendahl and M. O'Neill (Eds.), *Women and power in the nonprofit sector* (pp. 183–221). San Francisco: Jossey-Bass.

Office of Federal Contract Compliance Program, Revised Order No. 4, 41 C.F.R., Sec. 60–2.10 (1990).

Office of Personnel Management. (1993). *Revisiting civil service 2000: New policy direction needed.* Washington, DC: U.S. Government Printing Office.

O'Meara, D. P. (1994). Question the status of independent contractors. *HRMagazine, 39,* 33–39.

On board. (1995a, March 13–19). *St. Louis Business Journal,* p. 39A.

On board. (1995b, June 5–11). *St. Louis Business Journal,* p. 26A.

O'Neill, M. (1994). The paradox of women and power in the nonprofit sector. In T. Odendahl and M. O'Neill (Eds.), *Women and power in the nonprofit sector* (pp. 1–16). San Francisco: Jossey-Bass.

Oppenheimer, M., & Paguta, J. M. (1993). Reinventing public personnel management? Introduction to Forum. *The Public Manager, 22,* 7–9.

Ospina, S. (1992). When managers don't plan: Consequences of non-strategic public personnel management. *Review of Public Personnel Management, 12,* 52–67.

Ospina, S. M. (1996). Realizing the promise of diversity. In J. L. Perry (Ed.), *Handbook of public administration* (2nd ed., pp. 441–459). San Francisco: Jossey-Bass.

Overman, S. (1995). Preventing violence against health care workers. *HRMagazine, 40,* 51–53.

Page, C. (1984). *Employment agreements for managers: Guidelines for elected officials.* Washington, DC: International City Managers Association.

Page, P. (1994). African-Americans in the senior executive service. *Review of Public Personnel Administration, 14,* 24–51.

Pay raises at New York charities beat inflation. (1995, June 1). *The Chronicle of Philanthropy,* p. 35.

Pearce, J. L. (1993). *Volunteers: The organizational behavior of unpaid workers.* New York: Routledge.

Perry, J. L. (1991). Linking pay to performance: The controversy continues. In C. Ban and N. M. Ricucci (Eds.), *Public Personnel Management: Current Concerns—Future Challenges* (pp. 73–86). New York: Longman.

Perry, J. L.(1993a). Strategic human resource management. *Review of Public Personnel Administration, 13,* 59–71.

Perry, J. L. (1993b). Transforming federal civil service. *The Public Manager, 22,* 14–16.

Perry, J. L. (1995). Compensation, merit pay, and motivation. In S. W. Hays and R. C. Kearney (Eds.), *Public Personnel Administration: Problems and prospects* (3rd ed., pp. 121–132). Englewood Cliffs: Prentice Hall.

Perry, J. L. (1996). *The handbook of public administration* (2nd ed.). San Francisco: Jossey-Bass.

Perry, R. W., & Cayer, N. J. (1992). Evaluating employee assistance programs: Concerns and strategies for public employers. *Public Personnel Management, 21*, 323–333.

Perry, J. L., & Kramer, K. L. (1993). The implications of changing technology. In F. J. Thompson (Ed.), *Revitalizing state and local public service: Strengthening performance, accountability, and citizen confidence.* San Francisco: Jossey-Bass.

Personnel department eases access to best and brightest. (1995, April 1). *PA Times,* pp. 18, 2.

Places for People. (1991–1992). *Places for People, Incorporated: Twenty years at the heart of change.* St. Louis: Author.

Places for People. (1993). *Annual Program Evaluation, July 1, 1992 through June 30, 1993.* St. Louis: Author.

Polilli, S. (1993). Online with government. *Governing, 7,* 45.

Powell, W. W. (Ed.). (1987). *The nonprofit sector: A research handbook.* New Haven: Yale University Press.

Prager, J. (1994). Contracting out government services: Lessons from the private sector. *Public Administration Review, 54,* 176–183.

Pregnancy Discrimination Act, Pub. L. 95–555 91978.

Preston, A. E. (1990). Women in the white-collar nonprofit sector: The best option or the only option? *The Review of Economics and Statistics, 72,* 560–568.

Primoff, E. S. (1975, June). *How to prepare and conduct job-element examinations.* Washington, DC: U.S. Civil Service Commission, Personnel Research and Development Center.

Primoff, E. S., & Eyde, L. D. (1988). Job Element Analysis. In S. Gael (Ed.), *The job analysis handbook for business, industry, and government* (Vol. 2, pp. 807–825). New York: Wiley.

Probst v. Reno, U.S.D.C. NI11, No. 93–93345 (December 20, 1995).

Public library patrons check out books on their own. (1995, April 17). *Nation's Cities Weekly, 18,* 3.

Ramakrishnan, K., & Balgopal, P. (1992). Linking task-centered intervention with employee assistance programs. *Families in Society: The Journal of Contemporary Human Services, 8,* 488–494.

Ramanthan, C. (1992). EAP's response to personal stress and productivity: Implications for occupational social work. *Social Work, 3,* 234–239.

Ray, P. (1993, April). *Matching employee benefits to employee needs: AFSCME's experience.* Paper presented at the American Society of Public Administration's National Conference, San Francisco, CA.

Reed, B. J., & Swain, J. W. (1990). *Public finance administration.* Englewood Cliffs: Prentice Hall.

Regents of the University of California v. Bakke, 483 U.S. 265, 17 FEP 1000 (1978).

Rehabilitation Act, 29 U.S.C., Sec. 701–794 (1973).

Rehfuss, J. A. (1986). A representative bureaucracy? Women and minority executives in California career service. *Public Administration Review, 46,* 454–460.

Richter, M. J. (1994). A guide to emerging technologies. *Governing, 7,* 65–80.

Risher, H. H., and Schay, B. W. (1994). Grade banding: The model for future salary programs? *Public Personnel Management, 23,* 187–199.

Rivenbark, L. (1995a, February 20). Growing pains strain INS. *Federal Times, 31,* 4.

Rivenbark, L. (1995b, May 8). Back pay hits $86,000. *Federal Times, 31,* 7.

Robbins, S. P. (1994). *Essentials of organizational behavior* (4th ed.). Englewood Cliffs, NJ: Prentice Hall.

Roberts, G. E. (1994). Barriers to municipal government performance appraisal systems: Evidence from a survey of municipal personnel administrators. *Public Personnel Management, 23,* 225–236.

Roberts, M., & Wozniak, R. (1994, September). *Labor's key role in workplace training.* Washington, DC: American Federation of Labor–Congress of Industrial Organization.

Rocheleau, B. (1988). New information technology and organizational context: Nine lessons. *Public Productivity Review, 12,* 165–178.

Rocque, A. (1995, June 1). Pay raises at New York charities beat inflation. *The Chronicle of Philanthropy, 7,* 35.

Rose, L. J. (1995, May 18). Red Cross program in cash crunch. *St. Louis Post-Dispatch,* pp. 1, 3.

Rosenbloom, J. S. (Ed.). (1992). *The handbook of employee benefits* (Vol. 1). Homewood, IL: Business One Irwin.

Rosenbloom, J. S., & Hallman, G. V. (1991). *Employee Benefit Planning* (3rd ed.). Englewood Cliffs, NJ: Prentice Hall.

Rossheim, B. N., Kim, P. S., & Ruchelman, L. (1995). Managerial roles and entrepreneurship in nonprofit urban arts agencies in Virginia. *Nonprofit and Voluntary Sector Quarterly, 24,* 143–166.

Rowland, M. (1994, June 12). Nonprofits under I.R.S. microscope. *The New York Times,* p. F15.

St. Mary's Honor Center v. Hicks, US SupCt, No. 92–602 (June 25, 1993).

Salamon, L. M. (1987). Partners in public service: The scope and theory of government-nonprofit relations. In W. W. Powell (Ed.), *The nonprofit sector: A research handbook* (pp. 99–117). New Haven: Yale University Press.

Salamon, L. M. (1992). *America's nonprofit sector: A Primer*. New York: The Foundation Center.

Salamon, L. M. (1995). *Partners in the public service*. Baltimore: The Johns Hopkins Press.

Salamon, L. M., & Abramson, A. J. (1982). The nonprofit sector. In J. L. Palmer & I. V. Sawhill (Eds.), *The Reagan Experiment* (pp. 219–243). Washington, DC: The Urban Institute.

Salamon, L. M., Musselwhite, J. C. Jr., & Abramson, A. J. (1984). Voluntary organizations and the crisis of the welfare state. *New England Journal of Human Services, 4,* 25–36.

Sampson, C. L. (1993). Professional roles and perceptions of the public personnel function. *Public Administration Review, 53,* 154–160.

Schneider, B., and Konz, A. M. (1989). Strategic job analysis. *Human Resources Management, 28,* 51–63.

Schofield, P. (1992). Local government job ads: The good, the bad, and the ugly. *Personnel Management, 24,* 41–44.

Schuler, R. S. (1990). Repositing the human resource function: Transformation or demise? *Academy of Management Executive, 4,* 49–60.

Schuler, R. S. (1992). Strategic human resources management: Linking the people with the strategic needs of the business. *Organizational Dynamics, 21,* 18–32.

Schmidt, F. L. (1988). The problem of group differences in ability test scores in employment selection. *Journal of Vocational Behavior, 33,* 272–292.

Seeley, R. S. (1992). Corporate due process. *HRMagazine, 37,* 46–49.

Segal, J. A. (1990). Developing return-to-work agreements to avoid liability for negligent retention of dependent employees. *HRMagazine, 35,* 86–89.

Selby, C. C. (1978). Better performance from nonprofits. *Harvard Business Review, 56,* 92–98.

Shahar v. Bowers, CA 11, No. 93–9345 (December 20, 1995).

Shareef, R. (1994). Skill-based pay in the public sector. *Public Personnel Administration, 14,* 60–74.

Sheet Metal Workers' Local 28 v. Equal Employment Opportunity Commission, 106 S. Ct. 3019 (1986).

Sherer, J. L. (1994, March). Can hospitals and organized labor be partners in redesign? *Hospitals & Health Networks, 68,* 56, 58.

Sheridan, J. E. (1992). Organizational culture and employee retention. *Academy of Management Journal, 35,* 1036–1056.

Shibley, G. J. (1995). Teaching officers to serve seniors. *F.B.I. Law Enforcement Bulletin, 64,* 23–26.

Siegel, G. B. (1994). Three federal demonstration projects: Using monetary performance awards. *Public Personnel Management, 23,* 153–164.

Sims, R. R. (1993a). The enhancement of learning in public sector training programs. *Public Personnel Management, 22,* 243–255.

Sims, R. R. (1993b). Evaluating public sector training programs. *Public Personnel Management, 22,* 591–615.

Sims, R. R., & Sims, S. J. (1991). Improving training in the public sector. *Public Personnel Management, 20,* 71–82.

Sims, R. R., Veres, J. G., & Heninger, S. (1989). Training for competence. *Public Personnel Management, 18,* 101–107.

Sisneros, A. (1992). Hispanics in the senior executive service: Continuity and change in the decade 1980–1990. *Review of Public Personnel Administration, 12,* 5–25.

Skinner v. Railway Labor Executives Association, 109 S. Ct. 1402 (1989).

Slack, J. D. (1987). Affirmative action and city managers: Attitudes toward recruitment of women. *Public Administration Review, 47,* 199–206.

Smith v. Arkansas State Highway Employees, Local 1315, 99 S. Ct. 1826 (1979).

Smith, S. R., & Lipsky, M. (1993). *Nonprofits for hire: The welfare state in the age of contracting.* Cambridge, MA: Harvard University Press.

Snelling, B. W., & Kuhnle, J. H. (1986). When should a nonprofit organization use an executive search firm and when not? In INDEPENDENT SECTOR (Ed.), *Aiming high on a small budget: Executive searches and the nonprofit sector* (pp. 1–8). Washington, DC: INDEPENDENT SECTOR.

Sproule, C. F. (1990, April). *Recent innovations in public sector assessment* (Personnel Assessment Monographs Vol. 2, No. 2). Washington, DC: International Personnel Management Association Assessment Council.

Spurlock v. United Airlines, 475 F. 2d 216 (10th Cir. 1972).

Starling, G. (1986). *Managing the public sector* (3rd ed.). Chicago: Dorsey Press.

Stehle, V. (1995, May 4). Many groups worried about block-grant plan for states. *The Chronicle of Philanthropy,* p. 32.

Stehle, V., & Williams, G. (1995, May 4). Getting ready for the "contract." *The Chronicle of Philanthropy, 7,* 1, 30, 31–32.

Steinberg, R. J., & Jacobs, J. A. (1994). Pay equity in nonprofit organizations: Making women's work visible. In T. Odendahl and M. O'Neill (Eds.), *Women and power in the nonprofit sector* (pp. 79–120). San Francisco: Jossey-Bass.

Stene, E. O. (1980). *Selecting a professional administrator: A guide for municipal councils* (2nd ed.). Washington, DC: International City Managers Association.

Stoesz, D. (1988). Privatization: Prospects for unionizing social workers. In H. J. Karger (Ed.), *Social workers and labor unions* (pp. 97–108). New York: Greenwood Press.

Stop the violence. (1995, February 27). *International Personnel Management Association Agency News, 19,* 4.

Sundeen, R. A., & Siegel, G. B. (1986). The uses of volunteers by police. *Journal of Police Science and Administration, 14,* 49–61.

Swierczek, F. W., & Carmichael, L. (1985, January). The quantity and quality of evaluating training. *Training and Development Journal, 39,* 95–99.

Swift, E. W. (1992–1993). Glass ceilings and equity. *The Public Manager, 21,* 34–36.

Swiss, J. E. (1992). Adapting Total Quality Management (TQM) to government. *Public Administration Review, 52,* 356–362.

Tambor, M. (1973). Unions and voluntary agencies. *Social Work, 18,* 41–47.

Tambor, M. (1988a). Collective bargaining in the social services. In P. R. Keys & L. H. Ginsberg (Eds.), *New management in human services* (pp. 81–101). Silver Springs, MD: National Association of Social Workers.

Tambor, M. (1988b). Social service unions in the workplace. In H. J. Karger (Ed.), *Social workers and labor unions* (pp. 83–96). New York: Greenwood Press.

Tap into 3,000 city programs through the NLC examples database. (1995, January 16). *Nation's Cities Weekly,* p. 7.

Taylor, S. (1989). The case for comparable worth. *Journal of Social Issues, 45,* 23–37.

Thompson, F. J. (Ed.) (1993). *Revitalizing state and local public service.* San Francisco: Jossey-Bass.

Todd, C. (1994, October 2). Food pantries now feeding minds: Literary classes offer another way to assist those in need. *St. Louis Post-Dispatch,* pp. B1, B5.

Towers Perrin. (1992). *Why did we adopt skill-based pay?* New York: Towers Perrin.

Trans World Airlines, Inc. v. Hardison, 432 U.S. 63 (1977).

Travnick, J. (1994). Averting workplace violence. *Risk Management, 41,* 13–20.

Treiman, D. J., & Hartman, H. (1981). *Women, work, and wages.* Washington, DC: National Academy of Sciences.

Twomey, D. P. (1994). *Equal employment opportunity law.* Cincinnati, OH: South-Western.

Ulrich, D. O. (1992). Strategic and human resources planning: Linking customers and employees. *Human Resource Planning, 15,* 47–62.

Ulrich, D. O. (1993). Competitive advantage through human resources. In H. J. Bernardin & J.E.A. Russell (Eds.), *Human resource management: An experiential approach* (pp. 36–43). New York: McGraw-Hill.

Uniform Guidelines on Employee Selection Procedures. (1978, August 25). *Federal Register,* 43166, 38290–38315.

United Automobile Workers v. Johnson Controls, 111 S. Ct.1196 (1991).

U.S. Congress, Office of Technology Assessment. (1990, September). *The use of integrity tests for pre-employment screening.* OTA-SET-442. Washington, DC: U.S. Government Printing Office.

U.S. Department of Justice. (1994). *National crime victimization survey: Violence and theft in the workplace* (BJS Publication No. NCJ 148199). Washington, DC: U.S. Government Printing Office.

U.S. Department of Labor, Bureau of Labor Statistics. (1994, July). *Employee benefits in state and local governments, 1992* (Bulletin 2444). Washington, DC: U.S. Government Printing Office.

U.S. Department of Labor, Women's Bureau. (1995a, May). *Facts on working women,* No. 95–1. Washington, DC: Author.

U.S. Department of Labor, Women's Bureau. (1995b). *Join the Working Women Count Honor Roll.* Washington, DC: Author.

U.S. Department of Labor, Women's Bureau. (1995c, April). *Care around the clock: Developing child care resources before nine and after five.* Washington, DC: Author.

U.S. General Accounting Office. (1992, April). *The changing workforce: Comparison of federal and nonfederal work/family programs and approaches.* Washington, DC: General Accounting Office.

U.S. Merit Systems Protection Board. (1991). *Balancing work responsibilities and family needs: The federal civil service response.* Washington, DC: U.S. Government Printing Office.

U.S. Merit Systems Protection Board. (1992). *A question of equity: Women and the glass ceiling in the federal government.* Washington, DC: U.S. Government Printing Office.

U.S. Merit Systems Protection Board. (1993). *The changing face of the federal workforce: A symposium on diversity.* Washington, DC: U.S. Government Printing Office.

U.S. Office of Personnel Management. (1994, December). *Towards reinvention: A guide to HRM reform.* Washington, DC: Author.

U.S. Office of Personnel Management, Human Resources Development Group, Office of Executive and Management Development. (1995, Fiscal Year). *Seminars of the Management Development Centers.* Washington, DC: U.S. Government Printing Office.

United States v. Paradise, 107 S. Ct. 1053 (1986).

United Steelworkers of America v. Weber, 443 U.S. 193 (1979).

Vanagunas, S., & Webb, J. (1994). Administration innovation and the training of public managers. *Public Personnel Management, 23*, 437–446.

Vanneman, A. (1994, July/August). Youth worker salaries: Going nowhere, slowly. *Youth Today, 3*, 1, 4–5.

Van Til, J. (1988). *Mapping the third sector: Voluntarism in a changing social economy.* New York: The Foundation Center.

Vietnam Era Veterans Readjustment Act of 1974, 38 U.S.C.A. 2011–2014 (West 1972).

Vizza, C., Allen, K., & Keller, S. (1986). *A new competitive edge: Volunteers from the workplace.* Arlington, VA: VOLUNTEER—The National Center.

Walker, M. (1994, November 14). More people using employee assistance. *Federal Times, 30*, 37.

Wallace, M. J. Jr., & Fay, C. H. (1988). *Compensation theory and practice* (2nd ed.). Boston: PWS-Kent.

Walters, J. (1994a, November). The reinvention of the labor leader. *Governing, 8*, 44–48.

Walters, J. (1994b, December). The trade-off between benefits and pay. *Governing, 8*, 55–56.

Walters, J. (1995, July). The gainsharing gambit. *Governing, 8*, 63–64.

Walton, M. (1986). *The Deming management method.* New York: Praeger.

Wang v. University of California, SuperCt, Alameda County, No. 714915 (1996).

Ward, J. (1993, September). Privatizing public works. *America City and County, 108*, 48–53.

Watkins, B. (1992). Reassessing comparable worth: The Minnesota experience. *PA Times*, p. 8.

Watson v. Fort Worth Bank and Trust, 487 U.S. 977 (1988).

Watts, A. D., & Edwards, P. K. (1983). Recruiting and retaining human services volunteers: An empirical analysis. *Journal of Voluntary Action Research, 12*, 9–22.

Weissman v. Congregation Shaare Emeth, No. 94–1464 (8th Cir., 1994).

Werther, W. B. Jr. (1989). Childcare and eldercare benefits. *Personnel, 66*, 42–46.

Wexley, K. N., & Latham, G. P. (1991). *Developing and training human resources in organizations* (2nd ed.). New York: HarperCollins.

Wheeland, C. M. (1994). Evaluating city manager performance: Pennsylvania managers report on methods their councils use. *State and Local Government Review, 26*, 153–160.

Wheeler, M. T. (1995, June). Where are the leaders? *The Nonprofit Times, 9*, 26, 28.

Where things stand. (1995, October 1). *PA Times, 18,* 3.

Wiesen, J. P., Abrams, N., & McAttee, S. A. (1990, December). *Employment testing: A public sector viewpoint* (Personnel Assessment Monographs Vol. 2, No. 3). Washington, DC: International Personnel Management Association Assessment Council.

Widmer, C. (1985). Why board members participate. *Journal of Voluntary Action Research, 14,* 8–23.

Wilensky, R., & Jones, K. M. (1994). Quick response key to resolving complaints. *HRMagazine, 39,* 42–47.

Wilson, J. Q. (1989). *Bureaucracy: What government agencies do and why they do it.* New York: Basic Books.

Winsten, E. (1995, May 1). Plans unveiled to stem workplace violence. *Federal Times, 31,* 15.

Witt, E. (1989). Sugarplums and lumps of coal. *Governing, 2,* 28–33.

Wittig, M. A., & Lowe, R. H. (1989). Comparable worth theory and policy. *Journal of Social Issues, 45,* 1–21.

Wooldridge, B. (1994). Changing demographics of the workforce: Implications for the use of technology as a productivity improvement strategy. *Public Productivity and Management Review, 17,* 371–386.

Wolf, T. (1990). *Managing a nonprofit organization.* New York: Simon & Schuster.

Wurf, J. (1974). Merit: A union view. *Public Administration Review, 34,* 431–434.

Wygant v. Jackson Board of Education 106 U.S. 1842 (1986).

Yarborough, M. H. (1994). Use peer review for conflict resolution. *HRFOCUS, 71,* 21.

Zolkos, R. (1994). A guide to new pressures on pension plans. *Governing, 8,* 65–71.

Name Index

Subject Index